Live in the Moment, Including Zen and the Art of Healing

Live in the Moment, Including Zen and the Art of Healing

Ross Cribb

BOOKS

Winchester, UK
Washington, USA

First published by O-Books, 2015
O-Books is an imprint of John Hunt Publishing Ltd., Laurel House, Station Approach,
Alresford, Hants, SO24 9JH, UK
office1@jhpbooks.net
www.johnhuntpublishing.com

For distributor details and how to order please visit the 'Ordering' section on our website.

Text copyright: Ross Cribb 2014

ISBN: 978 1 78535 007 8
Library of Congress Control Number: 2014959593

A CIP catalogue record for this book is available from the British Library.

Design: Stuart Davies

Printed and bound in Australia by Griffin Press

We operate a distinctive and ethical publishing philosophy in all
areas of our business, from our global network of authors to
production and worldwide distribution.

CONTENTS

Zen and the Art of Healing

Dedication:
I dedicate this book to my loving family:
My parents Steve and Phyllis, and my brothers Steve, Ian and Geoff.

I also wish to acknowledge my primary spiritual teachers:
Helen Neufeld, and Dr. AlixSandra Parness.

An honorable mention goes to Jacob Goldfarb for his editing and insightful commentary of *Zen and the Art of Healing*.

And I also thank Daniel at Manuscript Magic for the polishing touches he contributed to the manuscript.

Last but not least, this book is dedicated to my dear friend Karen.

Author's Notes

This book is about enlightenment, but the point is to learn from—and enjoy—the journey rather than focus on the final outcome. It provides a practical explanation of enlightenment and a rational account of the healing process, which is necessary in some form or another in order to attain enlightenment. The theory presented in this book is a path to having a happier and more spiritual life, and from it I hope others will learn to enjoy the moment and will be inspired to heal the parts of themselves that prevent them from doing so.

As an introduction I will tell you that I am a graduate of an energy healing school, an ordained minister of a spiritualist church, and a student of Zen, all of which have played a significant role in my spiritual growth. I also have a BA in Philosophy and consider myself a rational, down-to-earth person, supported by my keen interest in science. In fact, the impetus for this book was to carve out a more useful role for the rational mind in spirituality, and to tie together ideas that seemed valid to me, but to my knowledge had not yet been incorporated into a holistic model.

I was born in 1960 as the youngest of four sons in a stable and functional family (thanks Mom, Dad, and brothers). I have worked in a variety of jobs, mostly in two main fields of employment: assisting troubled youth and business administration. I am married, have one child and reside in Japan, though I grew up in British Columbia, Canada. I also spent a year living in Korea teaching English, and I have traveled to many different countries.

As I began to write this book, I was a scared individual embarking on a new adventure, or perhaps more precisely, a new chapter of my *ongoing* adventure. In this book and in my life, I make no pretense that I am a refined individual, or that I have all the answers. My life has not been smooth sailing, but neither has it been the intense struggle I have seen others go through. I still wrestle with the human conditions of self-esteem; honesty; relationships; finances; fear; commitment; and common vices. For my entire adult life, I have also struggled with a chronic disease: ulcerative colitis.

One of the cornerstones of my journey towards joy and health is meditation, and more recently, writing has become another. I now believe writing is my ideal spiritual path, and the writing of this book has been a healing experience for me. As you read it, you will understand how vital meditation is to my writing and my life. A quiet mind has enabled me to appreciate the power of "Living in the Moment," leading to an ever-deepening sense of inner peace which I am able to maintain for longer and longer periods. Now I wish to share this knowledge with others so they can also experience the same joy and peace.

When I decided to follow through with my long-held ambition of writing a book, the writing happened slowly, and the initial product was more like a science textbook than a story. I quickly realized that a textbook-style book would have little chance of getting published, so I searched for a more interesting way to present the information. One day, the idea of having the main character be an aspiring author came to mind, and thus John Alexander was born.

Hence, the book is about a man's life as he authors a book, meaning there is a small book within the main book. This delivers my message in a clear and concise manner. I acknowledge it is implausible for the character to write at such timely moments, or to have the contents of his writing flow so easily and coherently. But by overlooking these shortcomings, the reader will be exposed to the overall process of writing a novel, which is a complex and labored task. Please note that I was writing the story as well as the theory (the inner book), so my actual writing time was much more than what is portrayed in the book.

As for the parallels between John's life and mine, there are many; however, John's story is not an exact retelling of my life. I felt free to change parts, add parts and omit parts. This is not an attempt to glorify my life; it just seemed easier to retell things I knew intimately rather than invent a totally fictitious character. The bulk of the alterations are to help in the telling of the story, and not falsely add drama. If some events strike you as implausible, there is a good chance they are actually true because there are only a couple of purely fictitious events. I have added the timeline of John's life at the end of the book to help clarify the sequence of events.

This was an ambitious project, partly because I am offering a brief explanation for the nature of the universe and the basis for human life. It is incomplete in that it is a sketch of a theory, and it does not cover all the bases, so to speak. One important factor to understanding human behavior that is not explained is sexuality. I am still attempting to understand this basic component; however, I felt it important to include a couple of chapters involving this subject for two reasons. First, the theory may be incomplete, but I didn't want the main character to be incomplete, so including his sexual nature rounds out his character. Second, because sexuality is such a reactive subject, I am providing you an opportunity to test my theory by including it. If you find judgments arising when reading these sections, you can explore the nature and origins of your reactions. I plan to offer a detailed explanation of sexuality in future writings.

Before letting you get on with the book, it may be helpful to say something about Enlightenment. Zen suggests that it is, by its very nature, indescribable. Enlightenment is the experience of the Now, where time ceases to exist, or where separation is transcended to become the "One." Enlightenment is indescribable because description is limited to mental concepts, and the experience of the One is not a mental experience. I believe that once you have a glimpse of the interconnectedness of the One, then you cannot help but be more compassionate about life and everything in it. And even being compassionate is limiting once you have truly experienced it, but the profound peace and tranquility that you will exude is an invitation for others to journey down the path of Enlightenment too.

This Oneness is what I believe religions are referring to when they say God. Mainstream religions in the West do not suggest that individuals can experience this Oneness, so obviously they do not provide directions on how to obtain it—but Zen does. And it is a simple and practical approach. Thus I have found Zen techniques to be invaluable to my growth.

Thank you for your interest in this book. I truly hope it can be of some help to you.

In service, Reverend Ross Cribb.

Chapter 1

Ordination

Sunday, August 19

As I look out from the veranda, the lake is as smooth as glass. In the pale light of early morning, it faintly reflects the distant hills and cloudy skies. In spite of the quiet feeling of pre-dawn, the intermittent buzzing of insects and chirping of birds are surprisingly intrusive. I also feel a sense of urgency because I have seen one person enter the main lodge, and I'm sure more will be coming soon. My chance for solitude is passing; the day will soon begin.

I have already spent thirty minutes struggling to find the magical serenity of a quiet mind, but it has been a restless thirty minutes. In preparation for the big event, AlixSandra had instructed us to take time this morning to reflect, but for me, the only reflection is on the lake. When at home, my morning meditations usually come easily and are generally pleasurable, but when away from the familiarity of home I find meditating a challenge. My resolve is fading fast, and the heavy feeling in my eyes tells me sleep will come quickly if I go back to bed.

I notice another worker approaching the lodge, signaling the impending hum of the morning's activities. I surrender; it is time to go back to my room. My accommodation is a room shared with another conference participant (I have financial constraints). This morning there will be no profound insights, no intense release of emotion and no experience of God's light to prepare me for today. Instead, a couple more hours of sleep will be my preparation for the day.

A few hours later I am walking on the path through the grassy courtyard to the main hall. I feel alert and buoyant, yet there's no denying a sense of uncertainty. As I walk, the inspiration of nature surrounds me. Looking at the trees, I can see more than their appearance; I can intuit their aliveness. And not only are they alive, but they are talking to me. I don't mean literally *talking* to me, but the vibrancy of their aliveness is a message for me to feel alive too. They have a certain power and a connection to the earth that is real and tangible to me. Trees have no doubts, no fears, no conflicting emotions—they are an expression of Nature, and their existence communicates a message of purity and harmony.

This is my experience as I walk toward my new life, yet I thought I would be more emotional. I often feel a connection with Nature, so that doesn't feel unusual, though today it is more acute. My heightened state of awareness is contrasted by my desire for clarity—to be free of doubts. On some level I know I am doing the right thing and that I must move forward, but I don't feel ready yet. I'm just a regular guy trying to make sense of my life, just as everyone else is likely doing. I want the security of knowing with my whole being that the step I am about to take is the right one.

Much of the drama I am expecting from today has already happened in bits and pieces. The intense emotion that accompanies such a deep commitment has been occurring over the last few months—today is just a moment to mark a transition. It is vital to mark it, because the rational mind likes external reference points to measure how things have changed. However, the *real* changes happen internally—not externally—and that process is less defined.

It is an overcast day, so I don't get the bright sunshine I wanted to highlight the occasion. Nature just is. I am at an Energy Healing Conference in Lake Geneva, Wisconsin, USA. The location is a small college campus that operates as a resort and conference center during the summer. It is a beautiful spot, and the conference has been fun, but today is the culmination of the event. Today is the day when the Inner Focus Church takes center stage. More importantly, it is the day when a few of us will be recognized for a new level of commitment to serve humanity. We are all servants, but not everyone is so willing to formally acknowledge that responsibility. Today is Ordination Day.

As I approach the veranda I see Russ and his wife Kim. Russ is a man who is on a similar journey to me. We met a few years ago while we were both enrolled in the Inner Focus Healing School. We soon became friends, and when we started doing our homework sessions together, our bond was cemented. In those sessions we revealed some of our innermost fears and secrets. I am glad we will be ordained together. Like me, Russ is uncertain as to how he will fulfill his commitment to the Divine. We each wrote a thesis outlining a vision for our respective ministries, but those are just words—action is *very* different.

In my thesis I talk about inspiring people to embark on a healing journey, and in so doing they can gain greater peace and joy. Part of my mission is to offer a rational explanation of the healing process. I am a firm believer that the rational mind can be incorporated into spiritual experiences. In fact, I want to appeal to the rational minds of conventional people and explain that energy healing is for them; it is not just for those "out there" people. In my thesis I mention that one way I hope to share my message is by writing a book—a dream I've had for a long time. However, not being a writer, I don't know if it is a realistic goal. As I attempt to start my book I am finding it much harder than I expected, but at least I have the theory outlined in my thesis as a starting point.

Another component of my ministry is to make Zen accessible and practical to those seeking self-improvement. I've often referred to the book *Zen and the Art of Motorcycle Maintenance* as my bible. Unfortunately, the author, Robert Pirsig, didn't do a great job of explaining Zen. I had to read the book three times before I had a clear sense of his explanation. I know it need not be that difficult.

When I step onto the veranda, Russ and I hug, and I am wondering if he is feeling any more certainty than I am. As we stand outside the hall waiting for the proceedings to begin, few words are exchanged—there isn't anything that needs to be said. His presence provides the encouragement I want, but I am also lost in my own thoughts—thoughts about how I arrived at this point in my life.

Given my personal history, this is a situation full of ironies and inevitabilities. My early life was marked by a keen interest in how the world works. Once I started school I learned to believe in science, and later used it to support my anti-religion views. During my insolent teenage years, I remember saying I was a devout atheist. How I used to love arguing with those I thought were misguided religious fools! However, while at university, I became disillusioned with science, and for several years wandered aimlessly through the academic landscape. In the end I graduated with a BA in Philosophy. In spite of it not being very practical in the real world, it seemed the only field of study that suited my quest for meaning.

My mind's search for answers also led me to explore an assortment of spiritual practices, such as yoga, tai chi and meditation. One of the more intense explorations was a seven-day Zen retreat. Fifteen years later I am still coming to terms with that experience.

The next phase in my journey was joining the Inner Focus Healing School, not with the intent of becoming a healing practitioner, but to further my personal healing process. It was during this phase that my life changed the most dramatically, and I started to get a sense of purpose in my life. And now, in an hour or so, I will be ordained as a Minister for the Inner Focus Church, which should give me a new sense of purpose.

There is a sense of destiny too; both my grandfathers were ministers (although they died many years before I was born), and my great-grandfather had the gift of healing, though it is rarely talked about in my family. Plus, I remember taking an aptitude test during my university days—the results suggested that my ideal profession was a religious leader first, a teacher second and a social worker third. Even though my father was a teacher and my mother was a social worker, I thought the results were strange because at that time I had no interest in religion.

And, oddly enough, I would still say I have little interest in religion. I am spiritual, not religious. I think people need to search *inside* to find the answers to life. Great prophets like Jesus and Buddha offered wisdom, but it needs to be internalized to be practical. A seeker is to contemplate that wisdom and create their own vision of a divine life in accordance with their heart's guidance. And I think Zen has much to offer in regards to accessing that inner wisdom.

I let these thoughts go as Russ and I enter the hall.

Soon, the ceremony begins. As a preliminary activity, AlixSandra, who is the founder of the church, asks previously ordained ministers to say a few words about the courage involved in their decision to become ministers. Listening to them and being familiar with a few of their personal stories, I know they are not doing justice to the courage involved in their decisions. Similarly, however, I would have little to say about the courage of my decision either; it just seems to have happened. In truth, all along I have been waiting for someone to tap me on the shoulder and say, "Sorry, you're not qualified for this. We've just been playing a little joke on you." But, in a matter of minutes, it will be too late; I will have gotten away with it. I will have fooled them into thinking I am a person capable of a spiritual mission. But I know I am capable—my doubts come from not knowing *how* I will do it.

The actual ordination proceedings begin. Russ and I, along with seven others, are assembled at the front of the hall. AlixSandra reads some scriptures from the Bible, words emphasizing her theme for the day: courage. I am feeling calm, and my lack of emotion allows me to notice the details of my surroundings. One of my fellow honorees is a florist, and he has brought dozens of flowers. The beauty of the lilies, irises, and roses, along with an assortment of enormous crystals and colorful banners, create an uplifting atmosphere in the hall. As I scan the audience, I briefly hold my gaze to acknowledge some of the familiar faces—people I have known since my early days at the Inner Focus Healing School.

AlixSandra's vision for the Inner Focus Church, and the school, is based on the premise that healing was one of Jesus' greatest gifts to the world, and something he taught others to do. In following Jesus' example, AlixSandra teaches healing, and in doing so helps to heal the heart of humanity. I now accept this as my path too: to teach and promote healing. The reality is that I know little of Jesus, and even less of the Bible. I acknowledge Jesus' life, but I am not intent on promoting *him*, just his mission of healing and his message of love.

The ceremony concludes, and I have a fleeting thought: "I've gotten away with it!" Next are the congratulations and hugs. A few group photos are taken, and I request one of Russ and me. As the celebration goes on, I am aware of several questions lurking in the back of my mind. Am I different now? Should I act differently now? What is my ministry going to look like? I don't have the answers, and I am content to leave these questions in the back of my mind. I know that, in time, I will find the answers I need.

Soon, things start winding down and people begin leaving the conference, returning to their homes and personal lives. I say my goodbyes as they leave, but I stay to help dismantle the conference paraphernalia. I'm in no hurry to leave because I fly out tomorrow; that's the cheapest flight I could get.

It is a pleasant last night at the resort. Somehow it seems appropriate to be alone on the first night of my new life—my life as an ordained minister. I have been alone for much of my adult life. Not that I'm a loner, but I don't readily make deep connections with others. I've had some involved, romantic relationships, but I've had longer periods without a lover. I don't currently have a girlfriend, and the people with whom I have a close connection live in other parts of North America, like Russ, who lives in the state of Arkansas.

As I lie in bed later, I think, "Am I any different today than I was yesterday?" I don't feel any different. Yes, I am happy with the day's proceedings, and I have some pride in that I am now ordained, but at a deeper level I still feel like the same flawed, doubtful person. I think what I was looking for was a sense of magic, and either it didn't happen or I let it slip by. There have been special moments in my life when things seemed perfect and I was at peace with the universe, occasions like scoring a crucial goal while playing a hockey game, or laughing so hard with friends that my stomach hurt or being moved to tears by the awe of nature while camping. Today was an exciting day, but it wasn't one of the magical ones. My mind was still distracted by my doubts.

I guess the key is to become so involved in the moment that I stop thinking about it. There is nothing for doubts or questions to hold onto when one is *not thinking* because questioning and doubting are activities of the mind. During these moments, one also loses track of time. I am coming to realize that the magic happens when one transcends the moment, and during those timeless moments life is truly enriched. My understanding comes from that same Zen retreat, where I had a moment of true insight. We all have had glimpses of timeless moments, but Zen training teaches us how to expand those momentary glimpses into prolonged looks, and it teaches us that every moment has that potential. Zen often seems contradictory and befuddling, but its aim is to train us to experience the magic of the moment, and the *longer* we can experience its *timelessness*, the richer our lives become. Time is a stumbling block in the way of living a joyous and profound life.

Though I don't yet fully understand this, and have even less of a sense as to how to explain it, I know timelessness is one message I want to convey with my book and my ministry. I want to rationally and methodically explain how to transcend time, and thus be in the moment. Towards this end, I know meditation and healing are practices that will help bring this into reality. Meditation conditions us to be in the moment, and a Zen attitude helps us apply this perspective to all aspects of life. Healing helps because it clears our minds of issues that take us out of the moment. The importance of meditation is a gift from Buddha, the power of healing is gift from Jesus and the art of living in the moment is the magic of Zen (Zen has no prophet). These two masters didn't invent these techniques, but they tried to show us how to use them—and now I want to continue this mission. I want to rationally explain how these practices can benefit us. These are not the only tools available, but I think they are the most effective and practical ones. The goal for my ministry and my book is to bring the light of rational thought to what are considered esoteric practices. Furthermore, I think scientific theory can support this position. Science and spirituality are working toward the same end.

As I entertain these thoughts I start to get overwhelmed with the challenge, and this is a great reminder for me to not get caught up in the imaginings of the future. I need to focus on my next step and have faith that things will fall into place. Thoughts about the big picture are OK, but it is crucial not to dwell on them. Life is in the Now, and not the future, so the more parts of myself—the emotional, the mental and the spiritual—that are in the present moment, the happier and more fulfilling my life will be.

And for this present moment I need to let this "stuff" go, or I will never get to sleep. If my mind has something to ruminate

12

about, it will just keep spinning and spinning.

In the morning I have to catch a bus to Chicago and then fly to Ottawa, Canada where I will spend a few more days with my aunt and uncle (I spent a week there prior to coming to the conference). After a few days in Ottawa, I will return to my home in Penticton, British Columbia, Canada (a town of 30,000 about five hours driving east of Vancouver).

I grab the book I brought, *The Kite Runner* by Khaled Hosseini. It is an engrossing yet easy read, which both occupies and relaxes my mind. Then, when I get tired, my mind will go from spinning to drifting so I can fall asleep.

Chapter 2

Dad and Elvis

Sunday, August 26

Coolness surrounds me, but I am not cold. Rather, the coolness emphasizes the coziness I feel while curled up under my blanket. We are having an unusual cool spell, so maybe that is adding to the strange feeling I'm having this morning. A fragment of a conversation I was having with my dad earlier is still floating in my head.

"What do you think I should do now? Travel?" I asked.

"Where would you like to go?" he countered.

Pondering my answer, I said, "Somewhere exotic, strange... I don't know, South America, or maybe Japan."

However, repeating the conversation in my head doesn't give it the same impact now as it did a few minutes ago. The words don't bring back the feeling of being with my dad. Instead, I open my eyes and my surroundings come into focus. My room is cluttered with yesterday's clothes, the pieces of paper that I scribbled on to capture my ideas and the dozen or so books that I have either partially read or had planned to read. It occurs to me that it is time for a major cleaning. Then it hits me, like a pebble bouncing off my chest, not hard enough to hurt, but enough to catch my attention.

"What am I going to do?"

If my first thought about today is a pebble, then those that follow are like rocks.

"I have no job, no money. I am wasting my life. This writing thing will never work."

Why do days have to start like this, with all this negativity? Why can't I just relish the freedom I have with no commitments or obligations? I am free to construct my day and my life any way

I choose. I can create my own reality.

I recall my dream again. I remember talking with my dad about Japan, but the dream is hazy now, partly because the memory is fading and partly because it is a dreamscape that isn't confined to the rules of physics. I can tell it is too vague to be of much use, so I let it go; however, there is a lingering sensation of closeness with my father. This sensation seems to be inter-mingled with the warmth of my bed. Emotionally I feel closer to my dad than ever before, obviously helped by once again living in the same town as my parents. When I returned to Canada after a year of living in Korea, it was an ideal time to change hometowns. My parents retired to Penticton, and I loved visiting there, so I knew it would be a great place to live. Plus, I thought it helpful to be near them as they get older.

Having let go of my negative thoughts, I just want to lie here for few more minutes. However, as much as I would like to, I can't really control my mind; I can already tell this morning will not be a fruitful one if I simply lie here thinking.

Once I accept it is time to get up, I realize I am actually looking forward to the next activity in my day—meditation. It has taken me years to feel this way about meditation. Maybe I should say *many* years. Now meditating is usually a place of calmness and tranquility, filled with all kinds of treasures and insights into my own life. Sometimes I tap into an infinite wisdom, and at other times I uncover the secrets I keep from myself. During meditation I can play with scenarios in my life without the burdens of emotional attachments. This allows me to see my life as an impartial observer. Meditation is how I have been able to navigate my complex relationship with Terra. I get to see my reactions to her objectively. Of course, the flip side is that it is much harder to lie to myself—I can't deny that I continue to have strong feelings for her. It has been hard having just a friendship with her when I want a more intimate involvement.

Recently, I have been feeling an added pressure to meditate. Well, not *just* to meditate, but to have *profound* meditations. Of course, it doesn't work that way; feeling pressure for insights inhibits the freedom and fluidity of the process. For me, meditation is about being unfettered, not about accomplishing tasks or having duties, but it is hard to let go of that pressure. It has been a week since my ordination, and I keep expecting to feel different, but I feel the same. I know my life *isn't* the same, and that I can't go back to my old self, whatever that means. It is funny how that one event, that at the time I didn't experience as being profound, could still encapsulate my whole life—all the struggles and pains, as well as all the risks and successes! That *one event* is a marker that will divide my life into *before* and *after*. My time will now be defined as *before* ordination and *after* ordination.

Now, not only do I have a piece of paper saying my life has changed, but I have a tattoo as well. It was an ordination gift to myself—a physical reminder of my commitment. I had been contemplating the idea for a while, and a couple of days ago I finally did it. Now I have "Live in the Moment" written with permanent ink on the back of my left hand. The uniqueness and permanence of the tattoo appeals to me. I believe it is a bold, yet subtle way to get my message out there. It was a tough decision, and in some sense it has felt more profound than even being ordained. This is my only tattoo, and I had to go to three places before I found someone willing to give me a first tattoo on my hand. It surprised me that tattoo artists were sensitive to the impact of having such a visible tattoo.

In this way, having made my transformation so visible, I cannot hide the real me anymore. Maybe that explains the added pressure I feel about meditation; maybe I am hoping it will help me understand what being ordained really means to me. Trying to ignore any pressure, I sit down to meditate.

Today's effort is rather benign. I end it with my usual

invocation: "I am the Breath of God; I Breathe the Heart of the Earth. I Breathe the Heart of the Universe. I am One with my Soul: I am One with my Self. My Inner Focus Heals the Heart of Humanity." It is a lovely way to make the transition from that tranquil inner space back to the uncertainty of outer reality.

As I get up there is stiffness in my knees and ankles. I suppose I expect these aches to magically improve just because I meditate. Doing something so spiritually beneficial must make my body suppler somehow. This thought leads my mind to trip over that sentence again: "I create my own reality." If this is so, why am I so broke, and why am I still single? The list of "whys" goes on. I have been down this road many times before, so I change my thinking before it becomes a negative cycle. In fact, there have been times in my life when things have worked out in such beautiful ways that I cannot doubt I had a hand in creating it. My move to Campbell River on Vancouver Island off the west coast of Canada is an example of how I created my reality.

Having grown up in the suburbs of Vancouver, living in a big city was the only lifestyle I had considered. After years of an uninspiring adulthood, I came to realize that I had been hiding in the comfort of my mundane life. The decision to move forward with my life prompted me to finish my BA, a four-year process that I had managed to drag out for ten years. After completing my degree, it was time to find meaningful employment; up to that point I had worked in construction and sales. My first conse-quential job ended up being in Campbell River, a small fishing town (population 30,000) on Vancouver Island. I was hired to work in a group home for troubled teens.

At that time I was a naive believer in the manifesting power of thought, so I actually wrote out a list of expectations for my living situation before moving. And it was not a simple list. I wanted to live on a large piece of land—an acre or more. I wanted my quarters to be a separate building, like a cabin, rather than an apartment or suite. I also wanted it to be close to work, and to be inexpensive. And if that wasn't enough, I wasn't prepared to be a dog owner myself, so I wanted the property owners to have a dog that I could walk. I even specified that it needed to be a large dog, because I'm not so fond of the little ones.

This is how my list of expectations manifested: I ended up living in a detached garage/studio situated on an acre of land overlooking the ocean. It was two blocks from work, rent was $200 a month and the owner had an Airedale dog that was starved for exercise and attention. It left no doubt in my mind that if a person is pursuing something intrinsically good for his soul, then powers come into play that support those efforts, and in turn, one's mind can affect those forces.

As I walk around my basement suite after my meditation, the soreness in my knees and ankles eases. I think, "What could be better for me than becoming an ordained minister? With that kind of karma on my side, I should be able to *think* myself into an incredible lifestyle." Then my mind hits the barricade on that road. "It is not becoming ordained that deserves merit, it is living a spiritually guided life as reflected by ordination—that what's important." And how spiritual is my life?

It's time to get on with my day and have some breakfast, so I boil some eggs. Free range of course. In the same pot I boil some turkey sausages, which may not be all that healthy, but I feel boiling them is at least a better way to cook them. As I cut a couple thin slices of rice bread, I can't help wondering if these dietary changes have improved my health. Regardless of the health benefits, I still enjoy this meal no matter how many times I have eaten it.

After breakfast it is time to work on my new "career." As I sit down at my desk, a wave of giddiness overcomes me. I am pursuing a writing career, and I feel truly blessed. I am following my long-held dream, a dream I am creating and living. There it is again: "I create my reality."

This is not to say that things are precisely as I want them, but I feel the exhilaration of knowing that my life is aligning with a higher purpose. I am doing something intrinsically good for my soul again, and I want my mind to influence the forces that are stirring to support me. Don't get me wrong—this is not carte blanche to wish anything I want—but I believe I can have some input as to what will come my way as I carry out this spiritual mission. I don't want to dwell on this now as I am likely to daydream my time away. This is my writing time!

I gather up all my notes and my ministerial thesis. Now, how do I actually start my book? I guess I start by writing...

Zen and the Art of Healing
By John Alexander

Chapter I: Energy Bodies and Universal Energy

I want to talk about something we often refer to as separate, but don't really consider separate—namely, the physical, mental, emotional and heart aspects of ourselves. It is very common to say, "My mind was somewhere else." And, when doing something with little enthusiasm, we say it was a "halfhearted" attempt. Have you ever said, "My emotions are all over the place"? Or had the experience where your body feels sluggish for no apparent reason? Considering parts of ourselves as distinct is how we sometimes feel and think, and I want to take this a step further. I am proposing that it is useful to take this informal distinction more seriously.

People have four fundamental Energy Bodies: the Physical, the Emotional, the Mental and the Spiritual. What I want to accomplish by introducing these four Energy Bodies is to provide another way to view our personal lives, and in doing so, encourage people to heal the parts of themselves that limit their joy and potential. My desire is for others to live happy, healthy lives and to experience a sense of peace in a more profound and spiritual way. One point that is worth noting, regardless of whether or not current scientific theory supports the idea of the proposed Energy Bodies—which I am suggesting it does—the model can still serve as a useful tool.

The characteristics of the Energy Bodies are evident in their names. The nature of the Physical Energy Body is what we commonly think of in terms of our bodies, like bones, muscles, organs, skin etc. The Emotional Energy Body relates directly to our emotions, such as happiness, sadness and anger. The Mental Energy Body is related to our thoughts, a principle component being one's beliefs. Finally, the Spiritual Energy Body relates to our essential spiritual nature, which has influence upon the natural realm. It is an intermediary between the physical and spiritual natures. I will explain in greater detail the function of the Spiritual Body as this book unfolds.

Though distinct, these Energy Bodies are superimposed and interrelated. A useful analogy is to consider air, which is comprised of several gases intermingling in the same space. The main gases are oxygen, nitrogen, argon, and carbon dioxide. Each gas maintains its distinctness as an independent chemical, but the molecules of each are dispersed throughout the same space. So it is with Energy Bodies: they are separate entities but occupy the same space.

With some writing done, now I can think about what I want to do with the rest of my day. I face this question most days as I am currently unemployed. Although I don't plan on going, tonight is the finale of Penticton's Elvis Festival. This may sound like a lame event, and I thought so too when it was first introduced, but it has turned out to be pretty interesting. It is amazing how many Elvis Presley impersonators there are out there, and how many are willing to come to little old Penticton for a festival. Leading up to the final contest, I'm sure some impersonators will be performing at various locations all over town; it could be a restaurant, a mall, a concert, a bar or even more unusual places. Over the years, the few impersonators I have seen have been surprisingly entertaining.

Penticton used to have a Peach Festival at this time of year, complete with a parade and evening concert. Many people would come, but as time went on it became more of a party weekend, with a higher percentage of younger people coming who had less interest in the city itself, and more of an interest in partying. The crisis point came a few years ago when a riot happened after the Saturday night concert. Subsequently, the city council decided that the Peach Festival was causing more trouble than benefit. A similar crisis had happened a few years earlier in Kelowna (a larger city about an hour's drive up the lake) with their Water Regalia Event. The Elvis Festival doesn't attract very many tourists, but it is good, honest fun, and the performers themselves add to the city's economy by renting hotel rooms and eating at restaurants.

Penticton's number one event is the Ironman (the swimming, cycling and running triathlon). Every hotel room in the city is booked for that event, and many residents rent out rooms in their houses. The participants and family members that often accompany them don't drink or cause problems, and are generally great people. Additionally, most athletes like to come a week ahead to acclimatize to our hot, dry summers. The whole community gets behind the event with thousands of volunteers.

Today I will ride to the park downtown; I'm sure there will be some Elvis performers entertaining the crowd. And in my mind, having done some writing, I have earned a drink while watching the show.

Chapter 3

Small Town Music

Saturday, September 1

After heading out of town on the highway for a few minutes, I turn onto a rural road. At the second street I turn left and drive the short distance to the end of the road. I can tell by all the cars parked around the cul-de-sac that this must be the right street, and the many people going into the house on the left signals it's the one I'm looking for. After parking my car I grab my small cooler of beer and walk cautiously towards the house. I feel unsure about my tattoo, but I tell myself that, if asked, I will explain my views on Zen without mentioning I've been ordained.

I go inside and look for someone I know, and though I don't recognize anybody immediately, the assortment of characters suggests I don't need to worry about formalities. There are some hippies, some country folk, some new-agers and some conventional-looking people. There is also a buzz in the air, which amplifies my sense of anticipation.

Two weeks ago I was delighted when I received an e-mail from Rick, an acquaintance of mine, informing me that he and his wife Julie were hosting a night of live music at their home. The feature performer was Valdy. I knew of him and liked his music, but it had been 20 years since I'd heard his name. Valdy was a rural artist that had two or three hit songs on the radio way back in the mid-70s. They were intelligent rock/folk songs with catchy melodies. I immediately replied that I wanted to come, and asked how to buy a ticket (which was 10 dollars). Rick said I could just pay at the door. Over the next few days I asked Terra and a few other friends to join me, but I had no takers.

So as I cautiously wander into the living room, I wonder whom I should pay. There are some familiar faces, but not people

I know by name or with whom I feel inclined to start up a conversation. A few select friends know about my ordination, and of course my family knows, but I haven't told a lot of people. I don't think anyone here knows.

Then I see Carol, a friend from the spiritualist church I attend and who introduced me to Rick and Julie. The two hosts are keen musicians and have performed at the church a few times. I chat with Carol for a few minutes and then ask her about paying for a ticket. She directs me towards a woman talking in the living room. I approach the woman, and when there is a break in her conversation, I manage to negotiate paying for a ticket. It is all pretty casual as things are done on an honor system.

With that task taken care of I head to the backyard as I was told that is where the performance will be. Exiting the back door I walk onto the patio and I am amazed to see that the house sits above a small ravine. There are four or five houses on the ridge surrounding the ravine, but this is the only one that has clear access down into it. At the bottom of a flight of stairs there is a flat grassy area the size of big yard. At the far end of the yard is a stage, beyond which the ground slopes off into uninhabited, rugged terrain. Benches and chairs are set up on the flat area, and some people have positioned themselves on the slope of the ravine. This is a natural amphitheater, ideal for live performances. I am in awe of the setup, and that it is a natural setting adds to my excitement.

Scanning the crowd of 50 people (in addition to the 50 I saw inside the house), I see Jeffery and Loro talking, two more people I know and enjoy. I make my way down the stairs to their location. Jeffery is a local musician, and I have seen him play a few times at local cafes and bars, but I got to know him because of a series of health treatments he did on me. After his years as a computer programmer he became a Rolfing practitioner. Rolfing is an alternative bodywork treatment developed in Sweden. Loro, who hails from England, is the main minister at the spiritualist church. I had told her I was planning to get ordained, and so when I greet them, she kindly asks about it. I tell her and Jeffery that I am now an ordained minister for Inner Focus Church. It feels odd to say it, but their enthusiastic response eases my embarrassment. They don't mention the tattoo—I guess they didn't notice it. After talking to them for ten minutes it becomes obvious that people are settling in for the start of the concert; and soon, Rick is on the stage making announcements. Jeffery and Loro head to where they have friends sitting, but I would prefer to sit on the slope of the ravine. I find a comfortable log to sit on next to a cute young couple. Valdy comes on stage shortly thereafter and the concert begins.

The concert was fantastic. Valdy is a seasoned musician, and he knows how to entertain a crowd. He has long since retired from his professional music career, but the performer in him never died, and he still takes to the stage occasionally. I gather he is a friend of Rick and Julie's, and came out this way for a holiday; Rick and a few others joined him on stage for the last couple of numbers. Rick invited those who were interested to join the jam session that will be happening in the garage, which is set up as a small studio. I didn't realize Rick and Julie were such avid musicians; their home is dedicated to the enjoyment of music.

People have brought a lot of food, and we are invited to enjoy it, but I feel awkward since I didn't bring anything. However, this doesn't stop me from sampling a few sweets. Over the next hour I start conversations with a few other guests; the high from the concert makes it easy to approach strangers. I'm sure the singing and socializing will go on for several more hours, but I have to drive, and the three drinks I've had is enough. If I stay longer I will constantly be fighting the urge to have another drink.

It has been a fabulous evening, and one that underscores the reasons why I like living in small communities. Getting to know good, honest people like Rick and Julie, as well as Loro and

Jeffery, is a privilege. They are all people who have lived in large cities, but choose to live in a small town. If you had lived in Penticton all your life you may be smart and know what you really want, but often it is the case that people haven't had the courage to pick up their lives and try something different. Choosing a place because it is where your heart is happiest is admirable, and choosing out of lack of ambition, or fear, is unfortunate. Having relocated several times myself, including once to Korea, I think it takes about seven years to really establish oneself in a new community. This is my seventh year in Penticton, and now that I am becoming acquainted with the local music community, it is a sign I am at home here.

I don't play any instruments, but I enjoy listening to music immensely, and live music is even better. When I was a young child, my parents had planned to have their four sons learn to play the piano. However, after struggling to get the oldest two to practice, they gave up on the last two sons learning music at all. The two of us took to sports instead, which we thoroughly enjoyed, but still I wish I had learned to play an instrument.

In an attempt to develop my musical talents, I tried to play the harmonica when I was in my early twenties. One Christmas I told everyone I wanted to learn, and found under the tree two books on how to play. One outlined a very methodical approach—to blow in this hole is the note A, to suck in this hole is a B etc. Then, using the scales, it provided a number of songs with increasing complexity to develop my skills. The other book was more of an intuitive approach. It distinguished between three types of notes: building, bridging and resolving. This method suggests building and bridging until it feels like it is time to resolve. I chose the methodical approach to playing, and over one summer of trying, I could haltingly play a few basic songs. That was the end of my attempt to become a musician.

These skills lay dormant for many years until one magical night while living in Campbell River. At the time, I was working in a high-stress job at a remote camp for young offenders. The day in question was one of our most stressful. A major incident had occurred the previous evening, and my co-facilitator and I— we taught the Life Skills program—had spent the day interviewing the ten residents. Being forthcoming with information is a major taboo in jails (they don't want to be labeled a rat), so it was very difficult to get a read on what had happened. By taking what little information we had, and then adding a little of what we *thought* had happened, we discussed it with one of the youth. He wouldn't specifically tell us what happened, but he would confirm what we "knew." For the youth, confirming information is different than giving information. We had the ten residents separated and went to each one individually, each time adding a little more conjecture to what the last youth had just validated. By the end of the day we had gotten the whole story of what had happened. We left work exhausted, but gratified.

After work, we were keen to unwind. Lorne, my coworker, owned a house and had a roommate—Wayne—but he was spending the winter in Victoria looking after his brother's house, who was on an extended vacation. Victoria is a four-hour drive south. On route to Lorne's home we stopped at the liquor store, and then upon arriving at the house we discovered that Wayne had unexpectedly returned for a few days. Wayne is a likable guy and easy to get along with, so the three of us ordered pizza and proceeded to drink and unwind for the evening. Eventually Lorne and Wayne began to jam, as both of them are casual musicians and often did this. I have even gone with them to some open mic sessions at a local café. I enjoy listening, but when it comes to a jamming session I always feel a bit awkward because of my musical ineptitude.

The release of stress, the alcohol and smoking a joint had us all in an altered state; we were happy, relaxed and totally oblivious to anything outside our own little world. Lorne sometimes plays the harmonica when he is jamming, and so there were several of them lying around. As Lorne and Wayne jammed, I cautiously picked one up and began blowing, trying to not interfere with their playing. After several minutes of trying to play quietly, I decided I was being foolish and put the harmonica down, but Wayne strongly encouraged me to keep playing. That little bit of encouragement was the permission I needed to really get into it. All of a sudden I recalled the book I had gotten for Christmas, but surprisingly it was the intuitive one that came to mind. I began to focus on building and bridging, and then eventually resolving, all in sync with the music they were playing. It became a magical scene where we were all jamming and grooving together. There was no tentativeness in my playing, as I was suddenly a blues harp maestro.

It was one of those definitive times of being in the moment. As part of my mind was listening to Lorne and Wayne's playing, I was simultaneously assessing whether I needed to build, bridge or resolve. Then, without a clue as to what actual note I was playing, I would find the appropriate tone. This was all being done without rational thought. I was aware I was doing all these things, but there was no sequential thinking occurring; the understanding was being done at an intuitive level. This is what I call being in the moment, and I am sure you are aware of it too. That night of playing the harmonica was one of the most enjoyable nights of my life. To be able to do something so competently, when I had not previously played at that level, required accessing a part of my psyche that I don't often use.

Music is such a good example because it is so universal, and it is easy to understand musicians, athletes and actors using this intuitive processing for their craft, but it is also true for doctors, chefs, teachers or just about any other profession. Being in the moment gets the rational part of our selves—the part that questions, doubts, and hesitates—out of the way of our performance. Visualization works this way too because it trains our body to react in certain situations, so when the real event happens we react immediately without needing to think sequentially. As Zen says, the mind is an impediment to Enlightenment.

Now that I am home from the Valdy concert, I need to get some sleep. I bought a CD at the event this evening, but I think I will save listening to it until the morning. With the joy of the concert still lingering in my head I get ready for bed, and I drift off to sleep soon after.

Chapter 4

One of My Pleasures—Bike Riding

Monday, October 1

The cool air caresses my face. It strikes me as odd that something I rarely notice is so soothing and pleasing. My attention moves from the breeze brushing my face to the air moving in and out of my lungs. There is a musty taste to it, but the scent is intriguing rather than unpleasant. The air also has a tinge of sweetness to it. Not in a sugary way, but in a gratifying way. My breaths are purposely slow and deep as they first fill my abdomen, then expand my chest, and finally lift my shoulders slightly. This is a yogic breath I learned somewhere along the way.

I am not in a formal meditative state, but my mind has that pure, clear quality. I guess I never really came out of that state after this morning's meditation. I feel in harmony with my environment and I feel like I am a part of it, not just an observer of it. The trees not only reach up into the sky, but their roots reach deep into the soil; they connect with universal energy and with earth energy. This mirrors humans; we are capable of such grandeur, yet we have a hidden side to us as well. And, like trees, I know my being is not limited by what we see (i.e. the physical body). Nature is balance and harmony, and at this moment, I feel this too.

This is one of my favorite places for connecting with nature. As I rest on my special rock, I have a majestic, panoramic view of Okanagan Lake. This is my usual turnaround point after the 50-minute ascent up the hill, though some days I will ride further. There are myriads of cycling trails through these hills—so many, in fact, that at times I don't meet another soul when I'm out riding. Mountain biking is one of the true pleasures in my life.

When I worked at the Penticton Alternate School (PAS), my

coworkers and I rode here occasionally, as well as a few other spots. We used to do a lot of things together in our free time, so much so that someone labeled us the PAS posse. Now we rarely ride together. Sometimes I ride here with Terra, but it is hard for her to make the time. So recently I have been riding alone. The solitude—or even the underlying sense of loneliness—can enhance the experience of communing with nature.

Today I came here because my morning meditation was particularly deep. I felt energized, but also in need of some time to integrate my insights. The solitude and physical exertion of riding are just what I need. In my meditation there was a sense of purpose that I have rarely felt before. Indeed, my life usually seems to be defined by a searching, a longing sensation, but this morning I trusted that writing is my life's purpose. There was also an element of surrendering to the process. I don't have to worry about fitting all the pieces together; it happens naturally. Surrendering means I don't have to outline my whole career, or even my whole book. I just have to follow through with today's requirement—or, more specifically, with *this moment's* requirement. Life has its own way of making all the little steps add up to a purposeful journey.

A richer sense of what ordination means comes to my mind. I have made a conscious commitment to be of service to the world; I am helping to heal the earth and humanity. And, as I move forward along my path, writing will become a cornerstone for my ministry. My ordination encourages me to trust in the process. If I dwell on the future or the past, I get sidetracked. But even when I get sidetracked, there are always opportunities to realign myself with my higher purpose. Events keep coming my way that lead me back to my spiritual path, whether or not I am conscious of them. However, when a person reaches a certain level of spiritual understanding, that purpose can be hard to avoid. At this level of awareness, a person consciously knows if they move away from his or her ideal spiritual path.

The story of how I became enrolled in the Inner Focus Energy Healing School is a prime example of being led back to my spiritual path. When I returned to Canada after a year of teaching English in Korea, I contacted Inner Focus and inquired about upcoming workshops. Previously I had attended two workshops conducted by AlixSandra, the founder of Inner Focus, and I knew spending some time with her could help me regain my balance. I went to Korea as an adventure, feeling in tune with the universe, but things had somehow shifted for me. The end of my time in Korea was particularly difficult, and after I came home I was in need of some spiritual uplifting.

AlixSandra's response to my inquiry about workshops was confusing. She said she had some great news—she was opening an Energy Healing School in Ottawa. This confused me because I was only looking for a workshop, not joining a healing school. And, even if I was interested in the school (which I wasn't), Ottawa, Canada, was still 2,100 miles (3,379 kilometers) away, making it a minimal advantage over attending a school somewhere in the United States. Disappointed in AlixSandra's news, I began looking elsewhere for a spiritual workshop to lift the gray cloud hanging over my head.

Over the next several months, I did not find the spiritual infusion I sought, and continued to struggle in a state of confusion and listlessness. I left Korea with the expectation that something significant was waiting for me back in Canada, but it hadn't materialized. As I mentioned earlier, upon my return I changed hometowns and moved from Campbell River to Penticton. I was unsuccessful in finding employment in my new location, and with no friends in the area (my mom and dad couldn't meet those needs), I found myself drifting along without reward or enjoyment.

Then fate stepped in and helped me move forward on my spiritual path.

I mentioned my aunt and uncle in Ottawa previously (having

stayed with them before and after my ordination ceremony), with whom I share a special relationship. Not long after returning from Korea, both of them were having some significant health challenges, so I offered to visit and assist with basic chores such as cooking, shopping and driving. After they initially declined my offer, my aunt's condition worsened, and I received a call from my uncle asking me how soon I could come. I inquired about how long they would need my help, and my uncle suggested two weeks, I think not wanting to impose on me by asking for a longer stay. After quickly checking some dates I said that would be fine, but I asked if it would be OK if I stayed a third week because I wanted to attend a workshop in Ottawa during that extra week. My uncle was pleased, and readily accepted.

So that was how I came to attend Module One of the Ottawa Inner Focus Energy Healing School, but how I decided to enroll in the school was more dramatic. At first, my intention was clear—I was attending Module One only. I had no plans to continue with the other eleven modules, which constituted the complete training.

It was great to see AlixSandra again at the module. The five-day workshop was intense, and I did my best to be mentally engaged. One afternoon, AlixSandra had asked for a volunteer to come up in front of the class to explore a personal challenge as a potential demonstration of a healing process. A couple of people had ventured forth, but the discussions did not progress sufficiently. After adjourning for a break I found AlixSandra alone and seized the opportunity to have a brief conversation with her. I wanted her perspective about my disease, ulcerative colitis. She asked me a few questions and then asked if I would be willing to share my challenge with the rest of the class. I said yes, without realizing how profoundly it would change my life.

When we reconvened AlixSandra called me up to the front of the room. She asked me to describe how my disease had affected my life. I was very candid in sharing my personal information, though I was emotionally detached from what I was saying. AlixSandra then asked me to describe some challenges from my childhood. She believes that diseases and suppressed emotional traumas are connected. Again, in a distant manner, I described a couple of incidents from my childhood. Finally I hit the trigger point of my emotional pain. I burst into tears as sadness overwhelmed me! My anguish was focused on times of feeling rejected by my family. AlixSandra had me work through my past trauma by having several classmates role-play various family members. It was the most intense release of emotional pain I had ever experienced!

In the midst of my own process, I was unaware of the rest of the class, but evidently my emotional release had triggered some of the other participants. They were also encountering their own past pains as they willingly let suppressed feelings surface. There were several clusters of people in the room, each with one person in the middle expressing their emotional hurts as they were supported by staff and classmates. Eventually things subsided and we began the process of honoring the healings (emotional releases) by bringing in light energy. To close, AlixSandra had everyone form a large circle and focus intently on a column of white light flowing through the center. Because I was the focal point of the healing process, she invited me to stand in the middle. The class continued to bring in light as they sang a song. I did my best to receive the love pouring into me.

That healing made a shift in my long-held feeling of loneliness. I didn't want to react merely from the power of that moment so I took a few days to reflect on my experience. After some consideration I had to admit that I now belonged to something—I was a part of the Inner Focus kinship. I enrolled in the school and I haven't regretted a moment of that three-year commitment.

It's hard to explain away as coincidences all the factors that came together for me to have that transformative experience at the workshop: my aunt and uncle living in Ottawa; the timing of their health crisis; my availability (namely being unemployed); my frame of mind (an important component of my willingness to share); and even the sense I had that, after Korea, something significant was going to happen to me. All these factors led me back to my ideal spiritual path.

Suddenly I make the connection between the courage AlixSandra had emphasized during the ordination ceremony and my own decision to become ordained. It took courage to get up in front of the class and show my vulnerability, but at a deeper level it was just me following my heart's desire to be healed. When circumstances come together that guide you towards wholeness and health, it is easier for the individual to dismiss the courage required to follow that path.

A shiver runs up my spine, bringing me back to the present scene. I am starting to feel cool. The exertion of my ride up the hill kept me warm for a while, but now that I am relaxed, the heat has dissipated. I have the urge to hurry back home; I feel grounded now and clearheaded enough to write.

When I get home, I put off showering; instead, I quickly get out my computer and start writing.

Chapter I, cont. (Energy Bodies and Universal Energy)

A second analogy that may be helpful in explaining the nature of Energy Bodies is to consider water. At room temperature, water is a familiar, clear liquid, but science informs us that water is composed of molecules, or more specifically, two hydrogen atoms combined with one oxygen atom: H_2O. When considering water as molecules of hydrogen and oxygen, one ponders water at a deeper level: the atomic level. Furthermore, science goes on to say that the atoms within molecules are made up of electrons, protons, and neutrons. This is the subatomic perspective of water. And, even further theorizing has led to a quantum theory where the subatomic particles are made up of different forms of energy (quarks, mesons etc.) that are governed by the strange laws of quantum mechanics. At each deeper level of interpretation there is a more universal quality to the energy that comprises the water, from crude visual observation to the base elements of all that exists.

In like fashion, the Energy Bodies range from the physically observable to the universal energy of the Spiritual Body. One sees only the densest energy—the Physical Energy Body—but next is the Emotional and then the Mental. Finally, the least dense is the Spiritual Energy Body. Each Body is energy of a different form, and each operates according to its own rules. The ideal state for each body is to have energy flowing within it without restriction, though restrictions are common. The potential sensations generated by having unrestricted flow, or complete fluidity, are relaxation in the Physical Body, joy in the Emotional Body, harmony in the Mental Body and compassion in the Spiritual Body.

One important way that the Energy Bodies differ from the analogies of air and water is how changes in one Body affect the others. Though they are distinct and superimposed, the Energy Bodies affect one another, but in imprecise ways. For example, when we are emotionally hurt, there will be corresponding effects in our Physical, Mental and Spiritual Bodies, but the degree and specifics of the effects will be different with every individual. Similarly, a change in a person's Mental Body will impact the Physical, Emotional and Spiritual Bodies. Some of the personal factors influencing the interaction between the Bodies are the degree of fluidity in each Body, one's personality, one's self-concept and one's self-awareness (or willingness to be honest with themselves).

Now that I have done some writing, I am feeling total gratification. Though it is hard putting my ideas into clear, concise words, I feel I am making decent progress on my book, but I wish it would go faster. I quickly catch myself; this is letting my emotional body get caught up in my mental body's activity, and my mental body is dwelling in a fictitious future. The book will be done when it gets done.

Now it is time to shower. I am feeling so upbeat that, after my shower, I may do some housecleaning.

Chapter 5

Understanding My Fear

Wednesday, October 10

My home is a sanctuary. Well, maybe not a sanctuary. But it is a fortress. I am protected from the evils of the world by its high walls and a moat; this is good, as I feel that the evil out there is especially strong today. The gray, concrete walls look very sturdy, almost impenetrable. The rooms are spacious — too spacious, in fact, given the sparse furnishings and barren walls. It is not a welcoming or relaxing environment, but there is no doubting its sense of security.

Suddenly, this sense of safety is being challenged. One of my confidants has broken my trust. It is either a close friend or a family member, as these are the only other occupants of my fortress. My anxiety increases! I feel fear closing in on me. I am afraid of being attacked, and not knowing who the attacker might be fuels a compulsion to protect myself. I secure myself in my room; surely it must be safe! My room's emergency devices spring into action — a steel wall seals the door and thick bars clamp down over the windows.

My body twitches as I slowly slip from this harried dream-state to my awakened state of consciousness. This was a familiar dream, and I remember that house, but this time I think it has gone further than ever before. I don't remember having a sense of betrayal by my inner circle of confidants, and I don't remember barricading myself in my room. My body has a film of perspiration and my heart beats heavily. The anxiety and drama of the dream still cloud my consciousness.

Immediately I connect the dream with the comments AlixSandra made in our conversation yesterday. I had called her to confirm she received the check I sent her for a wall hanging I bought on credit while at the healing conference. Really, the call was an excuse to talk to her, and we had an interesting conversation. She told me that spiritual initiations are opportunities to understand a deeper level of fear. Initiations are specific levels of spiritual understanding previously hidden by fear.

I must be experiencing a deeper level of fear. This now makes sense to me—the fear in my dream is part of my ordination initiation. But *what* do I fear? It has to do with my identity, I am sure of it. I am going through a lot of changes. Besides ordination, I am pursuing a new career, my friends are changing, my family relationships are shifting, I am considering moving, and then there are always the ongoing minefields of intimacy and sexuality. My life is in a state of flux.

It strikes me as strange that, on one hand, being ordained brings up fear, while on the other hand it alleviates it. Since ordination I feel a sense of responsibility—I must lead a pious life. What a joke that is! Since becoming ordained three weeks ago I have been doing all the things I feel most guilty about, like drinking, eating chocolate, seeking casual sex (which I am finding a challenge at the age of 44) and masturbating (or as Maria, my fellow IF minister, suggested calling it, self-pleasuring). It is as if I am *trying* to prove my unworthiness. However, I don't want to stop doing questionable things just because I am unsure of them; I need to understand on a spiritual level the merits of doing or not doing an action. The truth of an action does not come from ideas or judgments in the mind, but from how the heart resonates with each situation. The heart holds the key to every right action.

As I lie in bed, the frenzied thinking of the dream lingers, causing my mind to dwell on the "what ifs" and the "maybes" of my life. Living in fear of an imaginary future is, at best, a waste of energy, and is usually a recipe for distress. It is vital to focus on the present. "Live in the Moment" has become my mantra, and I can already feel myself calming down as I contemplate this simple statement. It amazes me how quickly my fear dissipates as I focus on the "Now."

How I came to know this stems from the experience I had at the Zen retreat 15 years ago. That experience continues to be one of the most profound and challenging experiences of my life! My fascination with Zen has persisted since that workshop.

At the time I had been living in Campbell River for only six months, and I was struggling to find harmony in my new life. With the initial excitement of my move wearing off, and not yet having made new friends, I felt lonely in my new home. In short, I was in the doldrums, and I was hoping a spiritual infusion would ease my gloom. I sought a similar solution years later when I was feeling down after returning home from living in Korea.

Prior to the workshop, my spiritual interests were varied, and Zen was just one of many practices that held a mild interest for me. Twice I had read Robert Pirsig's book, *Zen and the Art of Motorcycle Maintenance*, but I still didn't understand Zen. I knew it involved meditation, which at the time I was trying to make a consistent part of my life. Also, I knew Zen included studying *Koans* (befuddling statements), but otherwise I was very ignorant of the actual details of the practice. To be honest, the reason I chose the workshop was financial; most of the other ones listed in the spiritual magazine were double the cost of the Zen retreat.

The workshop itself shed light on the practice of Zen, but it also added to my confusion. Some events at the workshop have become pivotal to my life, and not understanding them has driven me to seek an explanation.

Zen retreats are silent—there is no talking allowed—and to emphasize this isolation, one is not even supposed to make eye contact with others. This means the energy that a person normally puts into social interactions (maintaining the self-image we project) is freed to be directed inward. As the workshop progresses, this continuous self-absorption creates an internal tension; one's ego is not comfortable with this intensive self-scrutiny.

Adding to the challenge is the use of Koans. These are puzzling sayings that one is to contemplate during the frequent meditation periods. One of the better-known Koans is, "What is the sound of one hand clapping?" By contemplating Koans, the rational mind is further taxed. When a person gets some insight about a Koan—and it does happen—the Roshi, or Zen master, will evaluate the insight and give guidance for achieving even deeper insights. This will hopefully lead to a *kensho*, or an insight into one's true nature. This is the goal for Zen retreats: to have insights into one's true nature. And many kenshos may lead to a *satori*, which is a full state of Enlightenment. Generally kenshos result from years of devout practice. Zen may offer a direct route to Enlightenment, but it is not an easy shortcut. As the Roshi explained during a lecture, Buddhism is akin to walking on a meandering path up the mountain, and Zen is like climbing straight up the cliff.

At my workshop I had a moment of insight into my true nature, and it came on day five of the seven-day retreat. Prior to that kensho I had had several insights while contemplating Koans, but this particular insight was of a different nature. It was not just an intellectual insight (though intellectual ones can be invigorating); it was a spiritual insight that I understood with my whole being! I had a tingling sensation throughout my body and a feeling of expansion. Later, however, I was disappointed when the Roshi assessed my kensho as a minor one, telling me that there are many on the path to Enlightenment.

The insight I had was about how the current moment I was experiencing related to all other moments, and in realizing this I was able to really enjoy the current moment as an entity in itself. Seeing the moment's relatedness enabled me to experience it in isolation. It was akin to seeing the forest through the trees. This may seem paradoxical, but it is in keeping with Zen's assertion that one does not use the mind to understand one's true nature. This is why Zen is so hard to explain; it is difficult to explain non-cognitive experiences, and kenshos are such understandings.

My kensho was a moment of peaceful joy that I had never felt before. However, the magic of that insight was not a lingering one, and by that night I was again struggling to make sense of my experience at the workshop. The ups and downs I was going through were dramatic, and I was having a hard time coping. I ended up leaving the workshop before it ended, feeling angry and overwhelmed.

Seven years after the event I started to write about my Zen experience because I was still trying to understand it. That retreat continues to be the impetus for my present exploration, and my quest was further stimulated by a holiday in Thailand while I was living in Korea. Buddhism influences Thai society, and the people's attitudes resonated with my ideas about Zen. It was during my idle hours after returning to Canada from Korea (and not long after my holiday in Thailand) that I began writing about the Zen workshop. And during that reflective process I garnered a clearer understanding of "Living in the Moment," inspired by the Thai people's approach to life.

I still don't understand the enlightened concept of everything existing in the *Now* (as Zen says it is not a rational understanding), but at least I can offer a partial explanation, namely the consciousness experiencing the alignment and fluidity of the Energy Bodies.

That initial insight into my true nature at the Zen workshop, and subsequent ones after that, have given me a vague understanding about the heart holding the key to the right actions. The fact that I am not acting in tune with my heart is evident from my dream this morning. However, this doesn't make me a bad person. Judgment Day is more of an internal process, not some god evaluating my life. When I die, a purer part of my consciousness—my soul—will review my life, and it will encounter any stuck energy patterns I have not healed, patterns from issues I haven't resolved. How I behave daily affects my stuck energy patterns, and not god's scorecard. So what is important is how I feel about my actions in the present, because this adds to, or takes away from, my stuck energy patterns.

That's how ordination has relieved my fear—I have a greater sense of trust that I am part of "god." I don't need to be perfect. Rather, all I need to do is to live my life honestly as it unfolds. After all, that's what my ministerial thesis is about: listening to my heart and taking a Zen approach to life, namely, "Live in the Moment."

Now, as I lie in bed this morning, I realize my mind has shifted from the agitated dream-state to one of my "thoughtful" moods. Ideas and feelings come and go, intermingling, sometimes connecting and sometimes not. As this is happening I feel a sense of playfulness and joy. The sound of the rain gently tapping on the window makes my bed feel even more inviting. Warm, cozy and relaxed, I notice that the anxiety from my dream has completely dissipated.

I feel a rush of excitement as I sense that my life is back on its ideal path. It confirms my recent life choices and my current project. If I can write this book, it will validate my life; everything else has been preparing me for this moment. The fact that I haven't followed a simple career path, the fact that I have so little money, the fact that I haven't planned anything for my future... this book can make all that go away. If this book happens, what a testament it will be to creating my own reality! People will stop thinking I am a failure.

That's it! The fear related to my ordination—the initiation fear—it's about letting go of other people's judgments of me. I am letting go of my need for their approval. I am ceasing to define my life through their eyes. Their judgments are *their* stuff; how I let those judgments affect me is *my* stuff. That's what I have control over: me, not them. The rush of excitement surges again! My trains of thought have come together—my ordination, the fear, being more independent, living in the moment, redefining myself—it all fits. An intense, peaceful feeling envelops me as my thoughts become suspended in time.

I relish moments like this when I lie in bed and let my mind wander as I ponder the meaning of life. I could spend hours doing this, but right now I sense I've come to a junction in my thinking. I can stay in bed and let my mind wander some more, or I can get up and start my day. What is required of me today? Nothing pressing, so maybe I'll start writing here in bed instead of doing my usual morning routine and the many other things that fill up my day.

I get up, grab my laptop and return to the warmth of my bed.

Chapter I, cont. (Energy Bodies and Universal Energy)

The most fundamental level of composition of the Energy Bodies is Universal Energy. In fact, each person, their consciousness and all other entities in this world are comprised of Universal Energy. To return to the water analogy, this would be adding another layer of composition to water where the elements at the quantum level would arise from a single type of energy. Science is still developing a unifying theory to explain the basic composition of the universe (one current theory I have read about is the M-theory, an extrapolation of String theories). Science explains that this fundamental energy is more stable in certain formations, or frequencies, and this gives rise to more complicated entities which could explain the development of the four Energy Bodies.

Another name for this fundamental state of energy is the Divine. There is a consciousness or innate intelligence inherent in this Divine Energy, but that intelligence is of a very different nature than mental thoughts. I will expand upon our relationship to the Divine in the next chapter. I believe that

Universal Energy—or the Divine—is the basis for the human concept of God (or gods), which might explain why compassion and love are common themes in most religions; these are ways of trying to describe the fundamental characteristics of Universal Energy.

The perspective I offer—that humans are comprised of four Energy Bodies—is an independent explanation. I am not attempting to do so here, but it may be feasible to integrate this idea with the ancient Indian interpretation of the body as a series of energy centers called *chakras*, as well as with the ancient Chinese view that the body has a network of energy meridians. I think all three interpretations of human-body energy dynamics have merit. Some of my theory is based upon the healer Barbara Brennan's book *Hands of Light*, where she suggests that there are Energy Bodies correlated with each of the seven main chakras in the body. She suggests that the lower three chakras relate to the Physical, Emotional and Mental Bodies, and that the heart chakra relates to the fourth Energy Body. She refers to the top three chakras as spiritual ones. For the sake of simplicity, I have chosen to explain the Heart and Spiritual Bodies as one Energy Body, but my theory could be expanded to incorporate different levels of Spiritual Bodies. I am not attempting a detailed correlation with Ms. Brennan's theory, as there are many significant differences.

To summarize, we can consider ourselves to be composed of four Energy Bodies: the Physical, the Emotional, the Mental and the Spiritual. The Bodies are distinct, yet superimposed and interrelated. Though each one affects the others, the subsequent effects are dependent upon the individual characteristics of each person. The natural state of an Energy Body is fluidity, i.e. its energy moving unrestricted. The Energy Bodies, as well as everything else, can be understood on a fundamental level as being comprised of Universal Energy, alternatively called the

Divine. Universal Energy has an innate consciousness that is sometimes described using the terms "love and compassion."

The feelings generated by this morning's insights, and by my writing, are invigorating. I get up and move around as I contemplate these ideas. As I think, new questions usually arise, but whether I explore them or try to finish my current train of thought depends upon my mood. Today, I am wondering about the nature of the effects between energy bodies. If I am emotionally hurt, what effect can it have on my other bodies? Maybe certain frequencies resonate together, similar to what happens with music. When a disturbance happens on one level— like the emotional body—there is a corresponding frequency in the mental body that is an "octave" higher which resonates with that disturbance.

This seems reasonable. I make a note of it and will think about it later. This train of thought is becoming too complex, and is clouding my thinking. Some fresh air will help clear my mind. I have learned to trust my thinking process; if the ideas are important, then it can be helpful to let them go, knowing they will come back to me later with more clarity.

I quickly wash my face, brush my teeth, grab a banana and head out the door to the mall. One thing on my to-do list today is to pick up some supplies for an upcoming camping trip. I am really looking forward to it.

Chapter 6

Hiking in Bryce Canyon

Wednesday, October 17

There is a loud beeping. I can hear Kim rustling in her sleeping bag as she turns off the alarm. Not yet aware of my surroundings, my only thought is about sleep. Kim and Russ don't seem to be as groggy as I am, because both of them start to get up. Grudgingly I think about getting up as well, but as soon as I feel how cold the air is I snuggle back into my sleeping bag. Kim and Russ are already sitting up and putting on their sweaters and jackets. We were warned that Utah is having an unusually cold fall, and the reality of it is adding to my challenge of pulling myself out of my sleeping bag.

The need to get moving finally begins to take precedence, so I fumble around for my sweater. Russ and Kim are now dressed, and are looking for their toiletries to have a quick freshen up before setting out. Kim is the primary decision-maker for our group, with Russ' and my blessings. She has done her research; she knows the places to go and things to do. She read in a book that watching the sun rise at Bryce Canyon is a must, so in spite of my objections, we are getting up before sunrise. Soon I am following their lead, and I head off to the communal washrooms.

The three of us are camping at Bryce Canyon, Utah, USA. We arrived in the early evening yesterday, having driven from Las Vegas. Like me, Russ and his wife Kim enjoy nature. They have spoken glowingly about their previous hiking trips to Utah, so I jumped at their invitation to go camping with them. It's a great opportunity to explore the state and to spend time together. Russ, of course, is a fellow minister with Inner Focus, and Kim is currently attending the Inner Focus Energy Healing School in Chicago. I know Russ well, and I like Kim, but I have only met her twice before at Inner Focus conferences.

They live in Arkansas and I live in Penticton, Canada, so the plentiful (and cheap) flights to Las Vegas, Nevada made it a sensible meeting place. Nevada borders on Utah. The other reason to meet there was because it is where AlixSandra lives, and she gladly opened her home to us as a base camp for the trip. Spending some time with AlixSandra was a fabulous way to start our holiday together!

In the end I decided to drive to Vegas because I thought it would save us the cost of renting a car. It also makes it practical for me to do some extra camping after Kim and Russ return to Arkansas, since they could only take a few days off work. Upon hearing that I was planning a trip to Utah, several friends asked me if I was going to Moab City, which I found out is a Mecca for mountain bikers. So I decided that, if I drove my car, I could bring my mountain bike, leave it at AlixSandra's and then pick it up again later. My plan is to spend a few days biking in Moab after I drive Kim and Russ back to Las Vegas.

The sky now has that predawn glow, so we must hurry to get to the canyon in time to see the sunrise. The campsite is on a plateau above the canyon, and it is a five-minute walk to the edge of the cliffs. When we emerge from the trees we see twenty or thirty people spread out around one particular outcropping. Kim informs us this is Sunrise Point, and it is reputed to be the ideal location to watch the rising of the sun. The sun is creeping up over the horizon as we find an open place to sit behind a low railing. The sliver of sun exposed over the distant mountains is a brilliant red, and it is glowing radiantly!

Bryce Canyon is famous for its hoodoos, which are unusual rock formations, pillars and outcroppings that rise up from the bottom of the canyon and tower five hundred feet above the canyon floor. The focal point of the canyon is a gentle arc of hoodoos and vertical cliffs that span about a mile. It is almost a sheer drop from the edge of the plateau to the valley floor. The cliff walls and hoodoos have numerous ridges and contours that form unusual shapes because of the unique composition of the earth in this valley. The exposed walls are layered with different types of stone, which appear as horizontal stripes along their vertical surfaces. It looks as if an architect has layered several different colors of rock on top of each other and then cut out the most unusual shapes to form the canyon. Earlier, Kim had informed me that thousands of years ago a huge plateau traversed what is now four states: Utah, New Mexico, Colorado and Arizona. With time, nature carved this massive plateau into many unique and spectacular canyons, one of which is the Grand Canyon, and Bryce is another.

As the sunrays strike the wall, each layer of rock takes on a different hue. The colors range from a rich, rusty red to a lustrous white. The glowing effect of these shimmering colors is awe-inspiring, and not a word is uttered by the many folks sitting on the edge of the canyon. I suspect the others feel as I do, awed by the splendor of nature. How could such beauty happen by chance? Such grandeur suggests intent by a creator! As an *idea*, I question whether this splendor implies a creator, but as a *feeling* this is exactly how I react.

The most dramatic effects last for about ten minutes, and then the increasing brightness of the sun bleaches away the drama of the varying colors. As the intensity of the moment fades, several of the other people wander off, most likely to get some breakfast, or possibly more sleep. Russ, Kim and I have a stilted discussion, but it is futile to try to describe the vision we have just shared. I thank Kim for making us get up at such an "ungodly" hour. Both of them understand the intended pun, the implication that these few moments could be a great example of God's magic. After a few more minutes of sitting, Kim and Russ decide to go back to the campsite. I decline the offer to join them; I would like a few moments of solitude to let my mind reflect.

The rocks of varying colors still make a wonderful sight, but they no longer have the glowing effects caused by the rising sun. The lingering feeling of euphoria encourages my mind to wander, and I know that spending time with Russ and Kim is adding to that feeling.

Strangely enough, watching the two of them interact reminds me of my parents. My thoughts turn to my mother. Of her four sons, I seem to be most connected to my mother, and I know one of my issues is my emotional enmeshment with her. This is partly because of our personalities, but it was also heightened by my father's emotional distance. I can remember times when I was a child, and my mother would be resting in bed, feeling overwhelmed by life, and I would sit and talk with her. I don't know what we talked about, but I'm sure it was my company that was helpful to her. She was a social worker, and was too easily caught up in the drama of her clients' lives. This left her feeling weighed down at times. I am sure coping with four sons added greatly to her challenges, but of course, at the time I couldn't see that part of it.

My intense emotional nature is like my mother's, and we share a compassion for others, but I get my desire to be different from my father. That sense of independence came in handy during periods of my childhood when I felt isolated. Unfortunately, it has also encouraged me to suppress the emotional part of myself. To allow the emotional side of my nature to resurface has taken years of hard work. I think the tension created by this internal conflict has been a main contributor to my disease, and helps explain why my health has improved as I have grown emotionally.

Everyone doesn't start out in life with the same capacities and tendencies, so there is no reason to think we should all have the same aspirations; but somehow I am convinced that our emotional state is fundamental. My thinking may be a reflection of my intense emotional constitution, but I believe our spiritual identity is directly connected to our emotions. We are all born into the physical world as emotionally centered beings, and the primacy of these emotions remains in spite of the later development of our mental bodies.

And so, when watching an awe-inspiring event like the sun rising on Bryce Canyon, we react to it in an emotional way. But it is even more than that—our emotional bodies become integrated with our spiritual bodies. Pure emotional experiences are Divine experiences, no matter how one chooses to understand the Divine. Our emotional bodies are our consciousness' door to the spiritual realm, and I think my emotional connection with my mother blurs the view I have through my own door. I am affected by her emotions. If I were not so enmeshed with her then I could have more compassion for her personal struggles rather than have them affect my well-being. Presently, her feelings often trigger me; I don't react independently of her emotional states.

Conversely, my bond with my father is one of longing, a desire to be more connected. It is a void in me that I hope he can fill. It is a false hope, however, because we are responsible for meeting our own needs. It is great to have loved ones, but at a deeper level, we are individuals. Others can help us by being supportive, but they also help us because we are easily triggered by them, and this in turn provides opportunities for us to heal. And paradoxically, it is when we achieve our full independence that we understand the interconnectedness of everyone and the world. However, at this stage it is not an emotional connectedness—it is a spiritual one.

As the sun continues to rise the temperature does as well, so I take off my jacket. Suddenly I realize that I am hungry. My reverie and subsequent reflections have subsided, so now I am ready to get on with the rest of my day. I will see what plans Kim has for today, but I'm already sure it will be hiking in the canyon. I get up and start walking back to the campground. My heart is warm; I am communing with nature and enjoying the company of some dear friends. For me that is as blessed as it gets.

Three days later we are now camping at the mouth of Zion Canyon in central Utah. The three of us spent the day exploring the grandeur of Zion, though the weather consisted of intermittent showers and sun. What makes Zion so spectacular is not the shape of the walls—they are almost flat—but the sheer vertical magnitude of them. They are expansive rock faces that rise 3,000 feet into the sky, culminating in sharp peaks. The names of some of these peaks are the Three Wise Men, the Weeping Rock and the Watchman. The river at the base of the canyon that carved these spectacles of nature is called the Virgin River. These names reflect the religious zeal of the Mormons that settled in the valley a hundred and fifty years ago. Religious or not, there is no avoiding the awe-inspiring feeling one feels as they gaze up at these giants!

In spite of it being late fall and the weather not ideal, the campsite is more than half-full. I can't help but notice a very attractive young woman settling in to the campsite next to us. She appears to be traveling alone, except for her dog. As she gets her temporary home set up, Kim, Russ and I go about our business of preparing dinner. We exchange a few friendly comments with our temporary neighbor. She asks about firewood, and we tell her none is available in the campsite, but that we bought some in town. I kindly invite her to join us later when we start our fire, and I am happy she accepts.

After cooking a simple but tasty dinner, Kim, Russ and I sit down for an enjoyable evening of relaxing by the fire. A little later, the woman and her dog join us. The dog is a chocolate Lab, and I can tell it is a skittish yet fierce animal, overprotective of its owner while being shy of strangers.

The obligatory introductory questions are asked. Her name is Karen, and she is en route to Colorado to do some advance scouting in preparation for moving there. She is single, a nurse by trade, but also a ski fanatic; thus, her desire to move to Colorado. My impression of Karen is of a charming, intelligent and independent woman. She accepts my offer of a drink and chooses beer; I am having vodka and grapefruit juice.

The casual conversation continues while we enjoy the ambiance of the fire. Soon, Karen asks us about our jobs. Russ is a chiropractor and Kim is a nurse, so professionally, the three of them have a lot in common. Russ and Kim are surprised when I say I am a writer. I don't want to mislead any of them, so I explain that this is a new ambition of mine and that I want to start the process of making it a reality. A good first step in creating reality is to "own" the desire, meaning one must act as if it is true. The flip side is that it is not good to talk a lot about the book because that can dissipate the energy from it. As the conversation continues, I divulge that Russ and I have recently been ordained. Similarly, part of my intent is to "own" this role, but I also hope it reassures Karen that she is safe with us. In the dim light of the fire it is hard to see her reaction. I realize this may frighten her as she may have visions of us as cult fanatics. Russ is a tall but kindly-looking man, and I hope it puts her at ease to know he is married. My personal hope is that she is attracted to me. Regardless, her dog is sitting attentively by her side to protect her should she feel threatened.

The evening has been pleasant, but ends as Karen, Kim and Russ decide it is time to call it a night. I had a faint hope that I might have some carnal company in bed, but it is not to be. Since there is more space at this campsite, I am sleeping in my own tent. I easily let go of any disappointment as I am happy with an evening of pleasant conversation and companionship. Rather than going to bed, however, I prefer to stay up and let my mind wander while gazing into the fire. Soon after, I mix myself another drink and get my Discman (I am resisting advancements in technology such as MP3 players and smartphones). It is a compelling combination of elements: sitting alone by the fire, feeling the spiritual inspiration of Zion Canyon, having a drink and listening to music (a favorite is an English band named

Coldplay and more recently Muse has become another). The desire to dance and emote spurs me into action. I quickly douse the remnants of the fire in preparation for a midnight walk. There is a trail that meanders through the flats of the valley floor, inviting me to revel in the mystic energy of the night. Soon I am walking, listening to music and sporadically breaking into dance, all the while reveling in the glory of my good fortune.

As I walk, the moon starts to peek over the tops of the mountains. The moon is late in rising here because it takes time to climb over the towering mountains. Minutes later I am amazed to see the moon is full, leading me to think some spiritually wise part of me—or God—is orchestrating an evening of mythical proportions. I continue singing and dancing as I stroll along the moonlit path at the mouth of Zion Canyon.

Not surprisingly, foremost on my mind is God. My recent ordination, and being in a valley with such religious overtones, sparks many strong emotions in me. My sense of being on a spiritual mission returns, and I remind myself that all I need to do is allow the magic to unfold. I don't need to make things happen, I just need to surrender to the process. Attempts to control events will inhibit the natural sequence rather than speed them along. My desire to find a purpose in my life has been instrumental in getting me to this point, but now that I have gotten to a place where my path is becoming clear, any new intent on my part will be based on fear and not wisdom. My ordination is teaching me about my fears: fear of change, fear of succeeding and fear of the unknown. These fears propel my personality to interfere with my soul's mission, with God's mission. My personality wants me to play it safe; it wants to protect me from being hurt, but it doesn't understand the suffering that comes from not living a full life. Taking risks and getting hurt allows for a richer, more joyous life. If while being hurt I can simultaneously connect with an old pain, then I have an opportunity to heal, and when I am healed I can have a greater appreciation of the present. This is counter to the personality's desire for safety and control.

I have reached the emotive phase of my evening ritual. As thoughts flow through my mind I periodically cry, but soon after I am laughing. The laughter expresses a connection with wisdom beyond my mind, knowing that in surrendering, I am living. The crying acknowledges my fears, releasing them so they don't inhibit my connection to the joy available in every moment. I continue this emoting for about thirty minutes until I feel the intensity of the process wane.

Unfortunately I am too drunk to really be grounded, and releasing my emotions has left me feeling drained. I turn off my music, sit down on a rock and let the silence envelop me. The silence is gradually replaced by the soothing sounds of nature: the breeze gently whistling in my ear, the soft rippling of the water from the distant river, the buzzing of an insect as it flies aimlessly by. Now that I am focusing on the present, I can feel the wind caress my face. I shiver slightly as the cool, moist air penetrates my clothing. These sensations bring me back to my reality. I am camping in Zion Canyon, and tomorrow, Russ, Kim and I are planning an ascent of one of the higher mountain trails. It will be a substantial climb, and if I don't get some sleep I won't be able to enjoy the hike. I head back to the campground, feeling elated but exhausted.

It was a welcome and intense release of emotions tonight, but I think the alcohol makes it an unnatural process rather than a true healing one. It feels like I pushed the stuck emotions out, and the effort of *pushing* means the complementary inflow of light was limited.

Back at the campsite I crawl into my tent. Now I am glad to have my illusions of solitude. I quickly fall asleep.

Chapter 7

A Job Interview

Tuesday, October 30

I feel lost, uncertain, confused. Actually, I don't know what I am feeling. Or is it that I feel so *much* that I can't sort it out? One thing I do know is that I feel like curling up in bed. Usually I like interviews, so why do I feel so strange after this one? I had done a reasonable job of communicating my background and how my skills fit the position; after all, I have previous experience as a job coach. The plan was to go bike riding afterwards, and so my bike and a change of clothes are in the car. I am in Kelowna, the bigger city an hour's drive up the lake, and there are reputed to be some great mountain bike trails here. But it is one of those cold, fall mornings where winter isn't far away, and my motivation to go is missing. However, it isn't because of the cold that I won't go riding; the coldness just reinforces my reluctance.

Is my muddled state because I don't really want the job in the first place? My vague plan was to allow myself six months of non-employment so I could write my book. After that I would find employment again—that is, if I *needed* to work given my blossoming writing career (ha! ha!). Currently I collect unemployment insurance (actually now called employment insurance; some bureaucrat's idea of putting a positive spin on being unemployed). Since I voluntarily left my old job, it was questionable if I would qualify for insurance. My argument to them was that the job itself was changing, and as a result I didn't really quit, I just wasn't as qualified. I think the real reason I am allowed to collect is because my manager told them my job was extremely stressful (several other staff at the agency have taken stress leaves).

Having passed that hurdle, a condition of collecting

employment insurance is that I look for work, but my heart is not into it. There is also money pressure because my landlady told me my rent would be going up next month. That will make it even harder to make ends meet.

As for my new, ideal career, it has only been three and a half months since I left my job, but I have to admit I have done very little writing in that time. I have started the book, but I have mostly been making notes. The instructor who taught the short writing course I took was right; she said six months is not enough time to write a book. One idea I had was to work in Japan if I still needed employment after six months, but at this point Japan looks like a dream rather than an option. I have applied for numerous jobs there via the Internet, but I am not getting any positive responses.

My mind returns to reflecting on today's job interview. This is the first interview I've had since my ordination and since getting my tattoo, so I'm still trying to figure out what to say about them. In my resume I note having a master's degree of ministerial studies, but I am reluctant to use the term "ordained" with it. I qualify the term "master's degree" by adding that it was issued by a non-registered educational organization (though Inner Focus Church is legally qualified to ordain ministers). As for the tattoo, I was surprised how little I thought about it during the interview. Even when it did pop into my mind, I didn't feel embarrassed by it.

As usual, the first question at the interview was, "Tell us a little about yourself." I could have just held up my hand in response, and that would have been a good answer. Having "Live in the Moment" emblazoned on my hand speaks volumes. I chose to take the conventional route and gave a conventional answer without mentioning the tattoo. I thought I would explain it when asked about my management style, but to my surprise, they never asked that question. So, in the end, I didn't mention my tattoo or my ordination. Maybe it is just because it is so new to me that I am expecting others to make more of it than is reasonable.

Part of the angst I feel is because I got so little response from them; I was having a hard time reading them. I've told my stories and anecdotes many times, and people have always been impressed. But the interviewers today didn't even react to my Life Skills Instructor story, and that's always been my ace in the hole, my guaranteed-to-impress story.

That sequence of events takes place when I was living in Campbell River and had been unemployed for many months (a regular occurrence in my life). I enrolled in a government-sponsored Life Skills Instructor Course (six months, part-time, two evenings a week and plus a full day on Saturdays). In this case the term "life skills" refers to cognitive life skills, such as communication, anger management, conflict resolution, assertiveness and self-esteem. It was near the middle of the course when I applied for a job with the John Howard Society in a specialized group home for young sex offenders. I sent in my application before Christmas, then went to visit my parents in Penticton for the holidays. When I returned, I had a message from the John Howard Society. They told me the society was starting a new program, and, having seen my application for the group home position, were wondering if I would be interested in applying for this new program.

The following day was Tuesday and I called them back and was asked to come in for an interview on Wednesday. This new program was working with young offenders (but not sex offenders) in a wilderness camp. Once the interview was completed, I was immediately offered a position. In fact, I was given a choice of positions: a youth worker, a recreation coordi-nator or a life skills instructor. Although I was still in the middle of my training, I was ecstatic about the opportunity to work as a life skills instructor.

They were pleased and wanted me to start the job the next

day, Thursday. It turned out the program was to co-facilitated by two people, and we only had two days to prepare the curriculum for the first batch of incarcerated youth who would be arriving at the camp on the upcoming Monday. The program was a wilderness residential camp where ten youths from jails around the province were sent for four weeks of training. The core of the program was the Life Skills Course, to be taught five hours a day, five days a week.

Obviously that first month was very chaotic, and the stress of it was more than the other instructor was willing to deal with, so she quit. The second month and second batch of ten kids was just as chaotic. Being short one instructor, I worked with several other people the society managed to free up from other programs they were operating. Each day I had a different instructor with whom to co-facilitate.

It is important to realize that with this type of life skills education, it is imperative that one component fits with the other components. For example, the ideas introduced in the communication segment need to be consistent with the ideas used in conflict resolution, where communication is crucial. The challenge was that each instructor I worked with had his or her own style and ideas about life skills. My job was to try to bring all these different ideas into an integrated, whole approach. Meanwhile, I was doing my best just to survive the stress of the job, let alone be an overseer of the curriculum. Managing ten incarcerated youth with no significant security measures—except that we were isolated in the woods—was very stressful!

All this was made even more difficult because I was still taking my training course and hadn't yet formulated my *own* ideas about how to prioritize and integrate the components into a cohesive package. The course wasn't just teaching us how to *instruct* a life skills course, it was requiring us to develop a curriculum too. It provided the components, but how they fit into an integrated program was part of the vision we were developing over time.

The third batch of kids was easier because the society managed to borrow one of the other life skills instructors for the whole month. The two of us worked as a team for that month while the society continued the process of trying to hire a new, permanent instructor, which they finally managed to do after the third month.

The newly hired person, Lorne, was a wonderful individual who taught me in areas where I needed to grow, and he turned out to be another one of those influential people who seem to come into my life on a regular basis. Lorne was the person with whom I had the amazing jamming session after a year of having worked together. Professionally, Lorne taught me much about understanding group dynamics and experiential learning, but on a more personal level he also taught me about integrity and taking responsibility for my own feelings. One cannot work in such an intense environment so closely with another person and not be changed by it. Lorne and I were both changed for the better because of the bond we developed. He was a great friend and source of support for the two and a half years I worked at the jail program. However, because our work together was so intense, we didn't spend a lot of our free time together.

The program also afforded me the opportunity to develop my own vision for the Life Skills program. Lorne gave me full rein over the details of the curriculum, which I chose to build around assertiveness. I envisioned all the other components supporting this overarching theme. To me, assertiveness is acting in a manner that focuses on respecting oneself while still being respectful to others. Communication, conflict resolution etc., when done well, reflect an assertive attitude.

About a year into the program, when the core staff had been established and the Life Skills curriculum had evolved into a coherent model, I became elated with my job. At that point I remember reflecting on the university aptitude test that indicated that my ideal career was a religious leader; I thought life skills was my religion—empowering lost youth with knowledge that could change their lives. It was the first time in my life that I had a sense of being in the right place at the right time. This was what I was meant to do with my life. Previous jobs had left me feeling as though they were a means to get to where I was going, but some mysterious and vague destination was my priority, not the jobs themselves. Working as a life skills instructor was a reprieve from my persistent sensation of *searching*.

Yet, in spite of the determination, perseverance and courage I demonstrated in that job, today's interviewers simply moved on to the next question after hearing my story. Usually, the people on the other side of the table come out of *interview mode* to acknowledge on a personal level that my accomplishments with the John Howard Society were impressive.

Is that it? Was I looking for their approval in the interview and I didn't get it? Now I am starting to get a sense of what I am feeling—I feel vulnerable. That's why I want to curl up, I want to get into the fetal position. Of course! An interview is about letting people know about myself, and I was pretty open and honest. The way the interview game is played, I'm supposed to paint a rosy picture of myself… but I guess I don't play that game so well anymore. In the interview, I was pretty direct about who I *really* am, rosy or not. That is what the tattoo does for me: it makes me accountable to *myself*. I have to be open; I can no longer hide the real me behind my persona.

With this realization, my body relaxes and my sense of internal turmoil has lessened. I still feel sensitive and fragile, but at least I know what I feel and why I feel it. I had opened myself up to those people and didn't get much compassion in return. I guess I have more personal work to do on not seeking approval from others.

As I relax, a bigger picture comes to mind, and I ask myself,

"Would taking this job be selling out?" I even called myself a writer when I was chatting with that girl earlier this fall on the camping trip. On the other hand, is it a coincidence that the job starts in January, which is when my self-imposed six-month writing period ends? Is some synchronicity happening here?

However, I know there's no chance I will have my book done by then. I let these thoughts go. What is more important right now is taking care of *me*.

After driving home, I go directly to bed. An hour later I get up from my nap and realize that I feel quite joyful. I have a sense of empowerment! I showed those interviewers who I really am, and I survived! It took courage to be my true self, so who cares whether they liked me or not? It's their loss if they don't hire me. If it is meant to be, then I will be offered the job, but I suspect my life is going in a different direction.

Now I should do some writing.

Chapter II: Zen and Enlightenment

As mentioned in the previous chapter, Universal Energy is the fundamental component of everything that exists. To understand the nature of Universal Energy, I suggest we consider Zen, an adaptation of Buddhist practices. Zen originated in China, and then migrated to Japan around the 14th century where it evolved into an influential spiritual practice. Three main schools of Zen evolved in Japan using somewhat varying methods for obtaining enlightenment.

I refrain from calling Zen a religion because it differs from most religions in some key respects. It has neither prophets nor sacred texts, and it does not proclaim any specific beliefs about the nature of existence. In short, it is a method and not a belief system. Though Zen does postulate Enlightenment, it makes no attempt to incorporate it into a structured analysis of existence, such as heavens, deities or rules of conduct. In spite of not being governed by rules of social conduct, Zen students tend to be very conscientious people. Zen posits Enlightenment as an attainable state, and provides a means for achieving it, but the methods offered are merely a means to an end. Although the practices have proven to be successful—as well as very arduous—there is no claim that they come from a Divine source. Zen ideology would not deny that there are other means of attaining Enlightenment, such as the more traditional Buddhist practices, but they are not nearly as efficient. Nevertheless, Enlightenment doesn't occur without the intent to make it happen.

In Zen writings, it is said that Enlightenment is an "understanding" of one's true nature, but this is not the common interpretation of understanding. Enlightenment is a state that transcends the rational mind. Ideas cannot describe the state because it is a non-cognitive state. In fact, Zen asserts that the rational mind inhibits enlightenment. The Zen practice of contemplating *Koans*—befuddling statements—is a practice that, in part, exhausts the rational mind, which then allows one to have insights into one's true nature.

To explain this, I suggest that our minds are conditioned to think in terms of language, which in turn imposes interpretations upon the external world. One is conditioned to interpret the external world in order to create an understanding of it; however, this mental understanding is limited by the very nature of the ideas it uses. For example, it is said the Inuit people of Northern Canada have about 40 different words for snow. They see qualities in snow that people from warmer climates don't see. Having words to describe things means people can look for those qualities. If we only have the word "snow," then we don't look beyond the initial impression of snow. Having the appropriate language prompts us to see the snow differently, and a lack of language prompts us to gloss over the finer details. Hence, language shapes our world.

Another example highlighting the difference between thought and understanding is intuition. This is a form of non-cognitive understanding; one is said to know something, but lacks a rational process for coming to this conclusion. Nature is abundant with examples, such as birds or fish returning to their places of birth without the mental capacity to know the details of their journey. Non-cognitive understanding is also related to many of our internal states. These states are understood either via experiential or spiritual learning. For example, words can only imitate the quality of emotional sensations or of the faculty of taste; internally, we have a much richer understanding of them. Another prime example is describing the sexual experience; words do not adequately convey the experience (though there is no shortage of words on the subject). One is to use this nonintellectual understanding when experiencing the true nature of Universal Energy; when fully understood, it is Enlightenment.

That's enough for today. As I put my computer away I decide to go for a bike ride after all. I feel more energetic now, and the coolness of the morning has eased. I quickly make a sandwich (with rice bread) and, after eating, get out my bike and head for the door.

Chapter 8

Don't Sweat Change; Moving

Thursday, November 8

There are three piles: things I am keeping, things I am discarding and things I haven't decided if I am keeping or discarding. Items move from one pile to the next and back again. However, I am pleased that the discard pile has a significant amount of junk in it; I am a bit of a pack rat.

I am sorting because of my sudden decision to move, in part because I don't want to pay higher rent, but also as part of my personal transformation. I am embarking on a new career and trying to formalize a plan for my ministry, so changing my home will help spur that process along. I know that if I follow my heart, circumstances will fall into place that will help me move forward. For example, it is good fortune that I am able to collect employment insurance even though I quit my old job. I have until the end of the month before I need be out of this suite. Most of my stuff will be put into storage. Where I will live is still undecided, but my sense is that it will be a temporary home. I have continued applying for jobs in Japan, and though nothing has happened yet, I'm sure an opportunity will present itself eventually.

It is great to have time to casually sort through all the stuff I have collected over the years. It gives me a chance to reminisce when items bring up fond memories. I am also surprised at some of the items I've hung onto; what was I thinking? Why have I kept old watches that don't work or broken video games? Not only am I discarding things, but I am clearing the stuck emotions associated with some of them. I am making space in my life for new things and more joy. For example, my report cards from elementary and high school are a link to those troubled times, and I don't need to hang onto them anymore. There is a part of me that thinks these report cards have sentimental value, but I recognize this as ego and fear of moving forward.

Without the negative emotional attachments of the report cards, I can admit their sentimental value is minimal. It is similar to looking at a car accident. We know it is unpleasant, but we look anyway. Hanging on to old pain can be comforting, such as using it to justify feeling sorry for myself. I can tell myself the world is conspiring against me and I am helpless to change it. It is not that I'm trying to erase my memory of those times; rather, I am trying to heal that part of myself. Once healed, the memories will be just memories, and not triggers to stuck emotions. Back then I was an emotionally injured person, and that is not how I see myself now.

Next I pick up some photographs of old girlfriends from the "keep" pile. I want to think about them again. They have moved from one pile to another more than once. Part of me says I should throw them out, but I want to be clear about my reasons for throwing them out. Why are they different from other pictures I am keeping? Just like the other pictures they chronicle a chapter in my life.

The problem is that these particular ones resulted in two explosive situations in the past, each when my girlfriend of the time saw pictures of old flames. Were their reactions simply because they were the jealous type, or did they have justifiable reasons for having a strong reaction? There is no question they really were irrationally jealous people, but blaming me for their pain was not likely to get the response they really wanted, namely the assurance that I loved them, and not some old girlfriend.

What I was really expecting of my old girlfriends was for them to be vulnerable, but I wasn't exactly willing to go there myself; we were both stuck playing out old patterns. That is one reason I want a new relationship: I want to know if I can be more vulnerable now. Can all the healing work I've done pay off? Now I see vulnerability in a different light: it is the key to transforming old pains and the door to a happier life. The pictures go in to the undecided pile.

As I continue sorting, I come across a certificate that Lorne gave me. The certificate was part of our year-end staff party where we gave each other acknowledgements of appreciation. The one Lorne gave me simply says: "Thanks for Being." The certificate brings back many fond memories.

As I reflect on it, one of the most amazing aspects of that job was the sweat lodge. It is common to use this Native American ceremony in jails, both for youths and adults, and our camp had a sweat lodge on the property. The office manager of the John Howard Society in the neighboring city was First Nations. His name was Wedlidi Speck, and he was a very spiritual man. Once a month he came to our program and conducted a sweat ceremony for our youth. I also had the privilege of participating in sweat ceremonies at his home sweat lodge, and they were enriching experiences for me. Plus I had previously participated in a few sweats through other connections with the Native community in Campbell River, so I have some familiarity with these ceremonies and a deep appreciation for them.

Unfortunately for our program, Wedlidi was a busy man, and on a couple of occasions he canceled the sweat ceremonies at the last minute. It was a big disappointment for our kids, and these youths did not handle disappointment well. We eventually sought out another Native leader to run our sweats, but we encountered some complications in getting that set up. In the end Lorne and I took over, offering our own version of a sweat. Our styles were quite different (his was casual and mine was serious), and soon I assumed sole responsibility for conducting our quasi-sweats.

It was important to me that I tell the youths this was not a traditional, Native sweat. I am not a Native and I have no formal training in conducting sweats. However, I drew upon my spiritual knowledge and offered the participants a healing ceremony. Mind you, this was before my healing school training, but still after some profound spiritual experiences, including the one at the Zen retreat.

Our program's sweat lodge was located in a clearing in the woods and was made of thin tree trunks arching across a fourteen-foot circle (4.2 meters). Cloth, old carpet and plastic were draped over the structure to make a thick covering. Historically, sweat lodges were covered with animal hides, but this is not practical now. The entrance also had a covering that was dropped down when everyone was inside. The height of the lodge was roughly five feet (under 2 meters) at the center, but less around the edges where the participants sat, which meant one almost had to crawl to move around.

There was a pit in the ground in the center of the lodge where glowing, hot rocks were placed. The rocks were heated in a fire that was started earlier that morning for the afternoon ceremony. Covering the ground around the pit were cedar boughs, which are what everyone sat on during the ceremony. For all the sweats I attended, people wore shorts, and a T-shirt if desired. Once everyone was inside and the doorway was covered, it was completely dark except for the slight orange glow from the hot rocks in the pit.

My ceremonies consisted of three rounds. A round is when all the participants sit inside for an unspecified length of time while some formal proceedings are conducted, and then everyone exits the lodge as new hot rocks are added for the next round. Once everyone is inside and the proceedings have begun, the rocks are doused with water at significant moments — usually every minute or so. The water is instantly vaporized and the stifling steam rises to the top of the dome. The hot, moist air gathers at the top and then slowly descends as it displaces the cooler air below. I always loved the sensation of a cloud of steam inching its way down my body. The periodic dousing of the rocks continues for ten to fifteen minutes, by which time the rocks have lost most of their heat. After a round's proceedings, everyone leaves for a short break while the lodge is prepped for the next round with new hot rocks.

For my sweats, each round was dedicated to some positive influence in our lives. It was optional for participants to express their thoughts aloud or to have a silent experience. Round one was for honoring the earth. I would ask the participants to think of something positive that either the earth or society had given them. The youth were always respectful of our prior request to not mention drugs. Round two was to honor people who had helped us in some way, and round three was to honor ourselves.

The seriousness with which the youth participated always impressed me; even youth that presented behavioral challenges throughout the program were appropriate during the sweat. The sweat lodge was frequently noted as the highlight in the course evaluations that all our residents filled out at the end of their four weeks. It was an honor to be able to offer a healing ceremony to a group of people facing many challenges in their lives. The significance of it didn't occur to me until later, but it was a place where I showed my vulnerability, and in doing so, I received many benefits as well.

This is why I feel it is a luxury to have time to sort through my things. I can reminisce about many wonderful experiences and let go of the not-so-wonderful ones. This isn't living in the moment, but that's OK. Often during the process I feel truly blessed, and I make an effort to stop and acknowledge this feeling when it arises.

Enough sorting—I am now in the mood to write. I file the certificate from Lorne in the "keep" pile and then grab my laptop.

Chapter II, cont. (Zen and Enlightenment)

To relate non-cognitive understanding to the Energy Body model, ideas are a tool used by the Mental Body to categorize experiences, but the ideas themselves are neither primary nor natural. Thoughts are pre-cognitive, but they become ideas when language is used to interpret them. Ideas are energy patterns which then become crystallized into beliefs and are stored in the Mental Energy Body or the mind. However, beliefs are not part of a fluid Mental Energy Body. In making thoughts into beliefs, we are "believing" that the ideas describe some permanent aspect of the world. This process conditions us to use language to interpret the world, but in truth, this is how our mind inhibits our understanding of our true nature.

To become Enlightened, one must experience the fluidity of the Mental Body, along with the other Energy Bodies, as one transcends language, beliefs and the Bodies' separation. A fully Enlightened person understands the common, daily interpretation of the world as a contrived separation of Universal Energy. The perceived separations are not intrinsic; they are *created* in order to achieve a different experience of the Divine. Our common view of the world as separate entities is an ignorant experience, but a learning one nonetheless. The value of the exercise is in going from being ignorant to becoming Enlightened. (Further explanation of the relevance of these separations is given in Chapters III and V.)

A non-thinking state of being is when one's consciousness is connected with only the fluid parts of the Energy Bodies, though some blockages can still be present. In an Enlightened state we are connected to all parts of the Energy Bodies, and they contain no blockages. Zen trains its students to "Live in the Moment," which is the process of connecting with the four Energy Bodies. This means having one's complete awareness focused on the task at hand, and not daydreaming or contemplating other ideas. This practice leads to compassion and

69

wisdom, rather than an accumulation of concepts of the world (thoughts vs. knowledge).

I appreciate that it is hard to think of the earth and the universe as contrived separation, but then, science is confronted with the same conundrum when trying to understand the origins of the universe. If modern science's String theory is correct, and there was some kind of big bang, how did it come about? Science has come up with some pretty wild ideas to answer this question, such as 10-dimensional space, or an almost infinite number of universes or the idea that our world is on part of a membrane of a multi-braned universe.

The fallacy of time and separation is not easy to accept, but to emphasize the invented nature of time I refer to the highly respected physicist and cosmologist Andreas Albrecht. In his book *About Time*, Adam Frank quotes Albrecht, "In quantum cosmology you have to decide which part of the equations describes time, explains Albrecht." And then Frank describes Albrecht's research, "The choice turns out to be arbitrary... In essence, the description of 'things' such as balls, rulers and elemental particles are exactly what scientists call the laws of nature. To his surprise and horror, Albrecht found that both time *and* the laws of nature rested on an ambiguous and arbitrary choice." (*About Time*, Adam Frank, p. 307) So when talking about the nature of the universe and the mathematical equations used by scientists to describe it, time is not a fixed idea. It seems unscientific to think that all this uncertainty has no bearing on our day-to-day lives.

To summarize, Zen is a spiritual practice that provides a few methods for obtaining Enlightenment, which is a non-cognitive understanding of one's true nature. I equate this understanding of our true nature with the experience of Universal Energy. Language imposes concepts upon our innate experience of the world, and when these concepts become adopted as beliefs, they are crystallized energy patterns in the Mental Body or

70

mind. These crystallized thoughts impose a subjective influence on our perception of the world, and thus alter our experience. Conversely, language is nonexistent in the state of Enlightenment, and one is aware of the full fluidity of the Energy Bodies as well as the contrived nature of their separation.

Having done some sorting, and now having done some writing, it feels like a productive day. Taking care of my well-being by doing some exercise would turn it into a great day. However, I will leave that for later as my need for food is more urgent—I am famished.

Chapter 9

A Sign of Things to Come; Another Interview

Tuesday, December 4

I feel very confident about this upcoming interview, not only because I am well prepared, but also because I feel a sense of destiny about the whole situation. After months of applying for jobs in Japan, it is hard to believe one might actually materialize! This does not seem like me creating my reality; I feel *drawn* to Japan. I sense it is meant to be significant to my writing career. Historically, Japan is the heartland of Zen, so there is that connection, but I also feel that the culture there will be influential to my writing.

Adding to this sense of destiny is this strange sensation I have while riding the rapid transit train. It feels like I am already in Japan, or at least in Asia. Vancouver is so much more multicultural now than during my youth, so it is not surprising that I am sitting among all Asian people on the train. As I look out the window, the scene is mostly trees and bushes, which could be many places in the world. There's nothing in my immediate view that distinguishes it as Vancouver, so for some reason I can't help thinking I am already in Japan. It is a strange sensation, and an exciting one.

I soon get off the train (which becomes a subway when you enter downtown Vancouver) and take the escalator up to street level. Today's interview is for an organization called Peppy Kids Club. It didn't seem to have much of a reputation; I found little written about it on the Internet. I did find one submission by a Peppy teacher responding to someone's query about the interview process. The teacher said the interview was basic, and the most important things were to smile a lot and to show that you can have fun with kids. My year of teaching English in Korea gives me confidence; I know I can be an effective teacher and work well with children.

I turn the corner and start walking the few blocks toward the building where the interview is being held. As I walk, a memory is sparked—a significant stage in my spiritual journey comes to mind. I had walked along this road while I attended a workshop in Vancouver, a workshop where the seed was planted for my spiritual mission. It was ten years ago, and at that time I was living in Campbell River on Vancouver Island. I had come to the big city for a two-day workshop called "Connecting with Your Higher Self." I had heard about the course (and its facilitator, AlixSandra) from Marcy, who was an acquaintance of mine, and who happened to be close friends with AlixSandra. Marcy and I lived on Quadra Island—a ten-minute ferry ride from Campbell River—and had become casual friends, meeting occasionally at local events. Our interests were similar, particularly nature and spirituality.

The Higher Self workshop was interesting, but not particularly eventful for me. However, for a couple of the participants it was a very intense experience. During the workshop, these students went through some strange internal episode where they were totally self-absorbed for close to an hour. As things progressed, the rest of us watched as AlixSandra guided them through an energy transformation process. She informed the class that these individuals were experiencing a Soul Merge. I had never heard of this—and certainly didn't understand it—but I could see that it was a profound experience. AlixSandra explained that when a person has cleared their body of enough energy blockages, Soul Energy can enter the body, at which point the person begins to live his or her life with a higher purpose. The blockages, or stuck energy patterns, are past traumas held in the body's energy system, inhibiting the natural flow of energy.

As fate would have it, on the two-hour ferry ride back to

Vancouver Island, I encountered AlixSandra, her husband Lee and Marcy. The two of them were going to spend some time with Marcy at her home on Quadra Island.

On the ferry, and during a subsequent meeting while she was vacationing with Marcy, I got to know AlixSandra a little more personally. Though she scared me immensely—I feared she could see past my persona to the real me hiding behind it—I knew she was a person who could change my life; she was another teacher being put on my path, and I vowed to take advantage of the opportunity.

Before she left to go home, I asked AlixSandra if I could book some personal healing sessions with her. She said yes, but suggested that a more fruitful use of my money would be to attend a Basic Training course, a five-day course being held in Las Vegas (where AlixSandra lives). It was a preliminary training course for people interested in joining her Energy Healing School. I had no intention of joining the school, but I got the dates, booked the time off at work and then waited for the workshop. I knew expectations often led to major disappointments, but regardless, I went to the Basic Training course with the intention of having a Soul Merge—even though was I still ignorant of the specifics.

If the seed for having a higher purpose was planted during that first workshop, then it was germinated during that second workshop with AlixSandra. Many of the particulars of it are lost to me now, but there are some prominent details etched in my memory, and in my soul. One day my ride to the hotel was delayed, so AlixSandra offered to give me a ride herself. As we talked during the drive, I told her of my intention to have a Soul Merge while at the workshop. She reminded me that it was not good to have such expectations, but also offered some advice: when I woke up the next morning I was to ask myself, "What is the one thing in my life that I don't want to look at today?"

The next morning I remember asking myself the question, but

I don't remember my answer, or even the subject matter. It may be something I am blocking from my memory, or it may not be an important detail. Regardless, I strongly believe that making that internal inquiry on that particular morning played a significant role in the events later that day.

After lunch we were scheduled to do complementary healing sessions with our partners from the previous day. I had been the healer earlier, so today it was my turn to receive a healing treatment. I felt unusually calm and focused, but I sensed some uncertainty from my partner. I tried to reassure her as we prepared to start. During the session I felt a sense of what I needed, and on a couple of occasions I guided her as to how to proceed, rather than the other way round.

Then came that unforgettable moment! We had reached a lull in our session, but I was keen to move on. With no clear reason why, I told my partner I was going to do some toning (singing a variety of single-note tones). I then started making a tone, and I felt a distinct tingling sensation as the sound resonated with my root chakra (a *chakra* is a central energy point where the body's energy channels intersect; the root chakra is at the base of the torso). I believe the sound I was making was quite loud, but I cannot say this for sure. Then, instinctively, I knew I needed to go up the scale, having each note resonate with the next chakra. I proceeded to do this toning in succession, moving up the seven main chakras of my body, feeling the intensity build with each step.

Normally I am not very aware of the kinesthetic sensation of flowing energy, but on this occasion, I could feel an acute pulsing in my spine. When I sang the final tone, resonating with my top chakra, I felt a surge of energy rushing up the length of my body and out the top of my head. At no time was there any discomfort or unpleasantness during the process. This toning lasted for maybe three or four minutes, with the finale being a minute more. It ended with a peaceful, joyous feeling; I was energized, yet calm and happy.

Soon afterward, AlixSandra came by and advised me to spend the next few minutes grounding the experience, which at the time I interpreted as focusing on energy flowing both into me and out of me in exchange with the earth. After the other participants had completed their individual healing sessions, AlixSandra announced as part of her summation that I had experienced a Soul Merge. Though I was unaware of it, I guess my healing had attracted some attention from the others. The class' applause only added to my immense sense of joy!

It was after my Soul Merge that I started to live my life with a clearer sense of destiny. A ray of hope had broken through my cloud of uncertainty and longing, which up to that point had been a predominant feeling in my life. It was not that I knew my purpose, but I was confident that I would *find* a purpose—that one existed for me, and that it would soon become evident. My life did not change dramatically after my Soul Merge; it was more of a gradual shift. I began enjoying things more, and my personal and professional relationships became more rewarding. It was a cycle of thinking positive thoughts and having good things happen, which then encouraged more positive thinking. Even when unpleasant incidents occurred, I began viewing them as opportunities rather than problems. It became a mission of mine to try to positively affect others. If I encountered a store clerk who seemed unhappy, I would try to get him or her to smile. That is one of the things I love about Christmas in particular; people seem to make a little extra effort to be pleasant, and I was feeling that Christmas spirit all year round. This joyous period of my life lasted about two years, and ended while I was living and working in Korea.

Before entering the building where the Peppy Kids Club office is, I put a bandage over my tattoo; I have found out that tattoos are frowned upon in Japan. It is ironic that something I did as my way of honoring Zen, a Japanese spiritual practice and part of my reason for wanting to go to Japan, could inhibit me from getting a job there. I enter the building and proceed to the third floor.

The interview goes well—I have great rapport with the interviewer, and we laugh a lot. She makes a comment that I demonstrate a good knowledge of ESL teaching methods (English as a Second Language). I tell her about my tattoo, but she says as long as I am willing to cover it when working, it isn't a problem. It will be two weeks before I find out if I am offered the job, but I am confident—some things are meant to be.

With the exhilaration of the interview lifting my spirits, I am anxious to get back to Andi and Martin's house—they are dear friends, and I am currently staying at their place.

I came to Vancouver for the interview, but I still call Penticton home. Doug, my old boss at the Penticton Alternate School, is going away for Christmas, and he asked if I would house sit for them. I readily agreed. Then Doug went a step further and offered his guesthouse as a temporary residence until I found new employment. He has a wonderful family; I enjoy conversing with his wife, Colleen, and interacting with their teenage sons, Callan and Drayden. Their guestroom is a small building, detached from the house, and I knew I would be comfortable there. Over the years it has been a brief home for an assortment of interesting people.

I will go back to Penticton in a few days, but it is great to come to Vancouver and spend time with Andi and Martin. I have known Andi since elementary school, and Martin is her New Zealander husband (they met somewhere while the two of them were traveling the world). I didn't start spending time with them until after I had moved away from Vancouver, but both of them are understanding of my quirks and appreciative of my lifestyle. My earlier thinking about my Soul Merge and my life's purpose, and now the prospect of working in Japan, fuels my current desire to be a writer. I catch the train back to the house, and as my two hosts are out, I take the opportunity to do some writing.

Chapter III: Consciousness, Mind and Personality

Prior to a person's birth, the Energy Bodies are not yet distinct; it is at birth that the Energy Bodies separate. And just as the newborn becomes separated from the mother, the illusion of the "person" being separated from the Divine starts. How the Physical Body develops over time is obvious, but the Emotional, Mental and Spiritual Bodies also develop with time. This is because these vibrations of energies—or densities—have a tendency to coalesce. As a person gains life experience and has emotional, mental and spiritual occurrences, these types of energies linger in the corresponding Energy Body and influence the person's life experience.

The Consciousness is separate from the Energy Bodies, and it is the life force of each person. It is the aspect of the self that does the perceiving, and via the will, it initiates actions. The consciousness is like an echo of spiritual energy. It begins as a reflection of the Divine Consciousness, but then functions as a distinct entity, and is ignorant of its relation to the Divine. For practical purposes, we can say the consciousness is generated at birth and always has a connection to the four Energy Bodies. In metaphysical terms, it is the "experiencer" and not the experience itself. In this sense it is like a container where information from the Energy Bodies is directed, but it is usually the case that only part of the incoming information registers in the consciousness. The parts of the information that get into the consciousness are what comprise the conscious experience.

As a newborn, the consciousness is based solely upon the immediate events occurring in the undeveloped Energy Bodies. Initially, one's experience is based in the Physical and Emotional Bodies, the latter being happy, unhappy or contented. The other two Energy Bodies have very primal perceptions and little influence. At this point the infant does not have the capacity to limit the information coming from the Energy Bodies. As the baby grows and the Energy Bodies become more complex, there is potentially less information from each Body being transmitted to the consciousness. The consciousness is ignorant that there are separate Energy Bodies or that the information it receives is likely limited.

During childhood, a person may be considered the composite of the four Energy Bodies, the consciousness and the mind. The mind is composed of one's memories and their personality, which includes a self-concept. As the mind develops it functions as a storehouse for the consciousness and the four Energy Bodies. The mind evolves as the consciousness creates the ability to avoid (tune out) its immediate situation. The functioning of the Mental Body facilitates this ability, and it uses the concept of objective time to alter one's perception.

That's enough for today. Andi and Martin are due home soon and I've offered to make a salad for dinner, so I had better get cracking. Both of them are excellent cooks, so I know we will have a delicious dinner, along with some wine. I get a head start by having a beer. My joyous frame of mind will only add to the evening's ambiance.

Chapter 10

A Party of One

Monday, December 31

The air is cold and crisp and full of electricity. The snow on the ground and trees had softened in the warmth of the day, and now the sharp night air has refrozen this top layer. This creates a coating of tiny crystals on the snow, and when the light hits it, the crystals sparkle like miniature diamonds; it's a memorizing effect. It may look peaceful, but it is hard to not to contemplate the dangers. Cougars (mountain lions) are known to be in this area, and if I fell and was seriously hurt, I could easily die of exposure, if not from the injury itself. It is likely that no one will be on this trail for a day or two. However, it is this element of danger that makes this adventure so exhilarating; I need to channel that energy into excitement, and not into fear.

It is New Year's Eve, and since I didn't have any social plans, I decided to make my own excitement. Terra is busy with friends, and I think that spending New Year's together is too intimate for the distance she is maintaining in our relationship. If two people spend too much time together or do activities that couples usually do, then outsiders will make assumptions. And it is not that she is actually concerned with what others say, but I think it is a guide for her not to let our relationship slip into uncomfortable territory.

Sometimes I hang out with the old staff team from the Alternate School, but not nearly as often as when I worked there. They have other plans for tonight: Doug is in Hawaii, Curt is partying with his biker buddies and Marsha and Tamara are doing the family thing. In addition to the PAS posse, there is Mary, who was a fellow employee at the John Howard Society in Campbell River. She moved to this area a few years ago, so we still meet up once in a while. Mary and I partied often back in the old days, but here our contact is intermittent, so I was reluctant to call her to see what her plans are. These are the only friends here with whom I feel at ease.

My mom and dad have gone to a party at a friend's house, but it's not a friend I know well. I could have asked to be included, and it would have been fine with everyone, but I would have felt like an outsider. Similarly, there is a function being put on by the Spiritualist Church, but it would feel like a bunch of people getting together that don't have anything else to do; it is great to have people to be with, but it is not the type of special event where you will still be talking about it years later. So it was a situation where I tried not to focus on the limitations, but instead looked for the opportunities. For example, if I don't have a friend to travel with, I will look for travel options that are better done alone instead of focusing on being friendless. Consequently, my lack of social plans for tonight led me to opt for a solo, cross-country night ski, which I am thrilled to do.

Having skied the 15 minutes of flat terrain, I am starting the ascent up the hill. It will be a good 35 minutes to get to the top of the hill, and then from there it is 15 minutes of glorious downhill. Finally, there is another 10 minutes of flat to get back to the parking area. I want to enjoy the wilderness and the sparkling snow, so I don't look into the trees too much; the penetrating darkness conjures up fictitious dangers. This is one of a couple of favorite routes for night skiing, and it takes just the right amount of time; a headlight illuminates my path, and the battery life is only an hour and a half.

Years ago I worked in a bicycle store in Vancouver, and at that time mountain biking had exploded onto the scene. Enthusiasts were always looking for more exciting and daring things to do. Night riding was one of the new fads, and a group of us at work often went for night rides. I was also a part-time university student, and the campus, Simon Fraser University, was on top of

Burnaby Mountain. So, one or two nights a week, I would ride up the mountain after work to attend class. Saving the bus fare meant I could have a beer in the pub after class. Taking the trail home through the forest at night was a highlight, especially after a beer or even occasionally smoking pot.

Years later, after my cousins introduced me to cross-country skiing, I decided it would be a great way to maintain my fitness when the mountain biking season was over. Biking is my main joy, but skiing has become a close second. The next year I bought some cross-country equipment and spent that winter developing my skills and exploring trails. Near Penticton there is a great Nordic ski center close to a big, downhill resort, but it costs money to ski there. I found some other trails closer to town— about a 20-minute drive—that were developed by a ski club (probably using a government grant). The area is just wilderness, with no services or buildings nearby. The trails themselves are not groomed or maintained, so I think the club has since been disbanded. Even a few days after a fresh snowfall I am often the first one to make fresh tracks; it's always exciting to be the first one to set the tracks.

One day it dawned on me that I could use my mountain bike light for night skiing. Doing it at night takes the joy and tranquility of cross-country skiing and adds the adrenaline and danger of downhill skiing.

I have finally reached the top of the trail where there is a small lean-to (a three-sided structure with a roof). There are fresh ashes in a small fire pit in front of the lean-to, so it is likely a family had a little hotdog cookout on their Sunday ski. Beyond that is a quick little flat ski to get to the downhill section. When skiing downhill on cross-country skis it is very hard to control the turns, so even a gentle slope is thrilling if the trail is curvy. It takes total concentration, and a little courage, to navigate down this section without slowing or falling. Plus, I can only see as far as my light shines, so that amplifies the challenge and thrill.

I make it down the hill without falling and then head for my car. Once in my car, I open a beer. I know drinking and driving is illegal, but one beer is not a real danger, and it is tough to beat a beer after skiing, especially when it is New Year's Eve. I know the police will be out looking for suspect drivers, so I will limit myself to one beer till I get to Doug's house.

As I drive, I feel satisfied that I have had a great evening, plus a sense of accomplishment; instead of feeling sorry for myself, I turned being alone on New Year's Eve into a positive. However, the night is not over, and it will be a challenge not to slip into sadness and self-pity.

When I get home I have another drink and then shower. I purposely waited until later to go skiing so I knew I would be on the trail when it was midnight. Now it is too late to think of doing anything else, but I *need* to do something; I am already fighting off the feeling of loneliness.

Even though there is snow on the mountains, it is not that cold at the city level, so I decide to sit on the patio and listen to music while I have my third drink. Doug and Colleen's house is on a hill overlooking the valley and lake, and the view is spectacular.

After that I decide to play darts. Doug is one of those lucky men who has a "man cave." It is a small garage that Doug originally planned to store his motorbikes in, but Doug and Colleen don't currently own motorbikes (maybe it's a retirement idea). So the garage had filled up with all kinds of junk; Doug is a worse pack rat than I am.

In the old days, after school on Fridays, it became a regular thing to go to Doug's house for a beer to unwind after a tough week at the Alternate School. One day Doug decided that the junk was of less value than the fun we had unwinding at his house, and the next week he gleefully invited us to come to his house on Friday to unwind in style. We found a dartboard, a mini fridge, an assortment of furniture, an outdated stereo and a

83

few posters on the walls (some of questionable artistic value). Over the years the empty space on the walls and shelves was filled with all kinds of "clubhouse" memorabilia. The many Friday nights we spent here were some of the best times of my life; we laughed, commiserated, joked, played, bonded and lived in the moment.

This evening has been a battle of keeping myself busy and engaged in what I am doing as a means of fending off the feeling that I am a loser because I don't have friends. This is a common theme in my life. I have always had people I am friendly with, but rarely have I had close friendships where I can spontaneously call them up and say, "Let's do something." If I were to call someone, it would expose me as a person in need of friendship. This is a hurdle I have yet to overcome, but tonight was a draw— I created enough fun and activity to counter the nagging voice. Now, finally, I am drunk enough and tired enough to go to bed without caring that I was alone on New Year's Eve.

The next morning I feel fine physically, albeit a little dehydrated; emotionally, however, things aren't so clear. This is because I am mostly tuned into my physical and mental bodies, though I'm sure there is a lot going on mentally that I am ignoring. Going cross-country night skiing is unusual—I don't know anyone else that does this, though I have taken Terra with me on two occasions—and this is what I focus on from last night.

It is 10:30 in the morning, and I am mildly hungry. I try hard to make meditation a daily habit, but it is easy to skip it when out of my routine (which I am because this is Doug's house). I have a piece of rice bread toast and then decide writing will at least alleviate some of the guilt from not meditating.

I start up my computer.

Chapter III, cont. (Consciousness, Mind and Personality)

When considering the interaction of the consciousness and the four Energy Bodies, the Physical Body is the anchor for all the other components. Because the Physical Body is the densest, it binds us to the physical world and facilitates the perception of oneself as a separate being. As long as the consciousness is connected to the Physical Body, one has an incarnate experience, but after death, the Physical Body remains and disintegrates while the consciousness and the other Energy Bodies are reintegrated into the Soul in the nonphysical realm. Thus, the Physical Body is uniquely different from the other Energy Bodies.

The Emotional Body is crucial for the consciousness, and can be thought of as a doorway through which the consciousness connects to the other bodies; hence, it is the primary experience of the consciousness. At times the consciousness may not receive information from the Emotional Body (when a person is essentially emotionally numb), and thus, the person does not have a genuine experience of the external world. It should be noted that the more turmoil there is in the Emotional Body, the stronger the personality tries to influence one's life and, when one's emotions are relatively peaceful, the personality's desire for control lessens. I will expand upon the personality shortly.

The Mental Body is where thoughts and ideas are processed, and these activities are the primary tool that the consciousness uses when interpreting the world. However, they are not the only tool, nor are they an essential tool. The Mental Body provides a means for the consciousness to organize its experiences. This organizing process is facilitated by the conception of time as an independent, objective part of the external world. It is important to note that objective time is a learned concept; Einstein explained that time is neither objective nor independent. Correspondingly, objective time also supports the false understanding of oneself as an individual entity. This sense of individuation, along with the consequences of traumatic events in the Emotional Body, help shape the constitution of the personality.

The Spiritual Body's contribution to the functioning of the person is to provide a broader understanding of life situations. In fact, this Energy Body contains the information that a person is merely an artificial separation that was created to experience its own Divinity and Free Will. The Spiritual Energy Body also has the information about the specific purpose for that particular life. A metaphor to explain the relationship of the Spiritual Body and consciousness is an image in a mirror. When a person first looks into a mirror, it enables him or her to see a new perspective of themselves. If it were possible for the mirror image to take on a life of its own and forget its relationship with its original body, then this is analogous to how people begin their lives on earth. The Spiritual Energy Body is that original body which is continually trying to make its mirror image—the consciousness—reconnect with it, and thus remember its "real" body. This will be explained in greater detail in Chapter V.

However, unlike a body in front of a mirror, the Spiritual Body does not control the consciousness or the other Energy Bodies. The Spiritual Body does influence the situation that a person encounters, but in an indirect manner. It does this in an attempt to allow the consciousness to fully realize its spiritual nature. And, when that understanding is sufficient, a person can consciously start to influence the physical world through his or her intentions.

Writing always takes me out of my doubting mind and gets me focused on the activity at hand. It is paradoxical that even though I am writing about abstract ideas, which are not directly connected to the moment, it still feels like I am in the moment.

The *act* of writing is being in the moment, and the actual subject matter is irrelevant to the process. I guess the physical and emotional bodies become subdued, and the mental becomes integrated with the spiritual body. Now I am left to wonder what to do with the rest of my day.

The motivation to go out is missing, so I watch some sports on TV. It isn't long before I find myself struggling to stay positive; the old judgment of being a loser is still gnawing at me. The genuine, underlying sadness is unconsciously being masked with anger and numbing. Last night's skiing and today's writing are usually enough to avoid this struggle, but because last night was New Year's Eve, there was extra pressure to think I should have been with friends.

An added element to this internal drama is my relationship with Terra. I resent the limitations on our relationship, and I resent my shortcomings with regards to her. If I were more open with her then I would feel different. My openness might not change how she feels or acts, but it would enable me to feel more comfortable with myself. If my actions are consistent with what I feel, then I'm content with the situation and I can let fate take over. However, not having done all I can do—namely, not having said to her, "I love you"—my fears have dictated my actions. My inaction is like a pebble in my shoe, reminding me with every step that I have not been true to myself. Allowing fear to influence my actions is another source of negative self-judging.

Again I catch my thinking and realize it is quickly spiraling downward. The anger is building. I am soon lost in my thoughts and again become engaged in a random, argumentative daydream. Perhaps as a diversion, I reflect on a period in my life when I was actively working through my anger issues.

When in my twenties, I was not a joyous person. My disease— ulcerative colitis—was troublesome, and I was either taking powerful medication (Prednisone, with its troubling side effects) or struggling with symptoms of the disease itself. There was an especially difficult sequence of events that is foremost in my mind. My girlfriend decided our relationship wasn't working for her, and this realization happened shortly after I lost my job. That had been the time I was working as a salesman in the bicycle store, which was a low-paying, non-commission job. And I was living in a small bachelor apartment above the bike store. So, being poor and in poor health, recently unemployed and newly single, it was not surprising that I was struggling with low self-esteem.

During this period I had a dear friend, Helen, who was helping me work through some challenges and grow as a person; "personal growth" was the catch phrase at that time. She lived in another province, Edmonton, Alberta, so we only met a few times a year. (Miraculously one of my brothers lives in Edmonton so I could conveniently combine visits.) Helen was a professional counselor, but she was also involved in energy work and parapsychology. I met her because she was a close friend of my girlfriend's roommate, and I attended an energy workshop she offered in Vancouver. Helen scared the wits out me because I knew she could see past my façade (like AlixSandra does), but after the workshop I was determined to work with her—I knew she could change my life. Once I started a conscious process of self-improvement, she was the first in a series of teachers that came my way. Working with AlixSandra at Inner Focus has been the culmination of this period. I know it is more than fortuitous that spiritual teachers appeared as I made an earnest effort to heal myself. My relationship with Helen was not professional; she had generously taken on a few protégés—my girlfriend's roommate was one, and I became another.

During one of her visits, Helen suggested venting my anger to see what lay beneath it. She said that sometimes she had her clients smash cardboard boxes as a means of releasing pent-up anger. There was a park near my home which was bordered by a creek, and on the other side of the creek was some undeveloped land which had an unused dirt road meandering through it. The road went through some bushes and ended at a chain-link fence at the back of a railway service yard. As a variation of Helen's suggestion, I came up with the idea of going down that road to where I had noticed an old tire, and hitting it with a baseball bat.

Every week or so I would take the bat and beat that tire with a vengeance. At different times the focus of my anger would be my brothers, my parents, my old school friends or my ex-girlfriends. It wouldn't take more than a minute or two before my anger would peak, which allowed me to connect with the underlying pain. Then I would cry for a minute or two before the anger would close in once again. This would prompt another session of hitting until I felt the pain return. For about six months I regularly did this "batting" routine. I had to replace the bat twice.

Another suggestion of Helen's was to use affirmations. For a month or two I made diligent use of this technique. For half an hour each day I would sit with a notepad and make a mark every time I said an affirmation. Out loud, I would say each statement 500 times, so with three affirmations it meant I was repeating 1,500 sentences for each sitting. One affirmation I remember saying was: "I love myself unconditionally." I now understand that this process altered stuck energy patterns in my mental energy body. Prior to this, my internal dialogue was to habitually repeat old messages imprinted from my childhood, messages that were detrimental to my well-being. Affirmations can change the unconscious routine of replaying old, negative messages, but it does not actually heal the core energy pattern. Affirmations just clear some of the habitual energy built up around the core pattern.

With the aid of these two practices, my attitude toward life shifted, resulting in much improved self-esteem. After this moderate transformation I made a concerted effort to finish my university degree and move forward with my life. I also quit drinking, which lasted for about three years. Another positive outcome was that my relationship with my parents and siblings improved because I wasn't being "triggered" as often when spending time with them.

One clear example of this growth was when all of us had gathered at my parents' house for Christmas. We often played board games when we were younger and continued to do this as adults when we had a chance. On this particular occasion I was winning the game, so my brothers teamed up to oppose me. This triggered old pains from my childhood when my brothers had periodically "ganged-up" on me. This time my growth enabled me to recognize the triggering and not slip into using old coping strategies.

There is minimal joy in the fact that my football team won its game today. This diversion has gotten me through the day without spiraling into negative thinking, but now it is time to get ready for dinner at my parents' home; I am glad I live in the same town as them.

Chapter 11

My Men's Group

Thursday, January 17

I am anxiously waiting my turn to check in. This is my biweekly meeting where a group of men gather to discuss issues relevant to our lives. The meetings start with each member providing an update of the developments and challenges in his life. I could have spoken up early and revealed my big news, but I am relishing the buildup. The downside is that it is hard to stay focused as the other men share their news. The check-in session reaches a lull where the men that were keen to speak have spoken, and those who are more introverted—or feel they don't have any interesting news to share—are graciously waiting for others to speak.

I have been in this men's group for three years. The group was an initiative of the local United Church (which my parents are active members of), and was later expanded to include a few non-church members. The other participants are doctors, lawyers, teachers, businessmen and some retirees. It has been a wonderful situation to challenge my vulnerability. It has been gratifying getting feedback acknowledging my honesty and openness; one fellow member said they always know how I am feeling. The group is extra special for me because my dad is a member—in fact, he invited me to join. It has enriched our relationship and added intimacy to it. It is through our sharing at the meetings that we often discover how the other person is feeling about certain events and challenges. Rather than regret that we don't share all of these details privately, I just appreciate that it happens.

Over the years I have been impressed with how much my father has grown emotionally. For example, when he retired and my parents moved from Vancouver to the Okanagan Valley, I saw my dad only a few times a year. On those occasions I started the practice of giving him a hug (my mom has always been the hugging type). Initially he was stiff when I hugged him, but soon it became reciprocal. Then, I was surprised some time later when he initiated hugging my brothers too. It was an open expression of affection that was new for him.

The lull in today's meeting is a good juncture for me to share my news.

"Well, I have some big news!" I say, venturing forth. After a short pause, I continue, "I have been offered a job in Japan! I start in April; soon I'll be leaving."

There is obvious excitement within the group. These men have become an integral part of my life, as I am part of theirs. I provide some of the details, such as Peppy having schools all over Japan but not yet knowing where I will be placed. And that the company teaches only children, and its classes are external to the regular school system. I also tell them that the job will include lots of commuting. I conclude my announcement by saying that I have signed a one-year contract. All of the men congratulate me, and they are happy for me—I know they get some vicarious pleasure from the adventure I am living.

When I was still working, after a meeting I would often go to the lake and park my car for a while. We meet in the early morning, so I usually had twenty or thirty minutes before I needed to be at work. It gave me a chance to reflect on our discussions, or emote if I felt particularly vulnerable that day. Now that I am unemployed I no longer go to the lake afterwards, but today I decide to drive there anyway.

As I sit in the car and look at the lake I find myself marveling at how everything is coming together. For a long time I have wanted to go to South America, so when I returned from Korea and was having trouble reestablishing a life in Canada, I started looking for employment in South America. The closest I got was a job offer from a school in Nicaragua. It would have been strictly for the experience, as the pay wasn't nearly enough to send money home. After careful consideration, I refused the job because of concerns about their health care system should my disease become an urgent problem. Once I found steady employment in the Okanagan Valley, I stopped thinking about working overseas.

The desire resurfaced when staffing cuts at the Penticton Alternate School threatened my position there. The dream of going to South America was still there, but I knew my chances of finding employment were better in Asia. Overall, my Korean experience was wonderful, but I didn't want to repeat an old adventure, so I began thinking of Japan as an alternative. I was enthralled by James Clavell's *Shogun*, which I read when I was a teenager, so Japan has always been of some interest to me. When I first went to work in Asia I applied for jobs in Korea, Japan and Taiwan (mainland China wasn't a major player at that time). Back then I would have been happy to go to Japan instead of Korea, but I was offered a job in Korea first.

There are other reasons for choosing Japan. One, my health is still a consideration, and Japan has a reputable healthcare system. In addition, I believe their culinary traditions will be good for my disease. Korean food was good for my digestion, and I think Japan's will be even better. My intestines do well when I eat a rice-based diet. In Canada I can eat rice at home, but when I'm running around town I am always tempted to eat convenience food, which in North America is primarily wheat-based. Wheat is one of the foods I have tried to cut out of my diet.

Another reason to go to Japan is that it will be profitable. It is a wealthy nation with a well-established ESL system. I have a debt to pay off (a financial debt, that is) and I need to be making payments on my loan. Part of my debt is paying for the healing school. Japan has a reputation for their unusual but honest business practices, and that is a definite consideration because of my contract difficulties in Korea; I had problems with two dishonest employers, including my last employer cheating me $1,300 from my final paycheck.

A third reason I mentioned earlier; it is the heartland of Zen. Buddhism migrated from India to other parts of Asia where it melded with the indigenous religions. In China, one of the variations that evolved was Zen. It was never an influential practice in China, but when Zen made its way to Japan it became established as a culturally significant practice. The prevailing Shinto religion and Samurai traditions were very conducive to the Zen approach to life.

The fourth reason is much more difficult to explain—it just feels right. I am not one to explore past life experiences, though I believe they are valid. I focus on my present situation because I believe my quandaries can be explained by examining my current life. It is OK for people to explore past lives when they have challenges that don't seem to fit with their current life. For example, I have a friend with a phobia of birds, and this might be explained by a past life experience as there is nothing in his present life to account for it. However, I am less sympathetic with people whose interest in past lives seems to overshadow coping with their present life. It's similar to technology where some technology can be an aid, but it is not good to make technology the focus of your life. It is plausible to think that Japan's draw on me may have something to do with a past life, but it is not my intention to explore it. What counts is that I am happy to be going there!

As I sit in my car, I am brought back to the scene in front of me as I hear the waves lapping at the shore. There is not much of a breeze today, so the rhythmical sound of the waves is gentle and soothing. The surrounding mountains have a dusting of snow but here at the lake there is none. I see a few birds hunting in the weeds for grubs, though at this time of year the pickings are sparse. It is an overcast day, but still a pleasant temperature; however, I do start up the car to help take the chill off.

The grayness of the day reminds me of the other emotion I feel about my men's group: sadness. Having shared with them my good news about Japan, it reminds me that I will be leaving them soon. That biweekly interaction has been one of the cornerstones of my emotional well-being. These men have given me compassion and validation. Even though I do not walk a conventional path, their acceptance has helped me feel like a grounded, likable individual. When I joined the men's group, I had recently completed my healing school training, and I was contemplating enrolling in the Inner Focus Church ministerial program not long after. The acceptance I felt from them encouraged me to venture further along my spiritual path towards ordination. It is a path I am sure I would have walked regardless, but sharing it with them has made it an easier and a more enjoyable journey.

Enough reflecting. Fortunately, I put my laptop in the car this morning, so I grab it from under the seat. I feel like writing.

Chapter III, cont. (Consciousness, Mind and Personality)

Another important factor influencing our experience of the world is the personality, which is associated with, but separate from, a person's consciousness. The personality is most closely related to the Mental Body, while the consciousness is most closely related to the Emotional Body. The personality develops over time and is, in part, the product of the consciousness learning to avoid emotionally painful situations. I believe the core of the personality is a collection of traits inherent in us when we are born, probably encoded in our DNA. Some examples of these innate traits are inquisitiveness, cautiousness, playfulness and being active or reflective. The Mental Body establishes rigid thought patterns on top of this base, which becomes one's self-identity. This mental self-concept is developed over time, is founded on the framework of memories and is greatly influenced by the familial environment. The mature personality is comprised of some innate characteristics, some learned characteristics and one's self-concept. As it develops, the personality exerts an increasing influence on the consciousness.

A person's life experience is via the consciousness, yet its perception is often based upon the limited information that the consciousness receives from each of the four Energy Bodies. The flow of information from the Energy Bodies to the consciousness is affected by a filtering mechanism, or perceptual "gauze," which is a function of the personality. This filtering is done in accordance with a person's innate personality traits and his or her self-concept, which in turn is reflective of his or her memories. An active personality will try to limit information that reaches the consciousness in accordance with its perception of the external world. Information filtered out is still registered in the mind, and hence can have a subconscious influence on the consciousness. Ultimately, the consciousness has control of one's experience, but it gets conditioned to allowing the personality to influence, and even dominate, the experience.

To summarize, an adult person is comprised of the four Energy Bodies, the consciousness and the mind, which in turn contains one's memories, the personality, including the self-concept, and other stored energy. The consciousness is the focal point of a person's experience, and is distinct from the Energy Bodies. It contains the experience a person has, but is not that experience itself. The consciousness receives information from the four Energy Bodies, the personality and the mind (subconsciously). It is, however, most closely associated with the Emotional Energy Body. The conscious information being relayed from the Energy Bodies may only be part of the energy flowing through any given Energy Body, and the consciousness may be unaware of the limited scope of information coming from any of the four Energy Bodies, such as being emotionally numb when missing much of the information for the Emotional Body.

As people grow from infancy, they become conditioned to using mental concepts to interpret and organize information. This organization of information helps form the personality, which is most closely related with the Mental Energy Body. The personality comprises some innate characteristics and a self-concept, which is based on memories. Information flowing to the consciousness becomes filtered by the personality, which acts like a "gauze." The filtered-out information is registered in the mind, which can have an unconscious influence on the consciousness.

Thinking about filtering, and the sadness I am feeling about leaving my men's group, brings to the fore another issue I am struggling with: Terra. There is sadness in leaving her too, though my leaving may also be a good thing for us—absence makes the heart grow fonder. With Terra, I can recognize my attraction to her—physical and psychological—but also notice that my personality is complicating my feelings. My personality thinks she would alleviate my sense of loneliness. There is a universal condition of wanting to be connected, and it is a strong motivator. Factors that may compromise our compatibility, or limit our intimacy, get filtered out. Unfortunately, when two people get intimately involved, their issues (energy blockages) inhibit the desired closeness. We protect ourselves rather than show our vulnerability, which later on emphasizes the discon-nection we feel. Over time, the initial giddiness of being together and of being in love gives rise to feelings of being alone because the other person doesn't seem to *really* understand us. As we clear our energy blocks, it enables us to be more open and intimate with others, which counters the loneliness, but we concurrently begin to realize that the connection we are seeking is not so much with our lover, but with the Divine.

It is time to move on, so I put my computer away. There are many things I need to do in preparation for going to Japan. I need to sort out health insurance, get an international driver's license, get some forms for Peppy as a requirement for my work visa and put more stuff into storage. And, because of the weather, at some point today I will go for a run on Doug's treadmill, in keeping with my fitness routine.

Chapter 12

A Slice of Paradise; House Sitting

Wednesday, March 12

Though the morning light has been evident for hours, the sun is just starting to climb over the hills, and its rays are dancing on the lake. The lake itself is beginning to lose that glassy calmness that it often has in the early mornings and late evenings. These are times when the sun is not heating the air and creating drafts, which in turn cause ripples on the surface of the water. I can see birds fluttering from tree to tree, singing songs as they go. The beach and shoreline are void of human activity; there are no man-made commotions to disturb this scene. My situation and I are the only exceptions as I soak in the hot tub on this cool but pleasant morning. The hot tub sits on the private beach of this wonderful home.

Jenny is lying lazily nearby; she is the cause of my good fortune here. Jenny is a golden retriever, and also the reason the owners of this exclusive home asked me to house sit. They are vacationing in the southern United States, a popular option for affluent, retired Canadians during the winter. After I'd stayed in Doug's guestroom for a couple of months, his brother-in-law asked if I was interested in taking care of their dog and cat. I said I would be happy to take care of Jenny and Bell, but I had no idea I was being invited to stay in a lovely home on an exclusive waterfront property. This is a lovely house without being opulent, and it is the only shoreline house on this acreage. There is another house several hundred yards farther back, but trees conceal it from view. This section of land is still an active part of the Okanagan Valley's history of orchards.

Even though the setting is as tranquil as one could possibly wish for, my mind is busily reviewing my situation. It is as if I am suspended from my life. I am enjoying it immensely, but there is a part of me that thinks I should be more in control. I am the central figure in this drama, yet I don't seem to be directing it. However, I don't want to question my good fortune in case that jinxes it; I want this dream to continue. In three weeks I will start my new life in Japan, and what is just as exciting, I am a week away from going to Thailand. Things have steadily been falling into place with less and less effort.

The trip to Thailand came about because, while I was making preparations for my life in Japan, a major earthquake and tidal wave struck Southeast Asia. It was a tragedy that inspired many relief efforts. While at a benefit concert I spontaneously decided that, prior to going to Japan, I should go to Thailand and volunteer my services. Thailand holds a special place in my heart because of a holiday I had there when I was living in Korea.

After some investigation I discovered that once the initial crisis passed, untrained help was not wanted. Now Thailand's priority is to reestablish its economy, and with tourism as a major component of their economy, I decided ten days as a tourist would be my way of helping.

It makes me smile when I realize how my affairs have come together in an orderly fashion. I quit my job; became ordained; had a great holiday in Utah; relinquished my suite; moved into Doug's guesthouse; found employment in Japan; chose to include a holiday in Thailand en route to Japan; and then found myself house sitting here. The hot tub on the beach is an unexpected perk.

This is why my mind is busy while I am relaxing in the hot tub. It is OK to be excited about my upcoming adventure, but I try not to get too emotionally caught up in the anticipation. If I focus on imagining the future, I miss out on enjoying the present, like being in this wonderful home.

Part of the magic of this fluid lifestyle (what I call "being in the flow of the universe") is that even when problems arise, they are seen as opportunities rather than problems. Ten days ago I developed an intense earache. The ache was severe and persistent enough that I was concerned I might not be able to fly. My regular doctor referred me to a specialist, but with my imminent travel plans I had to plead to get an early appointment. I was doing what I could to take care of myself physically, but I wondered, "What are the corresponding emotional, mental and spiritual components of this troubling earache?" Rightly or wrongly, I quickly came to the conclusion that the core of the problem was because I hadn't been open with Terra about my feelings for her. This spurred me into action, and I called her and set up a visit, which happened several days ago.

I didn't make a big to-do of it; I didn't bring flowers or do anything special. Instead, I calmly sat with her and told her about my earache, and how I felt the underlying issue was an emotional blockage. I said I believed the reason for the blockage was related to my feelings for her, and that I hadn't been totally open about how I felt.

Next, feeling anxious, I said, "I don't expect saying this will change things, but I need to say it. I love you." She said *thank you*, and then she moved the conversation onto another topic. I felt better about having said it, as it erased any doubts I had about her intentions toward me. Again, I am not positive of the cause and effect, but my earache has almost dissipated.

As this craziness unfolds, I have a sense that there is a purpose to these events. It is not that I am aware of an overall plan, but my choices are fitting into the mosaic of a larger picture. Somehow, the reasons or intuitions I have about each step along the way are in sync with a more comprehensive, purposeful plan. I only have glimpses of that master plan, but I am acting with faith that some higher power is guiding this process.

As I contemplate this, I decide writing will help ease the busyness of my mind. I get out of the hot tub and towel off. I throw Jenny's ball a few times, but now is not the time for us to play. I want to get down to writing while my mind is keen.

Chapter IV: Time and the Energy Bodies

Time, as it relates to the Energy Bodies, is an important concept to examine. First, let's consider time from an animal's perspective. They have no self-awareness and lack the ability to conceive of objective time, but animals obviously live and function adequately from day to day. So a being does not need a conception of time to operate in the external, physical world. I would suggest that an animal's experience is based purely in the moment, and is affected by how the world unfolds during the present.

For example, if a snake sees a small mouse and the snake is hungry, then both its senses and its instincts prompt the snake to pursue its next meal. The snake doesn't have a mental concept of how long it has been since its last meal, nor that another, bigger mouse is likely to come by in half an hour, in which case the snake could potentially wait to eat. The snake's experience is based upon its present physical state and its environment in that moment, so waiting for the next mouse is not a consideration for the hungry snake.

The situation is much more complicated for humans. A person's conscious experience of time is based on what his or her Mental Body has adopted as beliefs. If one is conditioned to think of time as an independent function of the external world, as people are taught, then that is how our consciousness interprets its experience. In supporting this, the personality alters our experience, via filtering, to try and make it consistent with the Mental Body's notion of how the world works. The result is that, to a certain degree, each Energy Body operates with its own sense of time. The consciousness can accept information from the four Energy Bodies, but also be ignorant that the Bodies' separate senses of time are not in sync. Stress occurs when our Energy Bodies' sense of time are not in sync. A person must also be attuned to all of his Energy Bodies to have a genuine experience of the present moment.

My mind starts racing again. When I think about a different concept of time for each energy body, I wonder how it relates to my life. The fact that I feel an inner peace, even though my external world is going through many changes, means I am in sync with my energy bodies. And because I am in sync, the steps I am taking are in tune with my spiritual path. I am following the lead of my spiritual body, which is presenting me with the opportunities I need to grow spiritually. Where is this path leading? It must be leading to my life lesson and the potential for healing my core blockages. Until our core blockages are resolved, they cause situations to repeat in our lives.

I start to think of the repeating patterns of my life. The main one seems to be feeling alone, related to a sense of rejection. I can trace this back to my early childhood. With three older brothers, I was always trying to fit in and keep up with them. From their point of view, they didn't want someone butting into their play who didn't understand and couldn't physically or mentally operate on the same level as them. I was often getting in the way of their games. That was the seed, or at least an early component, of my pattern of feeling like I am on the outside of my life trying to get in.

The core could go even further back than that. One energy healer has theorized that ulcerative colitis has its origins in the mother not being able to breast-feed her infant, which I have confirmed with my mother was a problem during my infancy. My life lesson about feeling alone started early in life, and an early sense of rejection is part of that lesson. Or, conversely, maybe the lesson is to learn how to be self-sufficient? And what could be a better situation to learn this than living alone in a foreign country?

My body is feeling very light as I am thinking this; I feel invigorated and alive! Even though I am sitting on the deck as I write, I have the same sense of freedom that I have when I am dancing or singing. In fact, I feel so lively that I get up and walk into the kitchen, for no other reason than to feel my body move. More thoughts come to mind and I want to write them down, so I return to the deck. However, as I grab my laptop again, I realize I am overwhelmed. This introspective thinking is a very intense process.

Some exercise will help calm my mind and relax my body. My bike has been put into storage in preparation for the trip, so I opt to go for a hike instead. Walking also helps me, particularly when I am hiking in nature. I remind myself that I don't have to figure out my whole life all at once. I can let the thoughts go and trust that if it is important, the thoughts will come back to me.

Jenny is also happy to be going out. We go to my new favorite hiking trail, about a 10-minute drive from the house. As I hike, I feel the wind on my face—its coolness is refreshing. There is a musty smell in the air, evidence of a heavy rainfall last night. My body relishes the exertion as I settle into a brisk walking pace. Trees always give me a sense of being connected to the earth, and this allows me to sort out my emotions.

I feel slightly lonely as I toy with the idea that I am walking with God. A memory of a healing session comes to mind, one I had when I was working with Maria, a fellow minister, and an earlier graduate of the Inner Focus Healing School. I was lying on my massage table (which we use as healing tables), and Maria was guiding me through the healing. As the session progressed, incidents from my past flooded my mind—times when I felt rejected by my family and friends. I felt myself reaching deeper layers of those same old hurts.

During the healing I had several releases of energy, which I expressed through crying, moaning and movement. This was followed by a sensation of being infused with a loving energy.

Even though I wasn't conscious of the thought, there was a sense that the pain I had been regurgitating had a deeper element to it. Soon I started to get an inkling of this deeper issue — I was feeling abandoned by God! When I had been silent for several moments, Maria asked me what was happening. I said I felt energy flowing into me, and that the word "communion" was coming to mind. She asked what that word meant to me.

I thought about it and methodically replied, "It means experiencing Jesus. In a sense, Jesus is in me and in everyone, so by seeing Jesus in others, I am reaffirming Him as part of me, because the world is our mirror — it reflects back what we are putting out."

As I recall my healing, I realize the deeper we go into our hurts, the less they are about personal traumas and more they are about spiritual lessons. With core healings, our soul is more involved than our personality, so the *result* is not focused on personal trauma, but on spiritual understanding.

I wonder what lies underneath my loneliness lesson. My Zen training immediately provides an answer — going deeper leads to Enlightenment, the ultimate experience of God, of *being* God. That was the first time in my personal healing sessions that I had a specific reference to Jesus, or any other spiritual master for that matter. I believe spiritual masters have lived, and that they each provided a vision of spirituality, but I have not limited myself to the teachings of any one particular master. I try to follow the core teachings of compassion and love, which I think are the essence of most religions.

As I hike up the trail through the woods, my legs have a slight burning sensation. I take this as a sign that I have walked far enough for today. I turn around and head for home, or at least Jenny's home. She seems ready to return home as well.

When I get back, I return to my writing, feeling grounded and alert.

Chapter IV, cont. (Time and the Energy Bodies)

To explain this in more detail, let's consider the four Energy Bodies. Time has no meaning for the Physical Body. Its state is based upon the mind and the other Energy Bodies, but it is most closely associated with the Emotional Body. An obvious example is being tense—a person may or may not be aware that they are tense. Even if the person is aware of being tense, he or she may be unaware that the current situation has triggered the recalling of a significant past event; thus, the person's physical state is unknowingly being influenced by the memory. It is often the case that one doesn't want to recall an unpleasant memory, and so he or she suppresses the awareness of being triggered. Instead, the person tunes out the physical sensations, or attributes their physical state to some other cause. In these cases, the Physical Body's state is more reflective of a time from the past and not the present. Another scenario could be that a person walks into a situation where people are upset, and the Physical Body intuitively tenses up in response. However, the person ignores this new tension and misses out on some important information about the present moment. Here, the Physical Body is in current time but the consciousness is not fully attuned to this fact. Note that influences can also go from the Physical to the other Energy Bodies.

The Emotional Body can also have an experience that is not connected to the present moment. The Emotional Body doesn't have a concept of time, per se, but its state is reflective of a particular time. The clues that give rise to the emotions in the Emotional Body may not be based in the present moment, so it can be caught reliving a past experience, or it can act as if it is involved in an imaginary situation. In both cases, the Emotional Body is not in tune with the present moment. Once again, this internal experience of a different time can go unrecognized by the person's consciousness.

Here's a hypothetical example: a man is having an argument

with his girlfriend, but his Emotional Body is not reacting only to this situation. The current situation triggers the recollection of past feelings, and those old emotions override the present, thus becoming the *source* for his experience. The sensation he is experiencing in the Emotional Body is being fueled by conflicts he had with his parents when he was a child. The strong reaction in his Emotional Body influences his Physical Body, too. Not being aware of this overriding influence is why people sometimes overreact to their current situation. The man may get very angry at his girlfriend, but the strength of his emotion is really stored anger from his childhood. The process of how the Emotional Body gets triggered into reliving a past situation will be explored in Chapter VI.

My thinking is interrupted by Bell, the cat, rubbing up against my leg. This also stirs Jenny from her slumbering. The cat's hunger and Jenny's subsequent hope for a snack too make me realize I am also hungry. As I check in with myself—looking at my physical, emotional and mental states—I realize I am not only hungry, but tired as well. It is not the kind of tired that requires sleep, but it is a tired that means I need to relax. The focus of writing takes effort, and prepping for my upcoming adventure has also been taxing. Feeling content, I put my writing away. I get the pets some food and then make myself an omelet. I feel happy and blessed. Later today I will go shopping for some last minute items I need for my trip. The running around is winding down, and the excitement is building.

Chapter 13

Revelation; Meeting a Thai Monk

Monday, March 24

The intense sound is one of the most prominent aspects of the whole scene, though in a situation like this it is hard to separate the perceptions of one sense from another. The crickets, bugs and other creatures are making a combined symphony of jungle noises. They are out of sight, but sound as if they are right underfoot. The air is humid and warm and smells of moist vegetation. The pungent scent of tropical flowers—probably orchids—drifts by periodically, but otherwise there is no hint of a breeze. The morning light is just beginning to penetrate the night's darkness, leaving my imagination free to conjure up all sorts of creatures that might still be lurking in the bushes. I am walking the short distance from my sleeping area to the main house. After being led to the second floor veranda, I join several nuns sitting in front of the Buddhist master. I notice two geckoes hanging from the ceiling, adding to the scene's exoticness.

As I sit, I am struck by the exceptional nature of my situation. I just spent the night in this Buddhist monastery in the jungles of southern Thailand, and now I am in front of a revered Thai monk of unquestionable wisdom. The intensity of my surroundings only enhances the intensity of my feeling of gratitude. How is it that I am fortunate enough to have an experience like this? Emotions well up in me; I can feel tears leak out of my eyes and slowly crawl down my cheeks. They are a small sign of the immense appreciation I feel toward this gracious, elderly man.

I am not sure how long I stay in this state, but I would guess a minute or two. As these emotions well up inside of me, the monk—also called the abbot—is talking to several of the nuns (he doesn't speak English). They all seem oblivious to me and my rapture. Later, I am told by my friend, Ester, that the abbot was confirming the various meditation techniques he had prescribed to the local nuns and me. She tells me he is confident of the appropriateness of the meditation technique he assigned me earlier. During our first meeting the previous day, he suggested I meditate while focusing on a small, white object placed three meters in front of me at eye level.

Eventually the intensity of my rapture wanes and once again I become conscious of my surroundings. I still feel grateful and humble for this opportunity, but now the situation feels more like just an extraordinary event, and not a life-transforming episode of a few moments ago. As I wipe the tears from my face I see everyone else settling into meditative poses, so I do the same. Then I am told it is time to meditate.

As I try to focus inward, my mind reflects on how I came to be sitting in front of this very learned man in a jungle monastery in Thailand. The decision to go to Thailand was a very sponta-neous one. As I said earlier, I was attending a local tsunami benefit concert when I decided to go. This intuitive, quick decision-making process is what I call being in the flow of the universe.

During my first trip to Thailand, the people's manners and actions made a strong impression on my heart. Their attitude towards life was a glimpse into the reality of "living in the moment." I attribute their attitude to Buddhist influences, but regardless, they struck me as happy and kind. On a number of occasions I saw the locals spend what money they had to enjoy themselves with no regard for how the next day might unfold. I, on the other hand, budgeted my money carefully; I was always planning for the next several days at least. In an attempt to adopt more of a Thai attitude toward life, I purposely came here this time without any specific plans.

The day before I was due to leave, as though foreshadowing the spontaneity of my upcoming holiday, I received an e-mail from Lib, my ex-girlfriend from Korea. Our contact has been sporadic since I ended our relationship by returning to Canada after my problems working there. I don't do the Facebook thing but I did e-mail her a month ago, saying I had work and travel plans in Asia. Her late but timely response informed me that she was flying to Malaysia, after which she would catch a bus in order to meet me in Bangkok. (Lib is currently living in Australia, and that was the cheapest route for her to get to there.) She did not mention any dates, but she was aware of how long I was going to be in Thailand. I looked forward to seeing her again, without knowing what a significant role our proposed meeting would play in my adventures in Thailand.

My cousin Al (Allan) lives in Thailand, and he is also an ordained minister, though for a different type of church than Inner Focus. He and his wife Terry operate a home for orphaned children; they have adopted thirty or so children, and they've also had four biological children. I had hoped to meet them again as I did on my first trip, but Allan said he might be away during the time I am here; he often goes out to remote areas to "spread the word of Christ."

My only plans when I arrived in Bangkok were the uncertain meeting with Lib, hopefully spending some time in a Buddhist monastery (I have the addresses of a couple of places), and a possible visit with my cousin. Not being fond of big cities even at the best of times, coupled with the pollution and intensity of Bangkok, I made the quick decision to head south. I would try to meet Lib en route; I didn't want to wait for her in Bangkok.

The day after I arrived in Thailand I boarded a train bound for Hat Yai, a seventeen-hour ride to the largest Thai city in the proximity of the Malaysian border. I hadn't been there before so it was a chance to explore somewhere new. The train left in the afternoon and arrived in Hat Yai the following morning. Internet access is limited during travel, so before leaving Bangkok I sent Lib an e-mail about meeting her in southern Thailand. My thinking was that once I arrived in Hat Yai I would check to see if she had responded to this latest development, hopefully before she passes by on her way north.

I saw no response from her when I checked my e-mail in Hat Yai, which meant I was free to spend time with Ester, a woman I had just met on the train. We had begun a conversation and found we shared a deep interest in Buddhism, though Ester's passion far exceeded mine. She is a woman nearing the age of fifty, who seven years previously had left her grown children, her home in Singapore and her well-paying and prestigious banking job to study Buddhism in northern Thailand. Ester's commitment to her faith was as strong as her transition was dramatic. She was diligently following the more than 350 precepts, or expectations, of a Buddhist nun.

She was keen to share her passion for Buddhism and invited me to join her at a temple where her teacher was visiting for a week. Miraculously, as if it had all been arranged in advance, I was granted permission to not only have a visit with the abbot, but to spend the night at the temple as well. This was a special privilege not offered to others; some of the locals would have loved the opportunity to stay at the temple. The visiting abbot has a large following, and many would like to be near him.

The chiming of a metal bowl signals the end of the meditation. My sense of gratitude for this wonderful man still fills me. The abbot's final advice to me is to be open to what Asia has to offer. Then Ester, the other nuns and I pay our respects to the abbot—three deep bows—and return to our respective sleeping quarters.

Not long afterward I am informed that someone will be giving Ester and me a ride into town; the temple has a water shortage, and only residents can continue to stay. Someone will be available to drive us into town in an hour, giving me a chance to make some notes about my meditation. Immediately I am struck by the question: "How can I express the intensity of the feeling I just experienced?" The answer comes just as abruptly—it was an aligning of my energy bodies. It was a healing experience where I released some stuck energy, but like the Zen approach, it was a healing where I didn't have any insight into the mental component of the process. (And, in Zen fashion, I don't feel it would be productive to dissect this release in search of some insight.)

Instead of making notes I decide to use the time to work on my book. Most of my luggage is being stored at the hotel I stayed at in Bangkok, but I am still carrying my computer with me. I get it out and start writing.

Chapter IV, cont. (Time and the Energy Bodies)

To continue with the exploration of time and the Energy Bodies.

The Mental Body also has an internal time function separate from the consciousness' experience of time. The Mental Body can independently imagine itself in non-current time and situations. The Mental Body also has the capacity to layer many imaginary components onto the base elements of the present moment. For example, one can perceive a benign situation as being hostile without any sound external justification for thinking of it that way. Someone in a current experience may look like a harmful person from the viewer's childhood, triggering all kinds of false perceptions which are based on old memories associated with that perpetrator and not on the current situation. All the while, the consciousness can be oblivious to the internal processes of the Mental Body and its misinterpretation of the current scene as hostile, and/or disassociate from the feeling of hostility.

The capacity of the Physical, Emotional and Mental Bodies to be caught in non-current time consciously or unconsciously affects a person's experience of the current situation. Subsequently, the consciousness can believe itself to be fully attuned to the present situation, even if the person's Energy

Bodies are not. Moreover, the consciousness can believe itself to be fully attuned to the present situation, yet not receive much information from its Physical Body, meaning in reality that it is not truly attuned to the present. When the Energy Bodies are out of sync, it is a subconscious stress for that person.

The Spiritual Body's sense of time is eternal. In fact, the Spiritual Body recognizes objective time as a contrived tool that both the Mental Body and the consciousness (out of habit) use to sort through their experiences. This understanding gives the Spiritual Body a compassionate perspective of events; however, one's consciousness often does not access this wisdom. When accessing limited aspects of the Spiritual Body, its influence on the consciousness can be detrimental. This happens when judgments influence our experiences, as judgments are held in the Spiritual Body. The extent to which the consciousness is attuned to information from the Spiritual Body is a reflection of how aware that person is of their life lessons. In addition, the spiritual health of a person is reflective of their capacity for a compassionate understanding of difficult situations. The more spiritually healthy a person is, the more compassionate they are in difficult situations.

To encapsulate, the Spiritual Body is nearest in quality to the Divine, and its sense of time is eternal. The Mental Body is next, and it utilizes an objective, external concept of time. This is because an external sense of time is necessary for the illusion of self-identity to be perceived, which in turn facilitates the "game" being played out in an incarnate life. Mental Body time is structured, while Emotional Body time is whimsical and subject to frequent changes. Hence, it is important that a person has a healthy Emotional Body to be able to focus on present situations. The Physical Body is affected by all of the other Energy Bodies, but it is the most closely linked to the Emotional Body; therefore, emotions have the greatest influence on the Physical Body. The time frame to which the

Physical Body is attuned depends upon what information is impinging upon it, be it from the environment, the consciousness, the mind or one of the other Energy Bodies.

It is time to return to Hat Yai, so I put my writing away. When Ester and I are dropped off I immediately go to an Internet cafe and check my e-mail. There is a message from Lib saying she is in Hat Yai as well. I say a thankful but sad goodbye to Ester. Though I have known her for less than 48 hours, and I don't expect to see her again, she has played an important role in my life.

The rest of my Thai holiday is enjoyable as Lib and I become reacquainted. We travel north to Phuket, and then several days later we met up with my cousin, who had since returned from his traveling. He is continuing his spiritual work and now runs a training center for others who wish to establish orphanages in third world Asian countries.

Later, as I take the bus to the Bangkok airport to go to Japan, I reflect on my holiday. The events and places are already becoming pleasant memories, but my time with the abbot will forever be imprinted on my mind. The time I spent with Lib also spawns some musings about my being single. It is fortunate that, though I don't wish to do so many things by myself, I don't let it stop me. I had planned my trip to Thailand thinking I would be alone, but ended up traveling with Lib. It was great to see her again and to see how she has matured as a person. She is involved with an Australian man now, so getting back together is not a consideration (though I wasn't thinking along those lines anyway). However, true to Lib's character, her relationship with her new partner is openly non-monogamous.

Chapter 14

Things are "Heating-up" in Japan

Wednesday, April 9

It has only been a week, but Japan is turning out to be as intense as Thailand. Today is the first day off since my training started six days ago, and it is a welcomed break from the long, grueling days—I need some tranquility and solitude. The training is fourteen days in Nagoya City, where Peppy Kids Club's head office is, and then I will start teaching in Fuji City. My plan for the day is to go to a Buddhist temple and meditate. It is a twenty-five-minute train ride from my apartment, and then a short walk. I had visited the temple briefly when a few others and I went sightseeing the day before training started. The buildings are simple, but the grounds are lovely, and occupy a couple acres. The buildings are on the upper plateau, and stairs descend through a bamboo grove to a lower section. A fifty-foot-high statue of Buddha dominates the scene at the bottom of the stairs. Beyond the statue is a cemetery with hundreds of headstones clustered together.

At the temple I proceed to the main building, hoping to meditate there, but unfortunately I find a monk talking to a couple of women. I wander the grounds looking for another prime place to sit. After a few minutes I decide that meditating in front of the big Buddha will be inspiring, so I go down the stairs to the lower section. I am alone at the statue, and I notice a couple of stone blocks available for sitting. After I sit down I focus inward and try to tune out the surrounding noises, but my attention is drawn to what sounds like a crackling fire. Finally, I give in to the urge and look. As I turn around, I see through the bamboo grove glimpses of a fire flickering away!

Not being familiar with the details of Buddhist practices, I assume the fire is part of some ceremony. I will have a better chance of ignoring the fire if I check it out; there may be some interesting proceedings to watch. I climb back up the stairs and walk in that direction. At the edge of the embankment I discover a small fire; however, it is just some forest debris burning, and not a ceremonial event. By the sporadic piles of branches and leaves I can tell someone has been grooming the grounds, but I do not see anyone tending to the fire. This strikes me as suspicious.

To make sure this is a planned fire, I start looking for the monk I saw earlier. A minute or two later I find him in one of the other buildings. Given the language barrier, it is difficult to explain my concern, but he is curious enough to follow me as I lead him to the fire. When he sees it, he jumps into action with startling speed—obviously this isn't a planned fire!

The monk runs over to a water tap and motions at me to start filling a bucket, then runs off to get another bucket. The water is coming out of the tap excruciatingly slow; it will take five minutes to fill the bucket! The monk is now running back and forth, scooping little dabs of water from a shallow water vessel that is part of a statue. He throws these little splashes of water onto the fire, but it is too little water to make a difference. My bucket is now about a third full.

The fire continues to grow and is spreading to the denser bamboo stalks further down the embankment. Now it is consuming an area the size of a car, but it is not yet a raging fire! Standing on the level section above the embankment, I am a fair distance from the heat of the fire, but I can see the tops of the flames. The most intense part of the experience is the periodic explosions; I hear one every minute or so. I have never experienced a war, but that is the first thing that comes to mind as I hear the loud bangs. As I think about it, my guess is that because the fire is burning bamboo stalks, which grow in sections, it must be airtight compartments of bamboo exploding under the intense heat.

It strikes me as inept to stand waiting for the bucket to fill, so I abandon the water tap and move closer to assess the scene. On the upper part of the embankment the bamboo is sparser, so it is the pile of debris near the top that is fueling the fire. I determine that the most useful action is to pull debris away from the pile in the vicinity of a nearby building. My thinking is that if I limit the fuel supply in that direction, the fire may stay clear of the building long enough for the fire department to arrive. The explosions continue, and I hope flying cinders don't burn me.

By this time a few other visitors have come to help throw water on the fire, but there is so little water available it isn't helping. The monk has attached a hose to the slow water tap and finds that the hose stretches to the edge of the embankment. As I continue pulling the debris away, the monk leaves the hose lying on the ground and runs off to do some other task. I scramble the few feet up the slope and pick up the hose, and then begin dousing the section of fire closest to the building. The water is still coming out agonizingly slow, but by covering the end of the hose with my thumb I create a small spray. I hope by concentrating the spray to a limited area, it may make enough of a difference to save the building.

The explosions are now happening every thirty seconds. They are frightening to hear, particularly since I am standing so close! I am surprised that the water I am spraying is stopping the spread of the fire, but I fear the fire will soon expand beyond my watering area. If the fire department doesn't come soon, there is not much hope of stopping the fire from attacking the building. It is now about ten minutes since the monk and I first started to combat the fire.

Within moments, I am very relieved to hear the sirens of the fire trucks! The firemen arrive, set up, and then douse the fire — surprisingly, very quickly. I am glad to take a spot at a safe distance and watch them ply their trade. One fireman, aware that I was fighting the fire, asks me in halting English if I am all right.

I say yes, but realize that I am feeling quite overwhelmed! Physically I am fine, but emotionally I am fragile. Lately my life seems to have been a series of intense experiences, and this is one more for me to process.

At this point I am still quite hot from the fire and exertion, so with my emotions welling up I decide to walk around to cool down. I pass the monk and a few of the other temple visitors that were part of the effort to fight the fire. Their expressions of gratitude are clearly visible on their faces and in their eyes; I was the only one standing close to the fire. It is a relief to me that we don't speak the same language—I don't feel like talking.

After cooling down I decide I should try to meditate again. I return to the lower section in front of the large Buddha, but I find it difficult to focus. The firemen are still causing a disturbance—not that there is any sense of urgency, but their walking around and discussing things is more than my concentration can overcome. The best option seems to be returning to my apartment with the hope that I can relax there.

When I get back to the apartment I try meditating, but it is difficult to get started due in part to the starkness and unwelcoming feeling of the apartment. It is used solely as a temporary residence for trainees, so its comforts are basic and minimal. Later I will discover that the housing Peppy offers it foreign teachers is even more sparse.

My next thought is to take out my computer, hoping that writing will help me relax. I begin typing, but my mind is not into it. As I sit, it is not long before Terra comes to mind. Having spent time with Lib and then having made a connection with one of the other trainees (though we have only gone out casually one evening), I am feeling lonely. The strangeness of being in a foreign country has me seeking something comforting. Without judgment, I let my mind dwell on Terra.

In thinking about our relationship, the question persists: "Why did I feel so inhibited with her?" My inhibitions are more

118

than just being confused; they are connected to her specifically. I know this because I have been carefree and humorous in my romantic relationships. At times I equate my level of comfort in a relationship with the presence of my sense of humor. When I am relaxed, my wit can be sharp. What is it about Terra that takes me to that *stuck* place? My guess is her anger. Her anger is very much like my mother's.

Let's figure this out. Terra triggers in me a stuck energy pattern of being hurt by my mother's anger. A coping strategy that I developed as a teenager was to become reserved and aloof to avoid this old pain. If I can release this pattern, I should be more carefree and playful around Terra, and I would think with my mother, too.

I suspect it will be helpful to write about this, not only to settle my mind but also to explain energy bodies. I go back to my computer.

Chapter IV, cont. (Time and the Energy Bodies)

For another example of how the consciousness functions, let's examine a hypothetical situation. Let's say I am in a relationship with a woman. In this relationship I am having trouble feeling relaxed. I suspect a factor inhibiting my relaxation is that, when stressed, this woman has a tendency to anger easily. However, I have made no conscious association of this tendency being similar to how my mother behaved when I was a child. It is likely that this woman has more similarities with my mother, adding to the subconscious association.

When I am with this friend, my consciousness believes itself to be attuned to the current situation, but often this is not the case. Sometimes I am aware of being tense, hence my consciousness is at least partially attuned to my Physical Body, but I may not know that the tension relates to my childhood. Emotionally, it is even more complicated because my consciousness is not very attuned to my Emotional Body. My

Emotional Body is experiencing a much different sense of time, and has been triggered into reacting as if I'm in a situation from my childhood, when my mother unexpectedly became upset. At that earlier time, my personality developed a coping strategy as a means of protecting myself, in that I became subdued when sensing my mother was stressed. My current experience with my friend's anger is not based on my brief history with her, as I have experienced her anger relatively few times. My reaction is based more on my history with my mother.

My Mental Body is aware of my friend's tendency to get angry, but makes no connection between her tendency and my mother's tendency. Furthermore, in this situation, my Mental Body is periodically projecting into the future because of my desire for a more involved relationship with this woman. This projection means that my Mental Body is out of sync with my current situation, which also creates tension. My consciousness is unaware of the Mental Body process that is causing this added tension.

As I write this, I feel fidgety. I try walking to continue this reflective process. The walking allows the energy to dissipate, but sitting allows me to concentrate on the flow of ideas and to make connections. Even in spite of these techniques I find my mind is losing focus, and I notice that my motivation to write is waning. Seeing my life from the objective perspective and making the connections between the various aspects of my life is intense, but I stick with it.

In terms of blockages in my energy bodies, how does this look? I have a stuck pattern in my emotional body. The pattern encodes traumatic childhood experiences with my mother. Corresponding blockages in my other energy bodies would be a belief that I will get hurt if I get close to an angry person (a mental body blockage), and a judgment that angry people are hurtful (a spiritual body blockage). There are many other conflicting beliefs and desires in operation, all underscored by my attraction to Terra. How these blockages manifest in the physical body could explain any number of ongoing aches and pains, including the earache I had earlier, but given we are talking about something as profound as intimacy, the physical blockage is probably resonating with the core of my disease.

This makes total sense to me. I feel a rush of energy in my body as I make connections between my theory and my life. Exploring this deeper, I would say my disease has its seeds in early traumas. If we consider the healer's theory where he suggested ulcerative colitis is connected to problems with breast-feeding, then my struggle with intimacy could incorporate a sense of rejection that started just after birth, if not sooner.

In terms of my body's physiology, the emotional rejection I feel is being mirrored by my body's immune system. Medically, ulcerative colitis is the body's immune system erroneously rejecting a part of the physical body—namely, my large intestine—as if it were a foreign substance, the why of this doctors still don't know.

The onset of the disease happened when I was fifteen. Whatever other childhood issues I had then, I think puberty, having a poor connection with my emotional body and feeling isolated brought my subconscious struggles to a crisis point. Something had to give, and in my case it was my large intestine. Where a disease manifests is unique to the constitution of each individual; I guess genetically I have a weak digestive system. This is consistent with stories I have been told about my early childhood. When I was very young I would get so worked up trying to fit in with my brothers that my dad would have to hold me in his lap for up to thirty minutes before I was calm enough to eat.

So if diseases are rooted in energy dynamics, and if I can create my own reality, it should be easy to change my disease with energy work. To elaborate: yes it is possible, but it takes energy—literally and figuratively. The easiest way to bring things into harmony is by aligning the energy bodies and releasing stuck energy patterns. This is an involved process that takes many, many years of devoted work. Things can change faster and more dramatically—it is called a miracle—but I need to explore this more before I can explain the dynamics of how miracles work.

I go back to my writing, picking up where I left off.

Chapter IV, cont. (Time and the Energy Bodies)

Spiritually, there is an unconscious dance occurring between both of our Spiritual Bodies; they are assessing how being intimate with the other person might facilitate learning life lessons. The dance executed by our Spiritual Bodies is not only due to the basic physical attraction between us, but also because they are assessing how that person's characteristics fit with our life lessons. The Spiritual Body does not consider the likelihood of us actually learning from each other, but simply the potential. As we get more involved, either one of us may become too wrapped up in our own fears to really achieve the intimacy needed for us to learn our lessons. The Spiritual Body is structured to create situations for us to learn, and then it is up to the consciousness to actually achieve this learning, in accordance with Free Will.

All the information from the different Energy Bodies is in the mind and available to the consciousness, but the consciousness is conditioned to attend to only a limited part of this information. The consciousness is influenced by the personality, which is primarily concerned with information that reinforces the person's self-concept and self-protection. This censoring of information reinforces basic beliefs, and this process is the personality's perceptual gauze. If a person is ignorant of their internal processes, the personality will often step in and guide the consciousness.

That's about as long as I can concentrate on this. It was a good session, and I have gotten some insights into my own issues. I am pleased with my writing, so now it's time to make dinner. This being a training apartment means it does not have a very functional kitchen, but then again, I am a pretty basic cook. Often I will simply put rice, veggies and meat—fish or chicken—in a pot and let them steam. It's simple, and with some sauce it's tasty enough, and easy on my digestive system.

Chapter 15

Life Begins Anew; ESL Teaching

Saturday, April 19

That wasn't so bad. I just finished solo teaching my first class at Peppy. During training we usually had an experienced teacher observing, but now I am totally on my own. My previous teaching experience in Korea gave me some idea of what to expect. I tried to have fun with the kids and keep them active by moving around the classroom. I was nervous and unsure of myself, but my general reaction is that the lesson went well.

Luckily, my first day of teaching is a one-class day. It's Saturday, and I have the next two days off before I start my first full week of teaching. With this job, a normal week is Tuesday through Saturday. The routine at Peppy is a four-week schedule; I will teach at a school one week, move to a different school the next week, and so on until after four weeks I begin the rotation again. For each week there are different students that come each day, so I will see my students once every 28 days. It will take time to learn their names and their personalities. For the three weeks between my visits, each school has a Japanese person teaching English to the students. I say "school," but the classrooms are often just a room in an office building, a vacated shop or even a small apartment. Peppy has more than a thousand small class-rooms all over Japan.

Today is my second day in Fuji City. I arrived around noon yesterday after leaving Nagoya City at 9am. The training ended on Thursday and our entire group (fourteen of us) went out for a celebration that night. It was a chance to say goodbye as Friday was "ship-out" day—the day when we were sent to our respective placements all over Japan. Chances are I won't see any of them again, except for one other trainee who was placed in the same prefecture as me. A prefecture is a small province or state, and with Peppy, each prefecture has monthly staff meetings (lasting a couple of hours) for the foreign teachers in that region. And, several times a year, each prefecture has full-day training sessions, some with the Japanese teachers and some with only the native English-speaking teachers.

To celebrate the end of training, we went out for dinner and then went to a karaoke place. I definitely had fun, but I don't want to make that kind of partying the norm. It could be an indication that I will be doing lots of drinking in Japan. From my experience in Korea I know it is an easy trap to fall into, a trap where your social life revolves around alcohol.

Where I was going to be placed was out of my control, but Fuji City seems to be a good location. Being at the foot of Mount Fuji should give me lots of opportunity to get out into the wilderness. I have yet to see Mount Fuji itself; since arriving in the city the mountain has been obscured by clouds. I am ignorant about the city, but my trainer warned me that just because Mount Fuji is revered as a spiritual icon in Japan, it doesn't mean Fuji City is pretty. He said it is a heavy industry town with lots of smokestacks. I was later told that there are over 300 smokestacks in Fuji!

Brad, who will be my boss, met me at the train station yesterday. He seems like a nice guy, though he is young—at forty-five, I am more than double his age. First, he took me to my apartment, and then we went to City Hall to apply for my Alien Registration Card (a requirement to reside in Japan). Next he set up my bank account, and finally he arranged for me to get a personal ID stamp. An ID stamp (*hanko* in Japanese) is used here instead of a signature; it is your official approval of a transaction. We also inquired about a cell phone, but the store said I needed my registration card first. Brad and I had plenty of time to talk while he showed me around town, and one of the things we discussed was Zen. Though he is not a follower of the practices, he did a presentation on Zen during one of the training sessions last year. Brad left around 5pm after my luggage arrived from Nagoya—the company saved me the hassle of dragging two large suitcases around by having them shipped here.

Yesterday I felt rough after Thursday night's festivities, so I didn't want to go out and explore at night. A wise decision considering I had to teach today, even if it was only one class. Tonight I will try to find the bar in Fuji that Brad mentioned. It is referred to as "Oz," which is short for "Land of Oz." Originally it had an Australian owner, but now a Japanese man runs it. I also heard about it from Jay, the teacher I am replacing here in Fuji— I met him briefly in Nagoya when he picked up his final paycheck from the Peppy head office.

However, finding Oz will be for later tonight; first I have several hours to occupy. Fortunately, the train ride home from my classroom is a simple one. Some of the classrooms we went to during our training were very difficult to find, with complicated train and bus transfers. One of the advantages Peppy has over its competition is that their classrooms are situated away from train stations and closer to where the students live, though I suspect the motivation is cheaper rent rather than proximity to clients. While walking the ten minutes from the train station to my new home, I stop at a grocery store and buy a prepackaged meal. I have a poor understanding of how expensive things are in Japan, but I think it costs around five dollars.

When I get home I quickly eat my meal—I am famished. It is 3 o'clock when I finish eating.

This is not an ideal time for me to write. I don't seem to focus as well in the afternoon and I am less creative, plus a full stomach is not good for thinking. I often use writing as a motivational ploy to justify some guilty pleasure, but today even this doesn't inspire me to get out my computer. I check the TV instead. There are ten channels, but I can't find any English-speaking programs. A couple of stations have English shows, but they are dubbed with Japanese dialogue. If there is a button on the converter that changes the dialogue into English, I can't find it. Though it is mildly interesting to see some of the weird, Japanese game shows on TV, I am not intrigued enough to watch them now.

Soon, I find myself just sitting and reflecting. I feel a sense of satisfaction—I made it happen, and now I am living in Japan! It has been fun getting here, and now my life begins anew. However, my teaching contract is only for a year, so it doesn't feel like I am establishing a new home—Japan is just an interlude in my life. I stop this train of thought as I realize this is not a "Living in the Moment" attitude. If I am dwelling on the fact that my current situation is a temporary one, then I am encouraging my energy bodies to be out of sync. This is not to say that I ignore the fact that I have a one-year contract—that is a reality. It is prudent to avoid buying any big-ticket conveniences such as a decent TV, stereo or even furniture (Peppy apartments are very sparsely furnished); when I leave, these items will be hard to dispose of and impractical to ship home.

If I consistently think about where I will be in a year, my consciousness will not enjoy the excitement of my current situation. The emotional and physical bodies will follow the lead of the mental body so there is no benefit in dwelling on my future. Sure I could actively look for a job via the Internet, but I don't intend to do this, so it is best not to put a lot of energy into thinking about a future job.

Initially, when I am outside doing things, all of it will be new to me, so it will be easy to focus on my surroundings. The bigger challenge will be to enjoy my home situation in spite of its simplicity. This is where making rituals out of routines can be helpful. One can easily get out of the moment when taking care of the necessities of life, such as cooking, cleaning or doing laundry. To help stay in the moment during these times, it is important for me to connect with my spiritual nature. A spiritual connection while doing the mundane transforms a routine activity into a ritual.

Now my spiritual growth is such that I have a strong connection to my spiritual body. I have worked hard to clear many blockages, and I have become acutely aware of the importance of being in the moment. It seems odd that knowing about energy bodies—a mental activity—helps me be in the moment, which is a state inhibited by thinking. However, the sooner I can mentally recognize being out of the moment, the sooner I can get myself back into it. The more I habitually use these techniques, the more joy I get from life. During the fire at the temple, I was engrossed in the experience. The fire had my full attention; I cleared debris, I picked up the hose and I responded only to the fire. The fire consumed my attention, and there was no opportunity to reflect on other events in my life.

Shouldn't all of life be like this? This is the essence of the Zen training, to "Live in the Moment." Where does my mind go when doing the mundane things in my life like washing the dishes? If I think about having a successful book, or how so-and-so mistreated me when I was eleven, then I am missing out on something. I am missing out on the joy of doing the dishes, and it takes wisdom to experience the joy of doing the dishes. If I focus on cleaning the dishes in the same way I focused on the fire, then I am living in the moment. It is the stuck energy patterns and the personality that propel us to divert attention from what we are doing.

Speaking of which, I need to stop ruminating and focus on *this* moment, but I'm not sure what to do. The thought of Oz crosses my mind. The lure of discovering a new place is enticing, and going there will be fun, but first I will force myself to do some writing. Writing when I am resistant to it can feel like a task; but my spiritual connection often becomes clearer when I start writing, and changes the task into a ritual. I get out my computer.

Chapter IV, cont. (Time and the Energy Bodies)

To review: the concept of time for the consciousness is usually based on the learned mental concept of an independent, external time. However, each Energy Body's functions can be based upon different time frames, though this variation is often not recognized by the consciousness. When the Energy Bodies are not in sync, it creates stress for the individual. The Physical Body is likely not attuned to its immediate environment when it is being influenced by the mind or by one of the other Energy Bodies. However, for the consciousness to be attuned to the current situation, its awareness must include the Physical Body's state, and that state must be in tune with the current situation. The Emotional Body can be caught up in past emotional experiences or be having non-current emotions based on mental imagining of future or past scenarios. The Mental Body can be in non-current time via false perceptions of the current situation or by being focused on a mental imagining. The Spiritual Body has an eternal sense of time, but this perspective is often not accessed. When the spiritual connection is limited, this Body's influence on the consciousness can be detrimental, and can result in negative notions such as judgments, which are rooted in the Spiritual Body.

Real life experiences are complex situations where the consciousness often tunes out parts of one or more of the Energy Bodies. The content of the consciousness varies over time, but in the moment it can be affected by the personality (which includes our self-concept) and the mind (which includes our memories). The consciousness is usually taught to consider itself as a singular entity, and unless educated otherwise, this misconception means the separate reaction of each individual Energy Body is not realized.

Writing is a struggle, so I put my computer away. The progress I have made may not be enough for guilt-free drinking, but I want to focus on the adventure of being in Japan. As I step into the shower in preparation for tonight, I am still thinking about my writing. Why do I have such a fascination with time? At university I wrote one of my term papers on the misconception of objective time. Starting in elementary school I have been a great admirer of Einstein, and later read several books about him. One book questioned why schools haven't changed the way science is taught, to reflect the new understanding of time created by Einstein's General Theory of Relativity.

There was also a personal experience which fueled my questioning of the common view of time and space. While attending university I went to a classmate's house party. Debra was a fellow student in a General Studies course titled "Altered States of Consciousness," and we have maintained a friendship to this day. At the party I had consumed a significant amount of alcohol, and I had also smoked some hashish. Unknown to me at the time, a few of the other partiers had taken acid.

As the evening wore on, there was a group of about ten people left, and everyone was having a great time. A shift happened as the gaiety continued, and we started communicating telepathically. I cannot explain how it happened, but I realized that we were communicating without talking. I remember telling a joke, and then part way through I switched to merely *thinking* the joke, yet everyone laughed when I came to the punch line. It was a seamless shift into this alternative form of communication, and though it was unusual, it also seemed natural. This intermittent telepathy lasted for less than thirty minutes, and then the magic was over. Soon people started leaving, but nothing was said about what had just happened. It is tempting to dismiss it as not having occurred at all, but that experience left me knowing that our personal existence is more than just our physical bodies; we have capacities that transcend our normal means of functioning.

Soon it is time to find Oz. I get ready and head out the door with a sense of anticipation. I will have dinner there as I was told the food is good. My new life in Japan has begun.

Chapter 16

Learning the Ropes of Japanese Society

Saturday, May 10

It is 6:30pm on Saturday night. I finished teaching a few hours ago, I've eaten dinner and now I am having a couple of drinks before going to Oz. I have been going there semi-regularly lately, limited by my finances. There are often several foreigners hanging out there; I have enjoyed drinking with them, and I am learning the ins and outs of life in Japan from them. There is a core group of about six people, including Brad my boss, and all of them have lived here for a number of years. They have created a fun and comfortable lifestyle for themselves and they plan on staying here for the foreseeable future. All of the guys speak moderate to fluent Japanese. Most of them are from Canada, and a couple are from the States, not that it makes any difference. For me, having studied French in school and having lived in Korea, I know the language part of my brain doesn't work so I have no intention to learn Japanese.

Suddenly my cell phone rings. Now that I have my Alien Registration Card, Brad got me a cell phone one day after a staff meeting. I am shocked to hear Mike on the other end asking me if I have plans for tonight (Mike is one of several guys I am getting to know at Oz). I say no. He tells me he and the boys will be by in 15 minutes to pick me up. They are going to his favorite festival in Japan, not too far from where I live.

I expect them to call again when they arrive, so the knock at the door startles me. Mike decided to come up and check out my apartment instead of phoning from downstairs (I live on the third floor). I gladly invite him in, and he says we only have a second but he wants to check out the "pad." He takes the short walk from the door, through the kitchen and into the main room.

Including the bathroom there are only three rooms as many apartments don't have bedrooms.

He says, "Hey, this is a pretty decent apartment, but you need some furniture, dude. I have a couch if you want it."

I shrug. "Yeah, well that's Peppy for ya. Having a couch means I have to get rid of it when I go, so I'll pass, but thanks."

I grab a few of drinks from the fridge, offer one to Mike, and then we head out the door. I climb into Hank's car (a new Nissan Pathfinder), and say hi to Gerry and Rob—all part of the Oz gang. A 15-minute drive later we park in a field along with hundreds of other vehicles. From there it is a short walk to the festival site, which is on a neighboring field. There are two rows of kiosks about 20 yards (or meters) apart with hundreds of people milling about in the middle. The booths are selling food, drinks, snacks, toys, clothes and some things I'm not sure about.

As we navigate our way to the other end of the kiosks—about 50 yards/meters—the space opens up and there is a stage on the right. There are about 20 drummers on the stage doing their thing. The drums vary in size from one to eight feet in diameter, and they all have some depth to them, so the sounds are deep and rich. The hitting of the drums is very dramatic and purposeful, and combined with the costumes and decorations, it is a captivating performance. I will find out later that taiko is a unique style of Japanese drumming that is both artistic and theatrical. I am enthralled by it, but I am told we are going over to the open field.

Now that we are out of the crowd, I notice that the field has three large poles, ranging in heights of about 15, 20 and 25 yards. On top of each pole is an inverted cone basket about 10 feet (3 meters) across at the top. I am told the baskets are straw and stuffed with fireworks. Each basket also has an object that looks like a Christmas tree sticking out of the top. We circle around the field and the poles towards the far side where there is a river embankment. The ground slopes up as you near the river, so it makes a great viewing area. There are several hundred people on blankets and tarps sitting on the hill, and I can sense this is going to be a memorable evening.

As we gingerly step by the various pieces of ground people have claimed, I hear Hank's name being called out. Soon I am introduced to Anton and Mark, another couple of long-time residents who hail from New Zealand. Both are married and have children. I was a keen rugby player at high school and at university, and since New Zealand is fanatical about rugby (similar to how Canada is about hockey) I am sure we will have something to talk about should there be a quiet moment. However, quiet is not likely to come any time soon; there is quite a buzz. Not only because of the crowd noise and drummers, but the air itself seems to have a buzz to it; I can feel the excitement.

We find space to sit on their tarp and they offer me a beer from their cooler, but I'm still drinking the ones I brought, so I decline. Japan doesn't seem to have any restrictions on drinking in public; I have seen people drinking on the streets and on trains, and alcohol is readily available at the ever-present convenient stores. I am told they even have alcohol vending machines on the streets, but I have yet to see one. I also haven't seen any inappropriate drunk behavior during my short time in Japan—a few drunks, but totally harmless.

Soon the show begins. I hadn't paid any attention to them before, but there are several fire barrels around the perimeter. A separate group of people that were previously selected are now taking fire sticks out of the barrels. They aren't actually sticks, but more like ropes with fireballs on the end of them. Hank says the proper English name for them is "fag." The ropes, or fags, are then twirled and launched in attempt to get them to land in the basket at the top of the pole. Presumably this will set the basket on fire. I am shocked at how young the throwers are; they seem like young teenagers, and there are about 40 them. Mike tells me the short pole is for the younger people. I am also shocked at how

134

dangerous this is. There is no fence or rail separating the throwers from the viewers; only attendants standing at the edge of the field keep the viewers from moving any closer. A bigger danger is that the throwers are making a complete circle around the pole; fags thrown from one side land near the throwers on the other. They may seem easy to throw, but the ropes are not coming close to landing in the baskets. My fears seem well founded because a couple of the fireballs have gone way off target, landing perilously close to the viewers.

It takes about 10 minutes for the throwers to get the hang of it—or maybe they have added some older boys into the mix—but some are now coming closer to the basket. Every time a fag comes close to the tower, the crowd cheers. After another 5 minutes, one lands in the basket. It is anticlimactic—nothing happens. The throwers continue throwing, and soon another fag lands in the basket, and finally a third. But if landing the fags in the basket was anticlimactic, soon things get extremely climactic.

Fire now starts to rise up out of the basket. The throwers are all ushered away and the real show begins. Gradually the fire builds until it ignites some of the fireworks stuffed into the basket. A few shoot off into the sky, followed by a short lull, and then a few more explode. Soon there is a plethora of fireworks shooting off in all directions. It is a breezy evening, and wind is blowing across the field and over the crowd. Miraculously, one firework shoots over our heads. It is probably 30 yards above our heads, but it seems perilously close. The fireworks soon diminish and then quickly stop. I am sure they put a lot of thought into packing the fireworks, but once the fire starts there is no controlling them. This is all shockingly risky.

I foolishly thought that was the show, but there is bigger drama yet to come. The straw basket continues to burn, and soon it is a massive fireball atop the pole that continues to get brighter and brighter. It hangs there for what seems like ages until, finally, a part of the basket collapses into a shower of sparks and smoke. I can feel the heat. The crowd gasps, as do I.

The rest of the basket continues to burn until, in a grand finale, the whole thing bursts into the air. The fire embers not only fall, but also rise because of the intense heat of the blaze. In a furious blast of light and heat, the fireball expands into a 30-yard-high plume. As I mentioned, the wind is blowing in our direction, and soon we have bits of ash falling on us; fortunately, it is only a small amount. I am stunned by the whole display and danger of it all.

Soon everyone takes a break as the coordinators douse the fire and prep the next pole. It is a chance for people to get refreshments, go to the toilet etc. In 10 minutes the process begins again, and then later, a third time. It was an amazing festival. I would have gladly paid money to see this, but it was free. After the last pole, the picnickers quickly pack up their stuff, as do the festival organizers. It is a mass exodus. We decide to go to Oz.

At Oz, everyone is still buzzing from the excitement of the appropriately named "fire festival." We have a fun time just hanging out and having a few more drinks. I enjoy getting to know Anton and Mark, but they are heading home soon as they live in a nearby city and the last train is at 11:00. I am on a natural high from the festival, but I am getting low on money, so I decide to call it an early night too. Gerry, a very kind soul, generously offers to loan me 10,000 yen (about $100)—the guy hardly knows me. Gerry says he knows that Peppy is slow to pay their new staff (probably because he is a good friend with my boss, Brad), and is happy to help out. Peppy withholds a month's pay, and then we get a monthly paycheck on the 25th of each month, so it is almost two months before we get our first pay. I decline, though I am grateful for the offer. I express my appreciation to the boys for the introduction to Japanese culture, of which they tell me there are many more opportunities to come.

When I get home, I watch some TV. There happens to be an American baseball game on, which is a nice treat. I feel that the rapport between the other guys and me is good. I am fortunate to have made some connections quickly; it took me months to establish a social life when living in Korea. I am sure the Oz boys and I will be hanging out quite a bit.

The baseball game ends and I decide it's time for bed.

The next morning when I get up, I am in a very upbeat frame of mind. It was a fabulous festival and I was with some new friends who are a lot of fun. Plus, I *don't* have any effects from over-drinking last night. I quickly prepare myself for my morning meditation. I haven't figured out a good setup for it yet, so I sit in a folding chair (the only chair I have). Ideally I would sit on a low bench, but the little bench I made for myself is in storage in Canada. The meditation goes well, but without any great insights into my life. Often while meditating I can see my life with an objective perspective, which helps me decide what I need to do to keep my life moving forward. Nevertheless, just having a focused, quiet mind for 40 minutes is of ample benefit.

After meditation, it is time to write.

Chapter V: The Soul

As previously stated, the world is composed of Universal Energy, or the Divine. At its base level, this energy is indistinguishable—all is One—and it is a benevolent consciousness. As an expression of its benevolence (love), this intelligence created a separation—a yin and a yang, to use the ancient Chinese terms. It is the contrast between the two that enables the conception of a separate existence. Further divisions of the Divine give rise to a Soul. The Soul is a level of separation, or individuation, of Divine energy that can enact Free Will. Creating a Soul and its ability for Free Will enables the Divine consciousness to "experience" its own Divinity. To illustrate, let's consider art. It could be argued that neither art nor music are necessary for life, but both seem to be an expression of the goodness of the world. And a world without art or music is both unfathomable and repugnant. God creating a soul is akin to God creating art.

I have described a person's consciousness as a mirror image of the Soul, and likewise, the Soul is a reflection of the Divine. The Soul still has a clear understanding of "The Now," or Oneness, but it also has the origins for the concept of individuality. With each further division of Divine energy, the capacity to understand "The Now" becomes more obscure. The Soul is the fulcrum where understanding the Divine truth is separated from ignorance of it. This is also the point at which the idea of objective time becomes necessary, because for Free Will to function, a personal consciousness must forget its connection to The Now. Creating objective time compels the person to forget The Now and to imagine individuality. When the personal consciousness utilizes its perceived Free Will to "remind" itself of its connection to the Divine, it enables the Soul to have the "experience" of its own Divinity, which was the purpose of creating the separations in the first place.

A parallel can be found in science and its ideas about black holes. A black hole is a region of space where the matter is so dense that its gravitational pull is too strong for even light to escape, thus its blackness. There is a perimeter around the black hole which marks the region between where light cannot escape the gravitational pull and where it can. This perimeter is called the event horizon. Our scientific concepts of time and individuation cease to exist inside the black hole. If one were to consider the converse of this process, where the Divine was a light so vibrant that no blackness (absence of light) could exist in its vicinity, then the perimeter (event horizon) is where blackness can first exist. This would be the domain of the Soul; the Soul is the Divine's event horizon. On the one side is the complete absence of darkness (acute awareness of the Divine), and on the other side is the possibility for blackness (a consciousness perceiving its separateness).

To highlight the view of reality as illusionary and not concrete, we can consider our day-to-day world vs. the world of science. In the 1600s, Newton developed his laws of motion for physics, which describe the functioning of objects in the material world and are based on the notion of objective time. These laws seemed accurate and were useful. Then in the early 20th century, Einstein proposed his revolutionary theory of time-space. Though it doesn't help the layperson to understand the world, science has revered Einstein's theories. His work also explained the limited scope and utility of Newtonian physics. The old physics are adequate for crude observations of "normal" objects, but it does not apply to the micro or meta-macro realms where matter interacts according to very different rules. Newtonian physics is too limited to explain the realms of stars or minute particles. Subatomic particles and black holes are even more obscure.

And so it is with Energy Body dynamics. The observable body seems to operate according to basic laws, but the other Energy Bodies function according to different sets of rules. We can function adequately using only the rules for the Physical Body (like Newtonian physics), but to understand beyond the crude physical, we must use different laws. Using the broader rules, the other Energy Bodies can and do influence the Physical Body and world. They serve as intermediaries between the Soul and the Physical Body. The physics of Newton vs. Einstein is also a parallel to Free Will and the Divine. Free Will works in the realm of day-to-day life, but on a bigger scale, it doesn't work. From the Divine perspective, everything is One, so any distortions created by Free Will will always get resolved (re-balanced). However, from the physical perspective, Free Will appears to be real because in that moment the consciousness can still choose which directions to move in. However, continually moving in the "wrong" direction is draining for the person and there is increased pull towards re-balancing. It is similar to willfully standing: eventually a person will have to sit down, but the moment they decide to sit is still a free choice.

Additionally, there are parallels between my Energy Body Theory and the Big Bang Theory. Scientists have theorized that just after the Big Bang, there existed only one force (akin to the Divine consciousness). Moments later that initial force divided into the four forces that science accepts today: gravity, electro-magnetism, and strong and weak nuclear forces. Of these four, gravity is inordinately weaker. This is similar to the four Energy Bodies, where the Physical Body is inordinately different, and the Divine is fundamentally primal.

I will leave further details of the scientific theories for the reader to explore, if desired. I mention them not to suggest that they prove the details of my exploration into existence, but to highlight that science provides some impetus for conjecturing the details. The conundrums created by my theory have parallels with the ones faced by scientists.

It has been a good writing session, but now my mind is strug-gling to stay focused, so I will stop for today. The joy I am feeling lets me know I am connected to my energy bodies; however, the lack of focus creeping into my thinking also lets me know that my connection to my mental body is not clear. Not that I am concerned; I am feeling joy, and that's what counts most.

It is a nice day outside, so I decide to go for a walk along a path outside my apartment. I put my computer away, grab a banana, and head out the door. As I walk, I find myself reflecting on today's writing. I can imagine the negative reaction of some of my science-oriented friends. I think what inhibits scientists from thinking about spiritual matters is that they have a strong bias against it. It is a reasonable area for thought and exploration, especially given some of the conclusions modern science is arriving at. But in Western society there is a long history of the "church" squashing and limiting new scientific ideas. The

Church feared that the ideas would impact their beliefs and perceived power. Also, scientists are people first and scientists second, so in practice, blockages in their energy bodies lead them to rationalize all sorts of unfounded biases. To compound matters, the nature of science fosters mental body functioning, usually at the expense of connecting with the other energy bodies. This supports the myth that scientific advancements are made by having an objective, rational approach, but the truth is that many new ideas came because scientists exhibited a dogged determination contrary to a rational approach.

Often I think that scientists have never had a profound spiritual experience that validates knowledge of a greater power. A near death experience usually changes a person's view of the world, and so can prolonged periods of meditation or a life crisis that shake up one's core beliefs. These kinds of experiences can leave one knowing that there is some form of divine consciousness underpinning the normal occurrences of life.

It is a beautiful spring day, and all these thoughts have me stuck in my mental body again, and not on the beauty of the day. As I try to let the thoughts go I notice the vibrant colors of the flowers and their fragrant aromas, and this pulls me into the moment. I will try to stay there and not dwell on ideas. And if my thinking slips, I will try to recognize it more quickly. This is Zen training for living in the moment.

Chapter 17

More Fear and a Hangover

Friday, May 23

I am feeling shaky and somewhat nauseous. It is mid-morning and I am on my way to the bank, knowing in the back of my mind that I have to teach at five o'clock today. The fresh air feels soothing, but it is not enough to cleanse away my sick feeling. It is not that I want to throw up; instead I feel queasy and unsure of myself. The physical symptoms are amplifying my shroud of uncertainty. There is a sense of vulnerability, and unlike when in a healing session, I don't feel I can change it. It is an unwanted and uncontrolled vulnerability, resulting in feeling helpless.

I am not one who gets hangovers like many people seem to experience them. I don't have headaches, it is extremely rare for me to get sick and I can usually function normally after consuming significant amounts of alcohol the previous night. The celebration at the end of Peppy training is a good example of excessive drinking but managing OK the next day. However, after last night's drinking, I am feeling horrible. It is rare that I would drink that much when I have to work the next day, but last night I got carried away. I was spending the last of my savings because I knew today was payday.

It evolved into a quasi-healing session, but one that was fraught with problems. I was at Oz for a while, and then went home feeling upbeat. But instead of going to bed, I chose to keep drinking and go for a walk on the path near my apartment. Walking this trail is becoming a routine, or maybe a ritual. The path is lined with a multitude of flowers and bushes, and later at night I rarely encounter another person. I usually listen to music as I walk and the songs induce all kinds of emotions. I may laugh at the magic of my life, and then soon after cry because I feel so alone. When in this state, I try to let my emotions flow unimpeded.

At best, I consider drug use—and I include alcohol as a drug—a shortcut in attempting to find different experiences. Many indigenous cultures use drugs for special occasions, often associated with initiations, so not all uses of non-pharmaceutical drugs are bad. In modern society, most recreational drug usage is detrimental, but in some cases it can have benefits. When not used habitually for escapism or numbing, you can have some fun, get some insights or emote with drugs. The psychiatric profession and pharmaceutical industry are based on this premise. However, I think for people with unhealthy Energy Bodies, drugs can be very harmful. Furthermore, I believe any *positive* state of mind you can experience while using drugs can be experienced by natural means, but to achieve those states by natural means takes effort—a *lot* of effort! It's analogous to climbing a mountain where the climb enriches the experience of the view from the top. One's appreciation of the view is not as great if one simply flies to the top. Taking drugs is, at best, trying to fly to the top of a mountain.

Some states of mind I have achieved during spiritual practices have far exceeded any illusions I've had while being high on drugs. These states of mind have come as a result of some very hard work on my part. For example, they came after days of meditation at a Zen retreat, after releasing some intense pain during a healing session or in a meditation after days of energy work at a healing school module. These are experiences that have lengthy preludes to them involving focused spiritual, mental, emotional and physical discipline. Drugs can be an attempt to get there in just a few hours without any concentrated effort.

In addition to stunting any positive experiences, there are high costs for taking shortcuts. One, the drug-induced experience doesn't get grounded. By this I mean it isn't a life-changing experience in the way a natural high can be. To see the world as interconnected while on some psychedelic drug trip may be a cool experience, but what do you make of it days later? When you see the world as interconnected after days of meditation, you become a more compassionate person. An experience is grounded when it is connected to your regular day-to-day life, and it changes you. That profound, natural high can be integrated into your normal life, while a cool drug trip is an experience that happened to you but doesn't become part of you. With drug use, you tend to think the spiritual insight emanates from the drug, and is not part of your personal world, and this encourages habitual use.

Another cost of drug use is the actual harm you do to your energy bodies. You literally put holes in your energy field. All the negative physical effects after a drug experience have similar negative effects on your other energy bodies. Being emotionally shaky, having a lack of mental clarity and experiencing a sense of existential longing (what's my life all about?) are just a few of the detrimental impacts of drug use on the various energy bodies.

Even knowing this, I still use alcohol as a shortcut. I am too lazy to do the work required to connect with all the emotions I hide from myself. So if I choose, while drinking, I can access some of those emotions and release them. Usually this release feels cathartic, but last night's session involved too much alcohol, and this morning I am paying the price. As I walk to the bank it feels like I have holes in my energy field, and this is enabling the fear to consume me. I am irrationally thinking that I will be put in jail because I don't have enough cash with me to buy a train ticket to get to work. This will be my first time withdrawing money from my bank, I am not sure how it is done and I don't feel up to the challenge. If I didn't need the money to get to work today, I would gladly leave it for another day.

I know these are irrational fears, but I still seem gripped by them. In the month and a half I have been in Japan I have been impressed by how nice the Japanese people are, yet now I fear they will abuse me, take advantage of me and mock me. My fear is amplified by thinking that I could be the victim of some random act of violence, like the story I heard about a man taking a machete into a school and killing some children.

My mind spins with irrational thoughts and my body is shaky and tense, but there is a part of me that knows I am experiencing the compounded effects of last night's drinking. I start to focus on bringing in light. The holes in my energy field are allowing fear to invade my thoughts, so to counter this I will work on filling those holes on an energetic level.

As I do this, Terra comes to mind, prompted I'm sure by some lingering effects from last night's emoting. She is a comforting thought, and I decide that I will e-mail her when I get back. I want to get some validation from her that I am not crazy. I don't mean the irrational fears I am having now, but crazy in trying to write a book, crazy in leaving my job and my home in Canada and crazy in trying to help the world understand how to be happy and how to heal themselves. This is the validation I am hoping to get from her. My momentary irrational fears are tapping into my deeper life fears, and I want to reach out to her for help.

During the last conversation we had before I left Canada, I told her we might never see each other again. For her I think it seemed melodramatic, but that wasn't my intent in saying it. I meant for it to be an ending, not in a fatalistic sense, but an ending to the type of relationship we had been having. I was tired of doing the emotional dance of desiring her and having hopes; even if she wasn't encouraging me, just the appeal of her personality and appearance kept me stuck in that state of longing. Leaving the country for a year is a chance for a different relationship. It is true that one possibility for our relationship may be not seeing each other again, but at least that would be a change. I couldn't continue feeling emotionally stuck—it was inhibiting my spiritual development.

But now, being in Japan during my emotional crisis, I find myself reaching out to her. I am looking for her to tell me that I am a good person, that I am not a failure. She can be my escape from my fears. I know that acting in this fragile, distorted state of mind is risky, but then, I am a risk taker. And what am I risking? Showing Terra that I can be vulnerable?

I negotiate the withdrawal of money from the bank without any difficulty; the clerks are very nice and helpful. Besides the tellers, the bank has a greeter that helps you get in the right lineup. Cheaper labor costs in Japan enable businesses to have lots of extra help. In fact, at most banks, you first see the greeter, then you proceed to one of the tellers, then once the nature of your business has been established, she (and they are all women) passes the documents to one of several people sitting behind the tellers. It is these people that do the "banking" while you are asked to sit. Once your banking is done, the paperwork is handed back to the teller, who then calls you to the counter again to complete the process. It involves many people, and to my surprise, the staff sitting behind the front counter don't have computers. Because it is a leading country in technology I was expecting Japan to be modern in most ways, but many things are still done with manual labor.

I return home quickly with Terra still on my mind. I grab my computer and walk to the park, which is where I can connect to a wireless Internet signal. I want someone else to convince me I am a sane, worthy individual. I want some validation from Terra.

Occasionally I share some of my strange experiences and ideas with family, friends, my men's group or even coworkers, and once in a while, with anybody who will listen. Most listeners seem to find my stories and notions interesting. However, what I am most longing for is specific feedback on my philosophy, and that always seems to be lacking. The one occasion I did get some insightful feedback was at a creative writing workshop. I took the course after I had left my old job, and it consisted of five mornings. The instructor, Luanne Armstrong, was amazing, and she was incredibly well read. She even had some specific knowledge of Zen. The positive comments and encouragement I received from her was the one time I had some external feedback that the project I was undertaking could have merit. The rest of the time I feel like I am walking in the dark. So now I am seeking some encouragement from Terra, and hopefully she will add some light to my ambition.

My hands are shaky as I write. I manage to produce a couple of short paragraphs explaining my state and my desire for some feedback from her. I debate whether it is wise to actually send the message; maybe just writing it is enough to shift my current feeling of vulnerability. My next thought comes with conviction: "No, it not enough to just write it; I need to send it!" I need to send it to help me move through my alcohol-induced vulnerability, but I also need to send it to have my relationship with Terra shift—in whatever direction that may be.

I click the *send* icon. It is done now, no going back. I have no idea when Terra will read my message, as her Internet use is intermittent. Nevertheless, at least now I feel better. Having sent the message, I go back home and resume working on patching the holes in my energy field. I want to regain my good feelings about my life in Japan.

Though this experience has deep spiritual implications for me, I am too fragile and sick to write about it now. I nurse myself for the rest of the day. I had planned to look at bicycles before going to work, but I can't manage it today. It is one purchase that I will make in spite of a bike being a hassle to dispose of when I leave. By the time I go to work, I am feeling much better. My classes go well, and I am satisfied I have done my job.

Chapter 18

Waiting for a Reply

Tuesday, May 27

It has been three days without a reply from Terra. I try not to focus on it and pretend it is not a big deal, but I can't fool myself. I want to know how she will respond. It's not about the immediate sense of vulnerability I was feeling that day—that is long gone—rather, it's about which direction our relationship will move. Will she respond to my neediness by reaching back to me, or will she move away?

To connect to the Internet, I have been making the walk to the park every day! Today, as I am strolling there, I feel quite upbeat. As I reflect back on that Friday morning when I e-mailed her, I realize I have comfortably gotten back into my routine. My life is rosy once again—in fact, I feel blessed. I am living in Japan, doing a job I enjoy, and I have the time and energy to write. It is the writing that makes my life so extraordinary; that is when I don't have a sense of longing or questioning. When I write, I am doing what I am meant to be doing; I am in sync with the Universe. When I write, there are no self-doubts, even though I may struggle with the ideas.

The anticipation builds as I sit on the park bench and pull out my computer. I turn it on and log in. Wow, there it is—a message from Terra! My heart skips a beat. I click on her name to open the e-mail. In my message to her I revealed my fear that people may think I am crazy for wanting to help the world, and I am anxious to see what she has to say.

Her response is a philosophical one. She correctly points out that I don't need approval from others, that what makes something worthwhile is the internal experience of it. She writes, "If it feels right, then that is all that counts, and what others think is not important." These words are very true, but they are not responding to my personal issues. They are not connecting with the hurt person inside of me; rather, they are appealing to the rational, thinking part of me. My heart sinks. I feel very alone.

I try to explain away my sadness. This is how relationships often are; I am looking for her to read my mind, or more to the point, read my heart, but it didn't happen. I thought I was quite specific in what I was asking of her, but we aren't communicating clearly. She said she knew I was looking for some specific response, but she didn't know what to say. All I really needed to hear was that she cared. And it is not that she doesn't care, but she doesn't understand how to touch my pain, or maybe she isn't in an emotional place where she can.

I recall one e-mail I received from her last year when she was traveling. In it she talked about being lonely, and my immediate reaction to her vulnerability was anger. I had wanted to see that vulnerable side of her for so long, but she was showing it to me in an e-mail when she was thousands of miles away! I wanted her to have the courage to show it to me when we were together, not when there was the safety of being in different countries. I replied to her emotional pain with some very philosophical comments. Looking back, it now strikes me as sad and ironic. But I can also see some humor in it; we both responded to each other's vulnerability with philosophical words, and not compassion.

Her words start invoking in me a deeper level of understanding: we are alone. It is great to have someone respond to our personal pains with sympathy and understanding, but in the end we still must transform our pain alone. Having someone walk with you to the door is helpful, but the door is our own personal threshold which no one else can cross. We are all connected in that we all have a door, but the doors themselves are all unique and individual.

I can't connect with it now, sitting on the park bench, but I know her response resonates with some deep emotional pain hidden in me. And if I have the courage to feel that pain, then my relationship with Terra will shift. What I really needed from her was not validation, but some emotional soothing. She has been the object of my desire for some time, and I have only myself to blame for being stuck. We are on opposite sides of the planet, and with a different response we could have felt more connected than we have ever felt, but that moment is gone. Now I must find the courage to move on and stop my fixation on her.

As I sit in the park I begin to *really* look at my surroundings. It is a beautiful spring day; the flowers, trees and grass all seem to have an extra vibrancy to them. I wonder why I hadn't noticed it before. They all serve to remind me that I am on a great adventure! The sadness of a few moments ago has left—buried in me somewhere—and the excitement I felt earlier this morning is back. I say to myself, "I am living in Japan, writing a book; life is a wondrous thing."

Still, I desire a relationship, but my expectation of that relationship has shifted; my partner will not have to be a mind reader. And when I do process this latest encounter with my pain, I will come out of it a more integrated person and enter my next relationship a little less needy. I also intend *not* to use drugs (namely alcohol) to access this latest encounter with my pain. I need the experience to be grounded, to change me, and not be some momentary shift that gets wasted.

Again, her words come back to me, reverberating; I am truly alone. But this is the paradox of life; you are alone in the physical sense, but spiritually you are intimately connected to every-thing—in a sense you *are* everything, so the concept of aloneness doesn't even make sense. When thinking, and hence using the mental energy body, you view the world from the physical body's earthly sense of separateness. When you do your thinking with your spiritual energy body, you view the world from the God perspective of Universal Energy.

This train of thought sparks some insights into Zen and the

practice of contemplating Koans. It makes us shift our thinking from the mental body to the spiritual body. Koans are paradoxical, because for a person to exist as a separate entity is a paradox; we are not really separate. The loss of separateness is also the loss of self. We are not our mirror image; we just get stuck thinking we are that image. Koans can lead us to an insight into our true nature, but the consciousness has to be connected to our spiritual body for the experience to be grounded. When we consciously think with our spiritual body, it changes who we are. How you act and how you think will be changed, meaning you will live your daily life differently and more compassionately.

My computer is already out, so in my vibrant state I decide to write.

Chapter V, cont. (The Soul)

When a Soul embarks on an incarnate experience, it creates the personal consciousness and the Energy Bodies. The four Energy Bodies provide the raw input for the consciousness experience. The consciousness becomes an actor in the play we call reality, and starts its performance being ignorant of its origins and of the Energy Bodies. As this play is acted out, the consciousness exercises its Free Will and sometimes creates energy blockages, though counter-influences are simultaneously created. This means the balance of the Divine is always preserved: when creating yin, an equal amount of yang is also created. This is also true for modern physics.

When an incarnate life is complete (meaning the death of the Physical Body), then the consciousness, the personality and the other Energy Bodies are reincorporated into the Soul. However, if the personality still has attachments to its sense of individuation—which are unresolved energy blocks—then these energy patterns remain with the Soul to be resolved in other incarnations. The unresolved energy patterns from one incar- nation manifest as life lessons for another incarnation, thus enabling the eventual resolution of the energy patterns. The Soul creates situations in the world to allow a person to resolve their life lessons. To put it another way, when the Soul is writing a play, it writes scenes for the actor (the incarnate) that relate to life lessons for that individual consciousness.

To summarize this chapter: There exists Universal Energy—the Divine—that is conscious and inherently benevolent. In a desire to express and experience its benevolence, the Divine energy starts a process of separation, eventually leading to the formation of a Soul. As part of the process of experiencing its benevolence and Free Will, the Soul creates the personal consciousness and the four Energy Bodies. This consciousness is ignorant of its origins and the Energy Bodies. The Soul then creates situations in order for the consciousness to exercise its Free Will. When the consciousness uses its Free Will to reacquaint itself with the Soul, this experience is the external expression of Divine benevolence. While expressing Free Will, the consciousness will create some energy blocks along with corresponding counter-influences. Eventually both will be reunited, but often not during that particular lifetime. In conjunction with other Souls, a world is created where these Souls can have incarnate experiences together. When a physical life ends, any of the personality's attachment to separation and past emotional traumas (energy blocks) remains with the Soul as life lessons for other incarnations.

That is enough writing for today. My current upbeat feeling makes me want to get some exercise to help me stay grounded. I have enough time to go for a casual bike ride before I start work at five (I bought a bike on Sunday). Fuji City has a beautiful performance center called the Rose Theater, and across from it is a large and diverse park. I think I will go explore the park, and then I can ride from there up the hill to my school. It should be a nice way to spend the afternoon.

Chapter 19

With Friends at a Music Festival

Saturday, June 7

As we cruise along in Mike's car I enjoy the taste of my Chu-Hi, a vodka-based drink and my alternative to beer. We are en route to a music festival somewhere in the foothills of Mount Fuji. I had to work today (Saturday), but Mike was kind enough to come down from the festival and pick me up after I finished work. Obviously I don't have a car, and in spite of public transportation being excellent in Japan, there are no trains or buses going out to the backcountry.

Hank is at the festival too. They are two of the guys from the Oz crew that I have gotten to know. Hank has been here the longest at ten years, and Mike six, but Mike had a stint back home in the States after his initial time in Japan. He finally decided Japan was the life for him. Both of them speak superb Japanese. I have enjoyed hanging out with them on many occasions, and we went to the fire festival together, but our friendship had been primarily at the bar. For some reason we don't call each other to arrange getting together.

When we arrive at the festival, Mike takes me to the place where he, Hank and their girlfriends, along with some Japanese friends, are camping. It's nearing dusk, so I can't see much of the surrounding area, but it appears to be a partially-wooded plateau with clusters of tents all over the place. It is a free-for-all with no organized camping plan, so people have found all kinds of quaint places to situate themselves.

Finding a nice spot under some trees, I begin clearing a place for my tent. Maybe it is because I feel like an outsider, or maybe it is because I am more comfortable being near trees, but I notice my spot creates some distances between me and where the others are camping. I don't feel bad about this. My independence can be a good thing, and I think tonight may be one of those times. I am not rejecting the others; I just feel like I don't have to try to fit in, in order to have a good time. I open my second drink as I set up my tent. While doing this, I hear the music; it is rock music, but nothing too heavy. I am far enough away that it's difficult to realize the lyrics are Japanese, so it sounds the same as a festival in Canada might sound. The noise is "music to my ears," and I look forward to a fun night.

After setting up my tent I join the group hanging out at our camping area. Hank is nowhere to be seen. Mike introduces me to a few of his friends, but I have found I can never remember Japanese names, so tonight I don't even try. None of them speak much English. I am surprised when they offer me a drag from a joint; I wasn't expecting to find drugs in Japan. I rationalize to myself that this is recreational use of drugs, where the fun from occasional use can compensate for the harm done to my energy bodies. I take a drag and then pass it along.

Over the years I have done some experimenting with a few drugs, mostly alcohol and marijuana, and I am quite content to use alcohol as my main drug. As the joint continues to get passed around, I take in my surroundings and tune in to the general feeling of the place. It has a hippie-type feel to it. Most people have a carefree, ragged look to them, and everyone is friendly and laid back. As I mention this to Mike, he tells me how lucky I am to be introduced to this subculture so soon. It took him years of living in Japan before he got to know the "hippie culture" in this country. The general population is very consumer orientated.

Darkness is encroaching when Mike suggests we check out the band. I grab my third drink, but I am also feeling some effects from the marijuana. We move over to the stage area, which is in the middle of a field. I am surprised to see a teepee-like structure which protects the stage from the elements. Japan is exposed to the Pacific Ocean, and so the weather can change quickly. The field is mostly rough-cut grass, and the area in front of the stage is dirt. There are currently about thirty people dancing. There is also a large screen to one side with some scaffolding in front of it, but at the moment the screen is blank.

As the effects of the joint become more pronounced, I feel both relaxed and excited. I drift away from Mike and move onto the dance floor. Usually it takes me a while to risk venturing onto the dance floor, but being a foreigner means I am already being judged, so I take this as license to act differently. If I am going to be judged, then I might as well make an impression as a free-spirited person.

Soon I feel absorbed in the music and the rhythm is flowing through me. I'm feeling free and happy. Off the dance floor I am limited by language, but dance is a universal language, so on it I am not so handicapped. After a short while I have the urge to be more animated, so I start clapping, in spite of no one else doing it. As I start, I notice a few odd looks from others, but I don't care. Actually it's not that I don't care, but my caring isn't strong enough to inhibit my exuberance. As the intensity of the music increases, I feel more focused and become more expressive with my clapping. As this is happening more dancers are moving onto the dance floor.

What I had mistakenly thought was a screen turns out to be very large canvas for painting; its size is about 6 feet by 10 feet (2 x 3 meters). Two artists have climbed onto the scaffolding and are now using mops as paintbrushes. There is an amazing three-part dynamic happening between the band, the audience and the painters. I have never seen painting as a performance art, but watching the two artists paint in conjunction with the festival atmosphere is captivating. As the music shifts, the audience's vibe shifts, and the painters' expressions shift. All three components are responding to and being influenced by each other. It is a magical ménage á trois. I'm feeling ecstatic to be participating in this alternative art form!

While I dance, I surprise myself by maintaining complicated rhythms with my clapping. At other times I quickly lost the rhythm because I made it too complicated, but tonight I am continuing a steady flow of intricate beats. When I am under the influence of nonalcoholic drugs, I sometimes have a greater trust of my intuition, so rightly or wrongly, I am not questioning my current thoughts—I sense a change happening around me. As I continue my clapping, some of my fellow dancers drift away, and others gravitate towards me. The people who are being drawn to me are enthusiastic dancers, and they are really allowing themselves to move and flow! I begin to sense that my clapping, my presence is a grounding influence for them, and this is encouraging them to be more boisterous. There is a fleeting thought that it is arrogant to think of myself as so influential, but I don't care, and let the thought go unheeded. I become more conscious of feeling connected to the earth, a feeling that encourages me, and possibly them, to let go even more. My rhythmic clapping continues, varying with a natural flow. The triad of earth, dancers and me is mirroring the triad of the dancers, painters and band. Everything is in harmony.

The dancing, my clapping, the music and the painting continue until a natural ebbing of the energy happens. Finally, everyone takes a break; the band puts down their instruments, the dancers disperse and the painters climb down from the scaffolding. The resulting artwork is an impressionist composition that reflects everyone's zest for life. Off-white spotlights and dozens of candles softly illuminate the canvas; it is an enchanting vision!

I walk toward one of the stalls to buy a Chu-Hi and then I find a nice place to sit. The cold can is soothing on my sore hands. Immense joy fills me as I reflect upon my situation. I am hanging out with hippies and dancing at a music festival in the foothills of Mount Fuji. I am feeling blessed and grateful for the good fortune life brings me. Life is wonderful!

Soon, another band begins to play, but now my mood has mellowed. The painters have put their pigments away for the night and the dancers are fewer in number. I would rather sit on the sidelines and watch than be a key component of it. I saw Mike dancing earlier, but I haven't seen Hank yet. The idea to seek them out crosses my mind, but I am content just sitting and having a drink, feeling happy and relaxed. Soon I find myself trying to explain my earlier sense of profound connection. I would suggest that I was in all four of my energy bodies at once, but how did being stoned influence that?

Being stoned — or drunk for that matter — enables one to avert some of the control the personality exerts on the consciousness. As long as the personality doesn't react with fear at the loss of control, then the high can be pleasant and insightful. The effect of drugs is to allow our consciousness to be free of some of the belief structures that shape our perceptions. For example, I grew up being conditioned that energy dynamics are not valid. My early indoctrination tells me that the world functions *only* via a direct cause-and-effect mechanism. However, the drugs can circumvent these beliefs and allow me to experience a different dynamic — that is, to feel the flow of energy that is not normally recognized. While dancing, I experienced an energy dynamic between the others and myself that I would have ignored under normal circumstances. And when the underlying energy flow is ignored, it often inhibits experiencing the joy available in that situation.

The drawback of being stoned is that the connection with the spiritual body is impaired. And without that healthy connection, the drug-induced experience is not grounded. Getting stoned can enable a circumventing of our belief structures (mental energy blocks), but it is the healthy spiritual connection that ultimately facilitates the release of those belief structures. When using our own resources to alter our belief structures, such as engaging in meditation or healing, the spiritual connection is healthy, and hence the insights can alter the structures and become life changing.

My thinking is interrupted as I see Mike and Hank coming toward me; it brings my attention back to the moment. Hank gives me a gentle punch and offers me a beer, which I gladly take as my drink is almost empty. I can tell he is feeling good too. Again, I express my gratitude to him and Mike for inviting me to the festival. Soon, they decide to go back to the camping area where they are meeting up with their girlfriends. I decline the invitation to join them. I feel like sitting in solitude, and letting my mind wander.

Half an hour later, the stage performers stop. The band is soon replaced by several small, informal groups of amateur musicians having jam sessions. Each group has a few musicians playing a variety of instruments, a few dancers and a few watchers. I migrate from one group to another, but don't feel particularly connected to the happenings. Deciding to call it a night, I return to the campsite.

Back at the campsite there is no sign of Mike or Hank but there are a few people quietly sitting around a fire; I'm sure they don't speak English even if I wanted to talk. They are friendly people, and would make the effort to communicate if I tried, but in my current state it will take more effort than I can muster.

From my experience in Korea, I know the friendships developed while in a foreign and temporary work situation are not like regular friendships. There is a need to share the experience of a strange culture with people that face similar challenges, and their company acts as a reminder of the comforts of home. Over time a foreigner will become more integrated with a new culture, but the initial reaction is one of strangeness. Friendships in this situation can be intense, but when one of the buddies departs—which is the norm in these situations—the connection is severed. The friendships I developed in Korea were strong, but the contact did not endure once we were no longer living in the same country (my ex-girlfriend Lib, of course, is different). It was the coping with the foreign culture that formed the basis for the friendship.

Let's consider food as a similar example. There is a longing for comfort foods because of the feelings associated with them (stuck energy patterns); having those foods is an emotional soother. So, like food, having friends that can relate is comforting. Too much change is a threat to my personality. A strong connection is developing with Mike, Hank and the others I have met at Oz, but I do not yet consider them *close* friends. We are having fun, but the bonds are not yet based upon acceptance of who we are as people. With them, I have not let my guard down. I have yet to admit to myself that I *desire* their friendship, and I have yet to show them any significant vulnerability. It feels to me that we should be closer friends, but emotionally I am not yet there.

The evening has wound down, so I take care of my bedtime chores and then crawl into my tent. I am glad my tent is secluded in the trees—it enhances my feeling of being connected to the earth. Content and happy, I quickly drift off to sleep.

Chapter 20

Celebrating Canada Day

Tuesday, July 1

My phone rings, shocking me out of my lackadaisical haze. It's 9:30 at night on Tuesday, the first day of my workweek, and I finished work an hour ago. On my way home I bought some curry rice from the supermarket, which I've just finished eating. I am settling into a routine of working, writing and meditating, with social outings either at Oz or hanging out with coworkers when our schedules coincide. Though not ideal, it is a pleasant lifestyle. I had intended to spend the night at home, so I am shocked by this call, particularly because no one calls me except my boss for work-related issues. So when I hear Gerry on the other end, it has a powerful effect on me.

"It's July 1st," he says. "Come on down to Oz, we're celebrating Canada Day!"

It hadn't dawned on me that today is Canada Day—I am not an overly patriotic person. I am proud to be a Canadian, but I feel patriotism often does more harm than good. Being Canadian has helped shape me into the caring person I am, but I acknowledge other countries also have great attributes and produce wonderful individuals. Hopefully we take the best from our country of origin and mold it into a more universal compassion for all people. The fact that it is Canada Day isn't what makes the call so significant; it's that I am being invited to celebrate it with friends. I quickly get ready and head out the door.

Tonight Oz is decked out with several Canadian flags. Muni, the Japanese owner, is wearing a Canada T-shirt, and there is a buzz in the air. When I was in Korea the Canadians outnumbered the other nationalities, and so it is with Oz, which is surprising since we are not a highly populated country. It is a fun scene of socializing, having a few drinks and playing darts. Though it is Tuesday night, tomorrow is some sort of national holiday, so the others have the day off. I don't, but it is another short day with classes starting at 6:15pm, so I am not concerned about tonight being a late night.

As the night wears on and the crowd starts thinning, I think about going home, but then Rob comes up to me and asks if I want to go to Hank's house. I say sure, knowing it is a common place to socialize, but I have never been invited. I am told Hank is waiting in the parking lot. This isn't because this is some clandestine operation, but probably because it was a last minute idea to include me. It is an invitation into the *inner* Oz family, or as I like to call them, the Oz crew.

Once we make it to Hank's house, I find that the gathering is a typical house party, but not something I was expecting to find in Japan. It is hanging out with the guys that is important to me, not the type of function. Having to work tomorrow curbs my enthusiasm, so I do little drinking for the rest of the night. We end up playing some poker.

I have mentioned some of the earliest events that contributed to my long-held sense of being on the outside of life looking in, events such as feeling rejected when trying to fit in with my brothers. However, there is another significant event from my youth that has had resounding effects on my life. It was when I was eleven-years-old and was rejected by my childhood friends. That experience scarred me deeply, and has been the basis of several of my personal healing sessions.

On that day, many years ago, I came to school thinking it was just another normal day. However, my life was about to change forever. My friends, two of whom were long-time neighborhood buddies that I considered best friends, all started taunting me. I was stunned by what was happening, and I had no idea *why* it was happening! In hindsight, I would say it was a moment that caused a split between my inner self and my outer reality. In essence, I shut down my connection with my emotional body. There was already a well-established rift caused by my common, childhood family traumas, but that particular loss of friendship was the final wedge that split my sense of self apart.

The taunting continued for the rest of that day, and for several more. Eventually the jeering petered out, and my former best friends and I settled into a new relationship: we no longer spoke. We were all in the same class at school and lived within a hundred yards of each other, so I had to work hard to avoid them. It was many months before I made an attempt to reestablish a friendship, but it was never the same for me. I never did find out why they rejected me that day, and I have found no obvious explanation.

That is how I lived the rest of my childhood, and a good portion of my adulthood, feeling alone and disconnected. When that happened to me as a young boy, I made an *unconscious* vow never to trust friends again. So now that I am being invited into the inner Oz family, I see this as an invitation to challenge my sense of separation. I am peeling away a deeper layer of my old energy pattern. One layer was healed when I connected with the Inner Focus family; and now, here is an opportunity to heal another layer. Part of me thinks that maybe I can let these guys see who I really am and that they won't reject me—that, just maybe, it is safe to trust their friendship.

Not being fully conscious of this inner drama, my rational mind tells me I am being silly in hesitating to accept these guys as true friends. "What is there to be afraid of?" But the healing of old wounds is not a rational process, and what happened to that boy—to me—on that day does not make sense. And hence using the rational mind is not how old pains get healed. Like a Zen Koan, it is a befuddling situation that requires a non-rational answer, and in fact, Zen informs us thinking can inhibit the process.

Hours later, with the sky just starting to show some signs of light, I walk home from Hank's house. The route home soon joins up with my usual late night walking path, and as is often the case, I am listening to music as I walk. I have a feeling of joy—I no longer need to feel alone—but I also feel some sadness. My walk is turning into one of my quasi-healing sessions. With the aid of the alcohol, I am connecting with my hidden emotion of loneliness.

As I stop to sit on a bench for a few moments, I am suddenly struck by a lost memory. It is not the memory itself that is surprising—it is understandable for this situation—but I am surprised by the clarity of the memory. In detail, I can see myself standing in the front hallway of our old house, fighting with my brother. As a child, my primary method for getting my way, and for venting my anger, was to rage. I would yell and swing my fists wildly until the intensity of the rage would overwhelm my opponent (generally one of my brothers). As a child, I was younger, smaller and weaker than them. On this particular day I was starting to rage against one of my brothers, but he wasn't being intimidated by my antics. I could clearly see the determination on his face to stay calm. As I approached him, he coolly looked for an opening, and then punched me in the face. After receiving three quick blows to my face, I made a hasty retreat.

Shortly after, I remember thinking that my raging wasn't working anymore, so I made an immediate decision to not get angry again. Not long after that event, I *convinced* myself that I could never get angry. This vision of myself as an emotionally inert person was reaffirmed a few years later when I read *The Fountainhead* by Ayn Rand. Her character was the epitome of what I was striving to become; for him, emotions were a weakness that inhibited having a contented, efficient life. The fighting incident that floods my mind is another piece of my childhood shutting down process. This incident was around the same time as the rejection by my friends. There are many layers of childhood traumas adding to my sense of rejection.

Now, as I connect with this memory of myself as an emotionally crippled person, I can feel my sadness dissipate into a white light. I know the sadness is genuine and intense, yet I am not immersed in it. The emotions trapped inside me are painful, and I need to face them honestly, but as I do this, I am not *immersed* in the pain. One way to describe this is to say there still needs to be a connection to the spiritual body, and getting totally lost in the pain interferes with this connection. There needs to be a connection to both for the healing to happen. As I have another momentary release—crying—it is brief and low-key and soon the process feels complete. On the last of my walk home I have a few more, less defined memories of conflicts with my brothers.

When I get home half an hour later, I am still feeling fragile. Once I am inside my apartment, I sit down and I find there is still a residual feeling of sadness. As it subsides, I feel energy flowing into my heart, and I settle into a state of peacefulness. The release of old pain has been smooth and measured, and now it is complete. Consciously, I bring light to my heart, filling the void left by the unraveling of that energy blockage. Next I shift into a state of gratitude. This subsequent phase lasts several minutes, and then this feeling also fades. I give thanks to God and to that part of myself that held that pain for so long, and thus this healing is complete.

It has been a long night, and I think sleep will come easily. Tonight's healing was more structured and I wasn't too drunk, so I hope it has a more lasting impact. Soon after I lie down in bed I fall asleep.

When I wake up it is just after 1pm. With a fresh sense of harmony and peace, I know this is an ideal time to write. So even before meditation and lunch (or breakfast), I decide to write.

Chapter VI: Energy Blockages

As stated in Chapter One, the natural state of Energy Bodies is fluid; however, blockages can and do occur. A blockage is a fixed energy pattern that prevents the normal flow of energy within a small part of an Energy Body. The blockage can occur in any one of the Emotional, Mental or Spiritual Energy Bodies, and will subsequently affect the other Bodies, including the Physical. Each blockage occurs within a unique set of circumstances, and hence the subsequent effects on the other Energy Bodies will be unique as well. The effects on the other Energy Bodies are inevitable, but the nature of the effects will always vary.

In the Emotional Body, blockages lead to hurt and fear (with anger and numbness being some secondary consequences). In the Mental Body they manifest as beliefs, and in the Spiritual Body they are judgments. Aches, pains and diseases in the Physical Body can be the effects caused by blockages in the other Energy Bodies. Most "core" blockages are held in the Emotional Energy Body, and since the consciousness is closely associated with that Body, the onset of these blockages in early childhood plays a major role in the development of the personality.

It is under special circumstances that a blockage is released, but until that time the consciousness experiences discomfort whenever it either is caught up in the blockage or is actively avoiding getting caught up in it. Both of these reactions limit the person from feeling the full benefit of a fluid Energy Body. Also contained in the blockage is some contextual information about the incident that prompted the blockage, and additionally it freezes the development of that aspect of the person's Energy Body. This means, in essence, that time has stopped for the person in regards to that issue. Hence, contained within the blockage is a potentially positive aspect of the person that cannot be experienced until the blockage is released.

For example, if a three-year-old boy has a major trauma involving rejection, then part of his emotional development becomes frozen, and he will not have full confidence in his independence until it is healed. At subsequent times, when he encounters an event that activates his sense of rejection, this blockage will affect his behavior. A person may even react to this "frozenness" by overcompensating, and aggressively show their independence, but it will lack compassion towards others. So, when either caught up in an old energy pattern or avoiding it, a person is, in a sense, reliving that old episode. This means he is not fully "in the moment." This discord is a stress on the person as a whole, and that stress can lead to various effects on the Physical Body. Short-term physical effects can be tense muscles and a decrease in the immune system's functioning; long-term effects can be chronic pains and diseases.

When the consciousness encounters a blockage, but then attempts to avoid it, the mind (and not the consciousness) continues to retain this information. Thus, the blockage can be unconsciously avoided. However, through a subconscious process, the blockage can still contribute to the person's experience. In consistently avoiding blockages, the personality can develop coping strategies. For example, one coping strategy is to become emotionally numb, causing the person's mood to be unusually flat or to become withdrawn when presented with a situation that is reminiscent of an old trauma. Again, this means the person is not attuned to all parts of his Energy Bodies, and hence is stressed by not being in the moment.

As I put my computer away, I realize that I am very hungry. Now is not a good time to meditate; I have thoughts running through my mind and it is mid-afternoon. I let myself off the hook and rummage through the fridge for something to eat. I have a bit of time before I must leave for work, so I will either read or see what's on TV.

Chapter 21

Individuals, Groups and Zen

Monday, July 21

I have to hurry to catch the train. It is 10:30 in the morning and I am meeting Jacob at 11:00. He is a fellow Peppy teacher that lives at the other end of the prefecture, so we normally see each other at monthly staff meetings or on training days. A difference Jacob and I share is that we both live alone in our respective cities, while our fellow Peppy teachers have a few coworkers living in same city. On training days all native English-speaking teachers from this area meet, normally in Shizuoka City, which is centrally located. After the meetings several teachers will usually hang out together, so we have gone out as a group in Shizuoka City a few times.

Jacob is from Toronto, and we share some interests—sports, philosophy, people, debating and a general knowledge and interest in the world. However, he is not much of a drinker, and DJing is a big interest of his (I have no idea of the DJs and bands he talks about), so we haven't made an effort to hang out a lot. On a few occasions, when not with a group, I have enjoyed just talking to him about life. On a previous outing for lunch after a staff meeting, we had an interesting discussion, and I shared some of my impressions of Japan. During this discussion I voiced a notion that the Japanese lack compassion. This sounds mean and judgmental, but I intended no malice in saying it, and obviously it would be an overstatement. My experience has been that the Japanese are extremely courteous people. That is a characteristic of their culture—to be nice to people—due in part to the fact that one's public image has great importance. It is ingrained in the population's psyche, and superb service is one thing foreigners always find extraordinary about Japan. But being nice is different from being compassionate.

One observation that prompted my speculation is how some people treat their dogs. Many owners have their dogs tied up all day on a five-foot tether (or shorter). Apparently these people lack any conception of the dog's well-being. Even if they are guard dogs, this is inhumane. If this sort of treatment were done openly in Canada it would create an outrage, while here it is ignored. This is by no means the case for all Japanese dog owners, but the percentage of what I would call uncaring owners seems to be vastly higher here, and the general public ignores it.

To explain this, I suggested that their approach to life tends to suppress the natural tendencies for compassion. Their upbringing emphasizes interdependence within groups, and is less encouraging of individualism. At regular schools (daytime schools, as opposed to Peppy's after school lessons), the students are in one class all day and the teachers move from one classroom to another. Though this reflects a greater value for the student over the teacher, such strong grouping breeds interdependence. The students eat lunch in their classrooms and they are responsible for its cleanliness, and classroom issues are dealt with as a group. And year after year, the same bunch of students move from one grade to the next. Interestingly, students are never held back regardless of their academic performance.

In some ways this is similar to communism, where group needs supersede individual needs, but communist societies have not evolved into compassionate ones. The Japanese are concerned with their personal welfare, and their competitiveness is apparent, but for them individualism is not paramount. Subjected individualism does not foster compassion. In contrast, I think America is the most openly individualistic society, and yet, on the international stage, it is the most generous. In the US the rights of the person often supersede society's. It may be another Zen paradox that individualism leads to more compassion for others, while obligatory group thinking doesn't.

As for adults, it is part of the Japanese mystique we hear about in the West that the employee and the company are enmeshed; the company demands devotion, and the employees give it. Surprisingly it is very uncommon for someone to be fired. By Western standards, most companies' expectations of employees borders on abuse. For example, with many salaried jobs, employees cannot go home until the boss leaves, even if the boss came in late and the employees have worked a ten-hour day. And the jobs being salaried means there is no overtime pay. The Japanese kindness and devotion to work are external norms, while the internal feelings may be very different.

What I hope makes my musing an observation and not a judgment is that it is not personal; I admire many things about their society. Somehow, Japan's lifestyle seems to work. It is a fascinating place to live. There is less crime, fewer social problems, and in general, people seem happier. The most marked improvement here is the fewer number of what I call angry people. In Canada, many people feel disenfranchised by society, and they lash out. These angry people commit crimes, abuse drugs, tend to be violent, and in general are *takers* from society. In Japan I hear other foreigners complain that this society is superficial because it is very consumer orientated; yet, I suggest this is better than the frequent despondency I see in the West. The Japanese are much more accepting of their circumstances, and hence are more content. Another wonderful aspect of their society is that honesty and trust are still prevalent; for example I can carry my backpack into stores without it being an issue, and it is easy to circumvent paying for train fares but the vast majority of people pay regardless.

This was the basis of my earlier conversation with Jacob. He seemed to agree with my observations that Japanese are not compassionate—or if he was not agreeing, then at least he understood how I could have that perception. When Jacob said he understood, it was reassuring. As I noted earlier, I am not inclined to talk with others about my perceptions and ideas, so to have a receptive audience was enjoyable. This is why I am keen to hang out with him again. We made a plan to get together on a day off, so today we are exploring a town located between us called Okitsu. Though not special, it was mentioned in one of the books I read—getting a Fuji library card has been beneficial, and the library has a reasonable stock of English language books. He was interested enough to check it out with me, so we are meeting at the Okitsu train station.

As I get off the train I see Jacob waiting. We check out the town map at the station and see several shrines and temples marked on it. The book I had read mentioned a Zen temple, so I was hoping to find it. It is not clear on the map which are shrines and which are temples, nor if they are Zen, Buddhist or Shinto. Part of the trouble is I'm not sure of the distinction between shrines and temples (possibly Shinto vs. Buddhism). Regardless, we head off in the direction where there are several religious establishments in succession.

Jacob is in his mid-twenties, and by all accounts an extremely capable man. He studied computers at university and achieved good marks. Upon graduation he chose to have an adventure in Japan rather than start a potentially lucrative computer career. As we walk, he confides that he has mixed feelings about his choice. Jacob has lived in Japan longer than I have, so he will be completing his contract soon; he is deliberating what to do when he goes back to Canada, which may be fueling his misgivings about having lived in Japan. Not surprisingly, I encourage him to be happy with the choice he has made. The crux of my advice is to appreciate and enjoy the moment.

To support my advice, I share a lesson I learned in my late twenties when I was working at the group home for troubled youth in Campbell River. In Canada, the government will take responsibility for youth living in very dysfunctional families. The youth becomes a ward of the court, which means the government legally assumes parental responsibilities. Group homes are one part of the government's system for tending to the needs of these displaced youth.

My employer and boss at the group home, Peter, was a few years my junior, but he was certainly my teacher about the intricacies of managing troubled youth. He had lost his parents at an early age and grew up as a ward of the court. He had many personal experiences living in group homes, and he knew the ins and outs of how troubled youth got their needs met. While working with Peter, there were a few occasions when he drastically changed the approach for managing some of our kids. Suddenly he would decide we needed to "get on the youth's case," when to me the individual seemed to be coping adequately. The youth may not have been doing great, but I saw no obvious sign that a change was needed. Invariably, these dramatic changes in treatment would result in the youth transitioning into a very upbeat period in his or her life. The youth would overcome whatever issue that was dogging them (not that it was enough of a problem for them to overtly act badly, but one that caused some internal anguish), and they would become genuinely happy for a period of time.

Peter was never able to explain how he knew the time was right for a change. In watching this process a few times, eventually I came to the understanding that it wasn't some magical signal from the youth that Peter was tuning into, it was more of a reflection of Peter's own psychological state. What seemed to make the change successful was the conviction that Peter was able to bring to the new approach. By his sheer strength of *will*, he made the change in treatment turn out to be beneficial for the youth.

What I gleaned from this, and what I am trying to impart to Jacob, is that choices aren't often inherently right or wrong; it is the attitude and conviction we have toward the choice *after* it is made that determines whether it is right or wrong. We have the power within us to determine the validity of a choice. The benefit of many of the choices we make is an evolving process, with us at the controls. If an option is clearly detrimental to our spiritual growth, or harmful to someone else, then our will cannot simply make it right, but when choosing between two unknown outcomes, our attitude is crucial.

The first shrine we encounter on our walk is not well maintained and not inspiring. After a brief exploration we move onto the next one, which is a short walk down the road. It turns out to be more utilized and worth some exploring. Both of these shrines have small buildings and statues for worshiping, but no offices or residences. Maybe that is the difference between a shrine and temple: the latter has people that live onsite. The map showed a third shrine 10 minutes further down the road, so we start walking towards it.

To relate this lesson to Jacob's situation, I tell him he has had many rich experiences while living in Japan, experiences that have given him a deeper understanding and perspective of life. His friends in Canada, or at least the ones that pursued a career immediately after graduation, lack his worldliness. The others are on a treadmill, and don't stop to reflect or even realize they have a choice; they are too busy running to perceive this imaginary treadmill. Yet, the carrot dangling in front of the treadmill is always out of reach. Jacob has made a step to the sidelines, but it is not the sideline of life, it is the sideline of the rat race. Unfortunately, he is not appreciating that the carrot is happiness itself, and not money; people often think that money will buy them happiness. Jacob fears that if he is on the sidelines of the rat race, he cannot make as much money, so he won't be able to buy as much happiness.

Jacob's quandary stems from imagining some fairy tale scenario about what his life would be like if he had immediately chosen to pursue a computer career instead of coming to Japan. It is a comparison between a life with some struggles and many rewards (the life he is currently living in Japan), versus a mythical life where he overlooks the potential struggles and only considers the possible rewards. And for Jacob, these imagined rewards are materialistic, even though he acknowledges money is not his primary motivation. Such is the allure of our imaginary lives; they don't even need to be in keeping with our own desires to seem appealing. This mental exercise prevents Jacob from appreciating the life he is living. He is not focused on the pleasures of his current life, and is instead engaged with some mental fantasy about something that isn't real.

The third shrine we encounter is much more elaborate and meticulously maintained. In front of the main building is a pebble garden which is so carefully groomed that there are intricate designs created by the rake's tines. We soon notice an English sign explaining that this is indeed a Zen temple, its origins dating back to the 1200s. I am excited to have found it. We spend the next hour walking around the grounds and exploring some of the buildings. There is a brief meeting with a monk, but he doesn't speak English. Jacob knows basic Japanese, but not enough to negotiate the possibility of staying at the temple for a few days. At some other time I might ask one of the Oz crew to help me inquire about this. This has been an enjoyable and uplifting exploration.

Jacob and I are now starving, so we head back to the main part of town near the station and settle on a noodle shop for lunch. It is a typical small Japanese restaurant of the type you find in every neighborhood of every city and town. The noodles are good, but nothing out of the ordinary.

The conversation gets back to my philosophy on life. Jacob asks if my theory means one should have no regard for the future. My response is that, indeed, having hopes and dreams are important. But one can imagine and plan for a future while not becoming emotionally caught up in those imaginings. Where our emotions are focused is where our energy is spent, and to find genuine happiness our emotions need to be focused on the present. Emotions based on non-reality, which is what the future and the past are, will not result in joy; in fact, they blind us to the potential joy of our current situation. If our present situation is not joyous, then mentally and emotionally escaping it will not bring improvements. Instead it will deplete our energy thus limiting our ability to improve our current situation. A change in attitude, such as looking for the joy in the now and having an open heart, will bring us opportunities for positive change.

If you are a happy person then you will have a happy life, and if you are an unhappy person then you will have an unhappy life. This may seem too simple to be worth saying, but it is a profound statement when thought of in terms of creating your own reality. Of great importance here is to not "put the cart before the horse," meaning that the attitude comes first. It is not a happy life that makes you happy, but your approach to life that brings positive events into your life. And the converse is that an unhappy attitude attracts unhappy events. To have a genuinely happy attitude we need to regularly focus on the present and find the good in it.

Jacob agrees that being happy leads to a happy life, but still counters that dreaming about the future is good and beneficial. I can't say I disagree, but I struggle to explain why having hope is beneficial. Maybe believing that you can change and being able to see yourself as a better person, as a happier person, helps the present. It is possible that "hope" is a process of trying to connect with your spiritual nature. It is a process of trying to use your ideal spiritual path as a guide and motivator for your present. That was one of the tragedies I often saw while working in group homes and jails—many youth had no hope. They could not see a different future than the troubled past they had lived. The ingrained problematic patterns from their pasts were dominant, and the youth felt they were destined to keep repeating those patterns. It was a sad situation.

Jacob resists when the conversation gets into creating reality and the nature of spirituality. He was brought up in the Jewish faith, and though he is not in total agreement with that religion, he still hasn't defined for himself what spirituality means.

It is time for us to part. Earlier we hadn't discussed any plans for this evening, but it turns out he is meeting up with another friend to do some DJing. I will head for home, feeling upbeat and happy.

When I get home I feel inspired by today's discussion and at having found a Zen temple. It is not convenient to visit regularly, but the possibility of staying for a night is exciting. For now, I will do some writing.

Chapter VI, cont. (Energy Blockages)

To offer an alternate explanation, each Energy Body can be thought of as a rainbow of colors. Each color represents a subclass of energy, so in the Emotional Body, each emotion would have a different color. When a current situation evokes a certain emotion, the consciousness is drawn to the color of that emotion. If there is a blockage along that color's path, the consciousness is influenced by it in one way or another. If one avoids the emotion—or color, in our analogy—then one becomes emotionally numb to that particular color. If one gets caught in the blockage, they lose connection with the current, external situation. The energy flow of a certain color can, in effect, go around a blockage. This means that the emotion is not totally inaccessible; it is a muted color. And going around a blockage is problematic because it starts to mix in other colors.

As one's life progresses, a core blockage usually becomes layered with both secondary and related energy. The related energy is a result of the repeated avoidance attempts by the personality, and over time the avoidance becomes a pattern in itself, encoding the coping strategy. The secondary energy is from situations of less intensity, but similar in nature to the

175

original incident. If this secondary energy doesn't get resolved (and it usually doesn't because of its triggering effect), it will get stuck in the same region as the core blockage. Thus, once the layering starts, the consciousness has easier access to the more accessible energy, and the core blockage itself becomes more remote.

In the Physical Body there are a few mechanisms by which blockages can create problems. Physical injuries, chronic pain and diseases can be caused by persistent stress or by repetitive behaviors when one frequently uses a coping strategy. For example, if one uses exercise to avoid connecting with unpleasant emotions, and this is done frequently, the pains from over-exercising are a result of the avoidance behavior. Similarly, poor eating habits can be a means to soothe emotional hurts, which can result in a variety of health problems. Also, using coping strategies means one is not in the moment, and hence, is stressed. This cumulative stress tends to affect the weakest part of a person's genetic constitution, such as the heart, digestive system or nervous system, leading to serious health conditions.

If we use the example of a person being hit by a car, then the cause of the physical injuries—the car—is obvious, and it is understandable that there are some correlating issues in the other Energy Bodies, such as being emotionally upset, creating beliefs and judgments about cars, drivers etc. In this case, the long-term injuries such as internal scar tissue or bone damage are energetically linked to the corresponding blockages in the other Energy Bodies. This linking is why prolonged nurturing of the Physical Body can initiate the release of blockages in the other Energy Bodies; healing the Physical Body can lead to healing the Emotional, Mental and Spiritual Energy Bodies. Therapeutic practices such as tai chi or yoga work, in part, with the Physical Body help to heal all the Energy Bodies. Also, practices like massages can help one connect with the related emotional, mental and spiritual blockages.

That's enough writing for today. The thought of a drink crosses my mind but Oz is closed on Mondays; plus I have to work tomorrow, so it will be a quiet night at home.

Chapter 22

Camping on Niijima Island

Friday, August 8

The gang is sitting on the beach, looking as if they haven't a care in the world. There's Gerry, Brad, Mike, his girlfriend Ayako, and Tano, a Japanese buddy of Jordan, who is out board surfing right now. They are all sitting in a row atop the sandy slope, watching the waves roll in. They have spent the last hour bodysurfing, and now they are relaxing on the shoreline, enjoying the scene. The sun is hovering overhead, radiating a strong but bearable heat. It is day three of our five-day holiday on Niijima Island, one of the many small islands that dot the coast of Japan.

Considering it is Obon Holiday—a five-day national holiday for honoring deceased relatives—I am amazed at how few people are here. There may be a hundred to a hundred and fifty people on the beach, but it is such a large beach it seems sparsely occupied. If this was a long weekend in Canada and we were at the beach, we would be scrambling to find space to lay down our towels.

After having a leisurely morning doing my own thing, I have come to the beach to join the others. The years have taught me that I function better if I have some solo time, which I wisely took this morning. Using one of the bicycles we've rented, I went exploring through the forest and along some deserted sections of beach. The solitude and exercise have put me in a joyful frame of mind. Adding to my joy is the fact that I am on a holiday and partying with the boys on an incredibly beautiful island off the coast of Japan. It has me feeling downright blissful!

I am also buoyed by the insight I had this morning. It makes perfect sense to me, but I will need to explore it again at a later time to make sure it is consistent. This is how my mind works—

my ideas can come at any time. During meditation is a prime time, but a peaceful walk in nature or lying in bed are also fertile thinking times. Once I have had a moment of inspiration I dwell on the idea, usually on many different occasions.

What occurred to me this morning is a distinction between learning lessons versus adopting beliefs. Jesus, Buddha and other prophets were wise, enlightened people who shared the wisdom of Universal Energy. However, after their lives were over other people were left to interpret their words and actions, thus distorting their wisdom. The mistake that has occurred is to adopt their messages as beliefs and judgments. A belief about compassion is not the same as an act of compassion. Beliefs are energy structures in the Mental Body (and judgments are structures in the Spiritual Body), and hence are counter to the natural flow of energy. Beliefs may be born out of wisdom, but the beliefs are connected to a specific time, and hence are not directly connected to Universal Energy. If the messages can be viewed as lessons, and not beliefs (or judgments), then the wisdom is fluid energy, and with effort, that wisdom can be accessed.

Why is it that even though the prophets preached about compassion, some followers of religions are not very compassionate? And in some cases, the adherents are extremely cruel, while quoting their savior's words to justify their actions. Actions based on rules allow the personality to subconsciously influence the choice. The personality makes decisions based on stuck energy blockages—trying to limit their own pain. So it believes that by avoiding pain, it is acting well, and how those choices affect others is of no concern to the personality. In order to be compassionate, one must consider each situation separately and find a heartfelt solution.

For example, say there is a natural disaster somewhere, like an earthquake or a flood. One compassionate response is to go the disaster area and physically help, and another may be to make a contribution, like money or supplies. A third response may be to focus locally; if going to the disaster area isn't practical, then acting locally is a good alternative. Some may feel prayer (or meditation, or sending light etc.) is a good response. It may be that you have so much stress that to dwell on anything more is overwhelming, and so you choose not to focus on the disaster, but use it as a reminder as to how precious life is. All of these are compassionate responses, so there isn't one good response; rather, the answer is checking internally, and then following your heart.

To simply ignore the disaster is not a compassionate response; this means you are emotionally numb. And one doesn't get to pick and choose which situations to be numb to; it is a general state of being. Hence, a numb person is also missing out on many pleasurable aspects of their life. It is worth noting that a very spiritually evolved person may not change their routine in response to the disaster. This is not because they are numb or indifferent, but that their life and their daily routine are already dedicated to helping the world. Their every action is based on being compassionate. The actions of the uninitiated are motivated by earthly desires, while spiritually evolved people have transcended them. So if you ignore the crisis, and you are still concerned with money, status, comforts etc., then you are numb as opposed to evolved.

It is not that churches have it all wrong, nor that churchgoers aren't good people, it is just that they don't have it all right. And it is counter to their philosophy to admit they don't have it all right, which compounds the problem. Christian doctrine is that Christ was the physical incarnation of God, which makes Christ omnipotent. Hence, anything he said must be God's wisdom. I prefer to see Christ as a person that over time gained greater and greater insight into God (or as I say, the nature of Universal Energy). This means that things he may have thought or believed earlier could later be altered when he had a deeper under-standing. Christians view Christ as a manifestation of God placed on earth, while I think Jesus was an earthly person moving towards godliness. Similar to my view, Buddhism is based on a "regular" man gaining the wisdom of God through discipline, meditation and searching.

The majority of religious people that I meet are caring people that have a genuine desire to improve the world, and this is great. It becomes a problem when they feel their religious views are a direct reflection of their God, which excludes similar ideas from other sources. When dealing with other religions, often the source of the idea becomes more important than the idea itself. This highlights fixed beliefs vs. fluid wisdom, and similarly morality vs. compassion.

One of the differences I see in Japan is that it is part of the school system's function to teach morality. In the West we consider this imposing a religious view on a secular school system. For us, morality is to be taught in the home or at church, but our modern society is doing a poor job of teaching morals, whether spiritual ones or religious ones. Going the next step and teaching students how to be spiritual would be considered outrageous, so we let our youth grow up handicapped. This relates to my experiences as a life skills instructor. In my way of thinking, components such as assertiveness, anger management and self-esteem are spiritual, yet they make no reference to religion or God. Teaching this "morality" to our youth would lead to a more compassionate and caring society. Unfortunately, religions want these kinds of beliefs to be attributed to *their* god and not just be spiritual wisdom.

Those were my insights earlier this morning, and now I am enjoying hanging out with the crew. The others acknowledge my presence, but are too relaxed to show any exuberance; their greeting reflects a "join the scene" attitude. I sit down and everyone leisurely watches the waves, the surfers and the scantily-clad women. After about twenty minutes I succumb to the urge to go for a dip in the ocean.

181

For a while I play at bodysurfing, and soon the others come join me. The waves are just right for this kind of surfing, with every fourth or fifth one having the ideal swell. For bodysurfing, you swim with an intense burst of energy just as a wave is about to crest, and if you have timed it right, you get swept along in the swell. Then there are several seconds of cruising along with the wave until you are unceremoniously dumped on the sandy beach. To the ocean we are just inanimate pieces of driftwood, and if you are not careful, the landing can be a scratchy crash. After an hour of bodysurfing, we again plant ourselves on the beach.

Sitting on the sand and enjoying the carefree feeling of being on a holiday, I am reminded of the beaches on Cheju (Jeju) Island in Korea, and more recently, Thailand. This makes me think of Lib, my Korean ex-girlfriend. I wonder how she enjoyed her solo time in Thailand. She had hoped to stay there for a few more weeks after I left for Japan, depending on how long her money lasted. The thought of her traveling makes me smile.

When I was in Korea, I met Lib in a jazz club a couple of days after I started working at a school on Cheju Island. For three months we had great fun, but then my job fell through—the second time this happened to me in Korea. At that point I had had enough of Korean-style business; I was ready to resume my life in Canada. Though it would have been a hasty decision, I was considering marriage because I didn't want our relationship to end. At the time I thought Lib would have accepted a marriage proposal from me, though now I think that was presumptuous of me. As a preliminary step I thought it would be a good idea for us to do some traveling. I knew from a previous extended trip (a friend and I bicycled around Europe) that touring around with someone can be a challenge. So before making a more serious commitment to Lib, I wanted to test our compatibility. I suggested we do some traveling together.

A second reason for wanting to travel with Lib was to honor

her courage. She was an independent woman living in a culture that thwarted her individualistic spirit. She has a university degree, a keen mind and is a hard worker, but because she was over thirty and thus past Korea's expected marrying age, many doors were closed to her. She hoped to escape Korea and possibly live in New Zealand, similar to a friend of hers that moved there. After living there illegally for five years, this friend was able to apply for a foreigner's permit. My thinking was that even if we didn't marry, the experience of being in a foreign country would be a step towards fulfilling her dream of living abroad. Lib had never been outside of Korea.

Lib wasn't working at that time and had little money, but I was happy to pay her way. We explored the idea of going to Tibet, since we had both dreamed of visiting there, but I was told traveling in China as an unmarried interracial couple was not practical (it may be different now, but at that time it was an issue). The next idea was to go to the Philippines. During the time we were contemplating this I made a phone call home and was told my dad had just been discharged after five days in the hospital. I was shaken. The nature of his problems was unclear, but he had been admitted for observation. The doctors did not find any medical reason to explain his condition. When I called, he was at home and feeling better, so there was no imminent sense of danger, but it gave me a scare to think I could have lost my father.

This prompted me to make a quick decision to return to Canada. I asked Lib to join me, choosing to show her Western Canada instead of the Philippines. She accompanied me as we visited with my parents, my brothers' families and many friends. We indulged in everyone's hospitality, and Lib was impressed with their kindness, generosity and openness. We also traveled to several of my favorite wilderness places that I had been longing to see again. The type of traveling we were doing didn't have the stress of traveling in a foreign country, but it did give me an indication that a more serious relationship with her would be hard work. Cultural differences are a challenge, and our situation was further complicated because she spoke only moderate English. Of course, my Korean was about as good then as my Japanese is now. In the end, I accepted that I was not adventurous enough to make such a risky marriage commitment.

It is getting hot sitting on the beach in Niijima, but rather than go back in the water, the boys decide to get something to eat at the local restaurant. I only ate a light breakfast a few hours ago, so I am famished. After eating, we decide to go to the onsen, which are spa-like establishments using natural water from hot springs. Japan is a series of active volcanoes, which means there are thousands of hot springs, so it is understandable that onsens are an integral part of Japanese culture. In the Japanese books I've read, every day after work men will either go to the onsen or have a soak in the bath at home. Depending upon the style of the onsen, there may also be a sauna room, a steam room and a variety of soaking pools, some with herbs added to the water. In most onsens the men and women are separated, and the soaking is done naked. The Niijima onsen is uncommon in that it is completely outdoors, and the genders are mixed, so the patrons wear swimsuits. It is also free, which is always a bonus in my books.

Sitting in hot water may not sound appealing on a hot day, but the guys who have been coming here for years know it is a good place to meet women. This is not a priority for me, but I will enjoy soaking in the hot pools. It's not that I don't desire women and sex, but recently I have come to the realization that if I focus on getting laid, it inhibits my enjoyment of other aspects of my life. That and my frequent sense of disappointment—or more specifically, sense of failure—were not helping me feel good about my life. What's more, my ability to pick up women in Japan is further hampered by my language limitations. So now I let sex happen when it lands in my lap, so to speak.

I have wondered about what role sex should have in my life, now that I am an ordained minister. I do not subscribe to the moral judgment that sex is a sin, but does that mean I should have casual sex? At this point, until I have a heartfelt sense of its inappropriateness, I will not exclude casual sex from my life. Sex is another prime example of where we need to learn the wisdom of past masters and not just try to follow some beliefs adopted from their words. Helpful guidance can be gotten from someone that has transcended sexuality, whereas someone simply suppressing sexuality (like, say, a priest or a minister) will express ideas influenced by their energy blockages and their personality.

Soon we arrive at the onsen, and in spite of it being free, it is one of the nicest onsens I've seen. I have been to a few here in Japan and regularly visited similar-style bathhouses in Korea, though I am not aware of Korean ones using natural hot water. The Niijima onsen has six outdoor pools of varying temperatures. The motif is ancient Greek or Roman with all the pools being made from stones, and there are a few concrete pillars around for effect. The locale is a craggy rock bluff overlooking the ocean.

There are only a few people here, but a group of three women catches the interest of the boys. We choose a pool perched on the cliff overlooking the ocean—the excess water from the pool simply spills over the edge into the ocean twenty feet below. Safety regulations are much more relaxed in Japan, as there is no guardrail around the pool. The other pools are more removed from the cliff, but there is one pool built up on a rock platform. It sits twenty feet above the main level of the onsen and has stairs that wind up the rock face. It looks enticing, and I am sure we will spend some time in that pool too.

After a quick soak in the pool the boys start up a conversation with the three women, and so we move to that pool. As I don't speak the language, I am just a casual observer. I settle into the water and feel totally relaxed. This pool is not particularly hot, so I let my mind wander, and soon I'm thinking about Terra. I have been thinking of her less frequently these days, yet I find she still stirs a longing feeling in me. I had hoped that over time our separation—and more recently our e-mail exchange over my drunken insecurities—would alleviate my desire for our relationship. I accept that she doesn't want an intimate relationship with me, but I am slower in letting go of my desires for her.

Suddenly I realize Brad is telling me that they are moving to the upper pool. The girls have decided they are "onsened-out," but there is a vague plan to meet up with them later tonight. We head for the stairs and then settle into the upper pool, which is significantly warmer. It has a magnificent view of the ocean and nearby shoreline. To the left is a beautiful beach that I hadn't seen before, and I can't believe it is completely void of people. Again, in Canada there would be throngs of people stepping over each other to lie on the sand. Japan is blessed to have so many lovely beaches that many of them can be deserted during a national holiday in the summer.

After we're done at the onsen, we explore the town again. There are only two main streets, but as with all Japanese cities, there is a maze of little side streets. The rest of the holiday includes karaoke at an izakaya (Japanese-style restaurant), attending a local festival at a small shrine and much more time spent on the beach and at the onsen. There was also an ample amount of alcohol consumed. It was a great holiday, and something we can reminisce about. Now I feel more connected with Gerry, Mike and Brad of the Oz crew.

Chapter 23

Reading Energy; a Training Seminar

Wednesday, August 27

I am nervous as I sit down. Placing my notes in front of me, I begin.

"Today I am going to talk about understanding the world by reading energy. Then I will talk a little bit about group energy, and finally I will explain how this can help you in the classroom."

Once I start talking my nerves settle, and thus begins my presentation at my company's training seminar. It is a glorification to call it a "training seminar," because it is not exclusively focused on training, and the word *seminar* is too formal a description. It is twelve of my fellow teachers and me, along with our two bosses—performance supervisors—one of which is Brad. We are all sitting on the floor in a Peppy Kids Club classroom; all teaching at Peppy is done while sitting on the floor. The room is appropriately adorned with alphabet posters, children's songs and animal cutouts. Previously, for training, the company would bring its foreign teachers from all over Japan to a seminar in Nagoya City, but recently—I think to save money—each prefecture has been required to design their own training program. Given that this is not the expertise of the performance supervisors, and that they are not given the time and resources to create a proper training seminar, it is understandable this is not of a professional caliber. We have each been asked to give a 30-minute talk, so I offered to do a presentation on energy dynamics. I also arranged for more time for my presentation; it is hard to say much in half an hour.

My presentation is going well, at least from my point of view. After starting, I am calm, organized and thoughtful. I use a three-pronged approach: one, viewing the world using energy dynamics is rational (scientifically plausible); two, it is innate; and three, it is something we all do to some degree, either consciously or unconsciously. The demonstration I set up doesn't work, but I am not disappointed. It is more of an excuse to have some fun with the topic than a serious attempt to demonstrate reading energy. I end my presentation with some closing remarks about how reading energy can help in the classroom.

As expected, some of my coworkers relish what I have to say, some ponder it and some are triggered by it. Ideas of this nature challenge our basic beliefs, and basic beliefs are not usually changed by rational discourse. In fact, the more deeply held the belief, the less rational we become when we get into arguments about it. I believe basic beliefs are more often changed through some emotional process, such as a healing or a dramatic event. Rarely does one approach it with an open mind, and then research and contemplate their beliefs. There is a strong emotional component to basic beliefs, and the personality has attachments to them—and both inhibit a rational approach to change.

Mine was the final presentation of the day, so with some final remarks from the performance supervisors, the seminar ends. As I am packing up my things, a fellow teacher approaches me and says he found my talk very coherent and rational. It is icing on the cake; his words are a confirmation of my inner reality. I ask a few of the teachers if they want to go for a drink, but either they aren't interested or they have other plans. In spite of this I head for home feeling happy and energized.

On the train going home I am in a contemplative mood, and I reflect on my presentation. Today was more like planting seeds rather than changing beliefs. Hopefully my fellow workers will be able to consider these ideas when working through some personal crisis. That is a more likely time to alter one's basic beliefs.

It may be helpful to make a distinction between core beliefs and basic beliefs, though initially both types of beliefs are acquired through non-rational processes. The most fundamental beliefs are core beliefs, which usually stem from a blockage in the emotional body that was created during childhood. Unconsciously, we make a snap judgment derived from the emotional pain, and the resulting belief is something that soothes us. So it is at the emotional level that the core pattern gets set, and that is the most obvious place for change to occur. Later, our logical mind creates rationalizations for the illogical beliefs; we fool ourselves into thinking we adopted the belief as a result of some rational process, or even deny we have the belief.

Basic beliefs are deep seated and adopted, but they are not as rooted as core beliefs. Only as mature individuals can we rationally adopt beliefs, and it is an involved process. Most basic beliefs are gained by an osmosis-like process where we assume the belief from someone of importance to us. They are adopted for psychological reasons, such as seeking approval, conformity or to emulate. These are subtler emotions, but still the belief has an emotional component to it. We are not aware of inconsistencies in these deep-seated beliefs because we do not examine them. These beliefs influence our attitudes, but usually surface independently during an argument or in difficult situations. In fact, the personality purposely avoids having basic beliefs examined for consistency because they serve non-rational purposes.

To give an example, you may have a core belief that people who love you cannot be trusted. Likely this belief would have been acquired as a young child when your parents or caregivers failed to resolve your emotional struggle during a traumatic experience. Generally when this occurs, the parents are too immersed in their own issues or do not understand the severity of what is happening, or they don't have the wisdom to help resolve these traumas. Years later, as an adult, you may have an argument with your lover about trust and emphatically assert that you trust them. And likely you believe your assertion is true, but at a core level you do not trust them no matter what they say or do. The lack of trust isn't about them; it's about you. The common belief—that one should trust one's lover—guides the person during calm situations, but it is the core belief that unconsciously guides their reactions during stress. And since you are not thinking rationally at this point, the contradiction in beliefs is not exposed.

Now I am engaging in a soother of a different kind; I am enjoying a drink on the train home, which is one of the things I love about Japan. I feel like celebrating, so I bought a beer on the way to the station. Soon my mind wanders. The thought that I am fulfilling my spiritual destiny comes to mind. Another aspect of my ministerial thesis was to give presentations about my ideas. In Penticton I had made a few presentations at the local Spiritualist Church, but today's audience was less aware and less receptive. Somehow it feels more minister-like to be creating new "awarenesses," rather than preaching to the converted.

My train of thought goes through several steps in quick succession. Thinking of my ministerial thesis and how it is slowly coming into reality soon leads to a tangential idea that *everything happens for a reason*. Counter to that idea is that sometimes things just happen, and it is our reaction to them that transforms them into significant events. One example of the latter is my earlier explanation of my boss' success at the group home in Campbell River. Peter would drastically change the approach we were using to manage some of the residents, and I interpreted the success that followed as happening because of the commitment Peter brought to his decision.

Conversely, there is an inclination to make a correlation between events and consequences where maybe one doesn't exist. The personal example that frequently comes to my mind is the possible connection between the quick deterioration of my life in Korea and events prior to the start of my problems. Somehow during my time in Korea, my fortunes made a dramatic change for the worse, and I am not sure why.

When I went to Korea, it was during a phase in my life when I felt in sync with the Universe—I had the Christmas spirit all year round. Unknown to me at the time, I would say I had a bubble of light around me, and when others came in contact with me they were positively affected by that light. It took constant effort on my part to keep the bubble inflated, but my mindset was such that the effort to sustain the bubble was easy. I kept thinking positively and my bubble of light made good things happen, which reinforced the positive thinking. The idea of having a bubble wasn't a conscious idea at the time, but it is a useful way to describe the experience.

It had been an easy transition from my Life Skills job at the youth jail in Campbell River to teaching English in Korea, even though I had no previous ESL experience. Initially the job near Seoul in Korea was a pretty good one, yet I had done little research or preparation. Many other ESL teachers I met in Korea did not have such good luck. I thought my good situation was a product of my persistent state of feeling blessed.

Furthermore, my attitude of being blessed helped me overcome many of the challenges of the job and of living in a foreign culture. Soon after I started, a second foreign teacher came to work at the school. She was less suited to the challenge and started feeling like a fish out of water. After only four months she skipped town and went home. We were working and living in similar conditions, but she gave up and left while I was having the best time of my life! Happiness is an attitude, and not a set of circumstances.

My joy continued until a shift started one morning about six months into my stay in Korea. One of the workers from the school came to my apartment and told me not to come to work that day (I didn't have a phone). It was a regular workday, and nothing had been said to me in advance. Later I was informed that immigration officials had come to the school and were checking work visas. That was how I found out my work situation was not legal!

The school I was at was new, and I was their first teacher, so only after I arrived could the school provide lessons. (I guess technically they could hire a temporary teacher, but tough visa restrictions means temporary teachers are hard to find.) The problem was that Korean regulations dictated that a school could not apply for a foreigner's work visa unless the business was already operating. My school's owner decided to circumvent this difficulty by having another school in the organization apply for my work visa, even though there was no intention for me to work at that location; each school was a franchise of the parent organization. However, a visa is valid only for the location specified on the paperwork, and the school I was working at was not the one listed on my work visa. All of this had been arranged without my knowledge.

That day marked the point when I began to struggle during my time in Korea. The shift most likely started earlier, but on a subconscious level. My boss proposed resolving this legal issue by meeting with an immigration official one night, presumably to arrange a bribe. I was adamant that my work situation needed to be legal, so instead, a few days later, he and I attended a small immigration hearing. It was all done in Korean, and I was represented by my boss. The result was that the school and I were each given a fine. My boss paid both fines (mine was about $1500 and the school's was about $4000). I asked my boss if this could affect my future employment chances, and he said no.

My boss wanted me to apply for a new, legal visa for his school. For my part, I was prepared to complete the one-year I had originally signed on for, but I wasn't prepared to sign a *new* one-year contract (a minimum work visa is for one year). Mutually we decided that I would continue to work for his school while he acquired a visa for a new teacher, and then once the new teacher arrived, I would leave. Despite the visa problem and my decision to leave his school, my boss and I still maintained a friendly relationship. This arrangement gave me a chance to look for other employment while still collecting a paycheck and living in the company's apartment. Up to that point I was having such a great experience that I was keen on staying in Korea.

I did find a second job, the one on Cheju Island, but the new employer encountered a series of obstacles in trying to get a second work visa for me. My old boss had been less than truthful when he said the fine would not affect my future job prospects. My fine meant I had an official record of teaching illegally, which didn't necessarily prevent me from getting a new visa, but it was a problem. The Korean system of business often included bribing, which my former boss had done with my first work visa, except only with the local immigration office (the visiting officials were from the regional office).

During the three months I was at my new school on Cheju Island, I made two trips to Seoul (an expensive flight from my new location) and one trip to Japan (an even more expensive flight), all in an attempt to sort out my work visa problem. In the end, my new employer didn't want to pay a bribe, so I was not granted a second work visa. To top it off, my second employer shortchanged me $1300 on my last paycheck.

Tired and discouraged, I'd had enough of working in Korea. This was when I traveled with Lib, my Korean girlfriend. Then, after moving back to Canada, I struggled to understand why my fortunes in Korea had changed so quickly. I still do not have an answer, but there is an event that persistently comes to mind when I look for an explanation. It happened while I was on my Christmas holiday in Thailand.

That holiday was an enriching experience, and as I have said, the Thai people spawned some ideas about living in the moment. Part of the reason for choosing Thailand was because my cousin lives there. As I mentioned, he and his wife are missionaries and have been running an orphanage there for many years. Al met me at the airport and I had a chance to visit with him, his wife Terry and their family—at that time about 15 children were living with them. It was inspiring to see their compassion in action.

After visiting Al and his family for a few days, they took me to a Thai resort they occasionally visit. His family enjoyed a day of fun at the beach, during which time Allan negotiated for me a reasonable rate at a modest hotel. In the late afternoon, he and his family returned to their home. I had the next five days to spend as I wanted before returning to Korea. My plan was to spend several days at the resort, then spend the last two days of my vacation in Bangkok. Traveling alone in Asia was a new adventure, and that holiday was very magical for me.

The day after I arrived at the resort, I was walking along the beach basking in the sun with a plan to do some snorkeling at a nearby outcrop of land. As I walked, I saw another foreigner sitting with several Thai people at a beachfront restaurant. Since this was a Thai resort area, I had not encountered other foreigners. We exchanged hellos as I continued walking along the beach. After snorkeling I made the walk back, and this time the other foreigner and I struck up a conversation.

Kurt was from Switzerland and had a Thai girlfriend, the woman that owned the beach restaurant. They would meet a few times a year, switching between meeting in Thailand and meeting in Europe. I spent the next few days enjoying Kurt's friendship and his local knowledge. I think he enjoyed having a native English speaker to talk to and someone who could appreciate his unique lifestyle. Kurt was fluent in several languages, including Thai and English.

After a fun evening of socializing Thai style with some of the locals, we met on the beach the next morning. It was then that he made me an offer that I was too intrigued by to refuse—did I want to go to a whorehouse? My reply had nothing to do with need, and was motivated purely by curiosity; I had never had a prostitute experience, yet I had often wondered what it would be like. Trying to ignore all the judgments I had about it, I was hoping to experience some of what Thailand had to offer. (This made the advice the Thai monk gave to me eight years later on my second trip to Thailand more peculiar—to be open to what Asia has to offer. Thailand is famous for its prostitutes.)

Being with a prostitute turned out to be an interesting experience, but it was not a sexually gratifying one. Having a woman offer her vagina to me without the usual prelude, and without creating sexual tension, was bizarre for me. I had never had sex with a woman that I hadn't kissed, and I found that kissing and caressing were a *necessary* part of my sexual enjoyment. Though I was somewhat excited, I did not find it a pleasurable experience.

Can I say this experience was the cause of my misfortunes in Korea? I am not sure if the event itself caused the shift, but I'm sure my reaction to that experience was an important factor. I felt very guilty afterwards. I know immeasurable suffering is caused by prostitution, but I am not sure if the act itself is immoral. At the time my thinking was that, even though prostitution involves many victims and causes great harm to many, it is still possible to think it may be helpful to some. This thread of rationale was enough for me to put aside my judgments.

Now I think that, yes, paying for sex could be mutually beneficial, but it would *not* be called prostitution, it would be more like therapy. And the practitioner would ideally have some training in healing. It is unquestionable that many payers would benefit from some sexual healing. As for the traditional prostitute-like interactions, it's possible they could happen with minimal personal damage to the participants, but this does not justify supporting an industry that is grievously harmful to so many. Perhaps we could learn a few things from Japan and the geisha philosophy. My understanding is that a geisha is trained in many arts forms (music, dance, conversation and more), and their involvement with clients, if sexual, is more encompassing than merely a sexual experience; it is a social arrangement that sometimes includes a physical component.

What is morality? Morality has to do with doing the right thing, but how is the right thing determined? Personally, I would change the discussion from morality to compassion. Morality suggests right and wrong, and compassion is more about personal responsibility. I am of the mind that there are some universal aspects of compassion and that we can learn to understand these tenets, but not so much from external sources; rather, it must come from going within. If we can cut through all the "garbage and baggage" in our minds, then determining appropriate action is attainable and clear. Having a religion give us rules of conduct involves many layers of interpreting a master's original intent, and the subsequent belief structures aren't as helpful as listening to your heart.

As for how my prostitution incident affected me while I was in Korea, my guilt would have had a negative impact on many levels. However, I have a hard time accepting that this event alone could have caused such a severe change in my fortunes. With all the work I had done to bring my unconscious motivations into my awareness, and with my frequent reflections on the experience, I don't think such a dramatic shift could be attributed to this event alone. Yet, it is hard to ignore this scenario when I cannot find any other basis to explain the subsequent problems I encountered in Korea. It was about a month after my Thai holiday when the immigration officials visited my school.

The next train stop is Fuji City. I end my reminiscing and grab my backpack. My frame of mind is buoyant as I am still relishing the success of my presentation! The presentation started me reflecting about my ministerial mission, and I ended up thinking about an experience with a prostitute in Korea. Destiny was part of my thinking, and the correlation between events, but I have lost my train of thought. Oh well—if there are any important insights I need to draw from these thoughts, I am sure they will surface again. For now, I let my thinking move onto other subjects.

When I get home to my apartment I feel like having another drink. It is Wednesday night, but I only have an office day tomorrow. Office days are non-teaching work days where we go to a nearby classroom that is not in use, and do lesson prep for five and half hours. We are unsupervised, so I don't have to be concerned if I am not alert. It is unfortunate that a celebration usually involves having a drink, but that is how I feel. To limit my guilt, I make a deal with myself—I must do some writing before having another drink. And if the writing goes well, I may even reward myself with a walk to Oz to see if any of the crew is there. They have a regular workday tomorrow, so they may not be there. However, first I have to do some writing, so I get out my computer. I also get out my notes from my holiday on Niijima Island. Now I am ready to write.

Chapter VI, cont. (Energy Blockages)

Continuing with the nature of blockages and Energy Bodies, a blockage in the Mental Body is a belief. These beliefs form structures in the Mental Body, limiting the flow of energy. This limitation forces one to view situations from a fixed perspective and ignore other interpretations. In particular, *beliefs* about spirituality actually remove people from the *experience* of spirituality. This is because one's consciousness is involved in these belief structures, and not in the moment. This can explain how so much pain and harm can be caused by religious organizations in the name of God when to do so is counter to the innate benevolence of the Divine. Beliefs and judgments are actually blockages of energy, and they inhibit one from connecting in the moment with Divine compassion.

Beliefs are closely related to judgments, which are blockages in the Spiritual Body. The difference is that a belief is inherently neutral, but a person often holds a judgment that a belief is good or bad. A belief is like a fact, and a judgment implies that the fact is good or bad. For example, I can believe that someone is often inactive, and then I can judge that indifferent belief as being bad and say the person is lazy. The distinction is often complicated because many English words are judgmental, so the neutral interpretation is hard to recognize (like the word lazy implying that being inactive is bad). Judgments inhibit forgiveness, and forgiveness incorporates the Soul's under-standing as to why someone acts in a certain way.

A significant situation where the distinction between belief and judgment is especially important is when one feels Vulnerable. Vulnerability involves suspending the desire and the belief that one needs to have control over a situation. The actuality of having control in a situation is irrelevant; it is the *belief* which is pertinent. When one negatively judges the belief of "not having control," it turns a benign situation into a perception of helplessness. Acceptance of the lack of control, which means the personality surrenders its desire for control, is in part Vulnerability. Not accepting or resenting a lack of control is negatively judging your Vulnerability as helplessness. Frequent judgments of helplessness lead a person to adopt a "victim's" view of the world, or a chronic sense of helplessness. The importance of Vulnerability will be explained further in the next chapter.

To summarize, blockages can occur in any of the non-Physical Energy Bodies, and are a fixed energy pattern that prevent the natural flow of energy. A blockage in one Energy Body will have some effect on the other Bodies, but this corre-lation is unique to each situation. As a person grows they are conditioned to avoid encountering the blockages, thus creating coping strategies to avoid connecting with the pain of the blockages. When the consciousness either gets caught up in the blockage, or engages in a coping strategy to avoid the blockage, then it is no longer in the moment. Having blockages means a person is not fully attuned to his or her Energy Bodies, which is a stress for the person. The blockage also means that there is a positive aspect of the person that is hidden within and is not being allowed to surface.

Core blockages result from childhood incidents that have a profound impact on the individual, and are usually held in the Emotional Body. Over time, these core blockages become layered with less intense emotional incidents of a similar nature and with the energy patterns resulting from the consistent use of coping strategies. The Physical Body can suffer from immediate injuries, from unhealthy behaviors involved in coping strategies or from the stress when a person is not in the moment. Emotional blockages are traumas of varying degrees, mental blockages are beliefs, and spiritual blockages are judgments. A judgment is a belief that has been assessed as good or bad. Of special note, surrendering the desire to control a situation is being Vulnerable, and resenting not having control is helplessness.

I put my computer away and grab a drink. Writing has added to my earlier feeling of gratification, so I am keen to go to Oz—the payoff from the bargain with myself.

It turns out to be a mellow night at Oz, but this doesn't dampen my spirits. After a couple of drinks I decide to leave, preferring instead to stroll the now familiar walkway near my apartment while listening to music.

Chapter 24

Watching Sumo

Monday, September 22

Soon after waking up I sit down for my morning meditation. After 40 minutes there are no great insights but it was a pleasant sitting. It is now 8 o'clock and I have a bit of time before I need to get moving; a group of coworkers and I are going to a sumo tournament today (called a *Basho* in Japanese). I am really looking forward to it. I have watched several tournaments on TV and I am starting to understand the intricacies of it. It is very popular here, and seeing it live should be another insight into the Japanese psyche. I'm not hungry, but I grab a banana anyway.

Having meditated, the next "should" that follows is that I should write. I push this thought aside. This leaves reading a book or watching TV to kill time. Most of my reading is done on the train while going to work, or while at work before starting my lessons. I haven't been to the library recently, but I have borrowed a book from a fellow teacher—it's OK, but not one that is holding my attention. Strangely, I don't want to watch TV either, so I am at an impasse.

I am feeling upbeat, not only because of having meditated and going to the sumo tournament later today, but I had a nice surprise on my casual bike ride yesterday. While I was out exploring the east side of Fuji City, a district called Yoshiwara, I came across a local festival. It is amazing how many there are in Japan; during the summer as you travel on the main train line, at least one of the cities, if not more, along the track is having a festival that weekend. You always see some people on the train dressed-up in the traditional Japanese clothes.

Not only does it surprise me that there are so many festivals, but also that the locals are so committed to them. Compared to

Penticton's former Peach Festival, there is much more community involvement both in running them and supporting them. And there is a real emphasis on children. The one I was at yesterday had the usual festival booths (food, toys, more food, festival paraphernalia—based on Shinto I think), but it also had a stage where kids were performing traditional dances. In Canada you would never find this, well maybe somewhere but I never encounter it. It is yet another example of the tradition/ritual heritage of this society.

Finally I decide I really should do some writing, and hopefully getting out my computer will increase my motivation. Writing will at least give me some compensation for the drinking I know I will do today. I start my computer and open up the document called "my book."

Chapter VII: Healing and Vulnerability

Healing is the process of releasing stuck energy patterns. For standard healing to take place, the person must be willing to be Vulnerable. When Vulnerable, the consciousness simultaneously connects with the past trauma (or some of the stuck energy surrounding the past trauma) and the timeless wisdom of the Spiritual Body. To access the wisdom of the Spiritual Body, the personality must be willing to surrender its desire to control the current situation. This surrendering by the personality is a key feature of the state of Vulnerability, and of healing.

As previously stated, energy's natural state is to flow, so when a blockage forms there is always an inclination for it to unravel. Healing doesn't have to be intentionally sought, because if allowed by the personality, the process will start to happen of its own accord. As a preliminary step in healing, there needs to be some conscious awareness of the blockage, and the Soul attempts to this do by creating situations that trigger a core blockage. This triggering energizes the blockage, and this is the first phase of healing. However, if the personality reacts negatively, then the triggering may lead to engaging in avoidance techniques (such as numbing, busyness, worrying or anger to name a few).

Connecting with a past trauma is an emotionally painful process, but not nearly as painful as the personality fears. It is the fear and the coping strategies employed to avoid the pain that compound the problem. Healing is more manageable when one knows not to get caught up in the fear. Nevertheless, the conscious connection to the past trauma does require one to experience some of the pain involved in that past experience. It takes courage to be willing to face this pain, but then once the willingness is there, one does not have to become fully immersed in the pain. In fact, getting too involved in the pain of a past trauma can be an avoidance technique of the personality. Melodrama can impede the healing process, because this weakens the Spiritual Body connection, resulting in the desire to be healed being diverted.

The healing process can be initiated in other ways as well, and the individual need not be fully conscious of the details of each step to have a release. Besides the conscious act of the person becoming Vulnerable, stuck energy can be released by an intense emotional experience or by miracles. Intense emotional experiences can, in a sense, dislodge the stuck pattern. This new traumatic event serves as a "wake-up call," which may or may not be heeded. With this type of healing, one is not usually fully attuned to the process, so some of the accompanying learning of a life-lesson can be missed. If this is so, the Soul will continue to "arrange" similar situations in the future to provide the opportunity to fully learn the lesson. Miracles, on the other hand, mean that the Divine Energy has been engaged for some unconscious reason. How and why this happens, I do not fully understand, and so I will not try to explain it.

As mentioned earlier, other means for initiating healing are practices such as meditation, yoga or tai chi. Also, nurturing the

Physical Body, with its connection to blockages in the other Bodies, can bring enough energy to the blockages to begin the healing process. Since major blockages in one Energy Body have corresponding blockages in the other Bodies, any Body is an access point for healing issues in all the Bodies. Of course conventional counseling is another means for healing, but I think it is not nearly as effective as energy healing because of the involvement of the personality. Drugs (including pharmaceutical, psychiatric ones) are another avenue for healing, but they are a very problematic means of healing, because drugs also damage the Energy Bodies, and inhibit grounding the healing experience. Also, drugs don't necessarily bring about healing of core blockages.

As for conscious healing practices, different cultures have developed their own methods, so there are several ancient and esoteric practices, such as the Chinese acupuncture points. However, as modern society begins to understand more about the healing process, newer healing techniques are being developed. Many traditions and societal functions stem from the desire to be healed. In modern Western Society, events such as music concerts, sporting events etc. provide a mild form of release. During these events, a person is likely to be "in the moment," and he or she can express some emotions more readily, both of which help to reduce stress.

As is often the case, once I start writing, I really get into it. I am pleased with today's effort. Now time is short, and I must hurry to get ready.

Soon I'm out the door and heading for the station. Many Peppy teachers have Monday off and since it is a weekday, there are lots of tickets available for the tournament. One of my fellow teachers speaks Japanese well enough to have purchased a few. To save money we decided to take the local train (as opposed to the bullet train) to Tokyo, and I will join up with them at Fuji station. My coworkers are scattered from one end of the prefecture to the other, so as the train moves from west to east we will accumulate teachers along the way.

On the train, Japan's lax liquor laws tempt us, which means some of the boys are getting a head start and having a pre-noon beer; I join in. By the time we arrive in Tokyo, several of us are feeling good. After negotiating the web of subways that intersect all over Tokyo, we get to the station near the arena. We will have lunch nearby and then go inside the arena. The wrestling started early this morning, with the junior ranks competing before the "big boys" start at 4 o'clock.

I am familiar with some of the tournament's proceedings, but there are also many things I haven't a clue about. As with many aspects of Japanese life, some things are done simply because that's the way it has always been done, with no one stopping to ask if still makes sense. For example, the wrestling is done on an elevated platform that is 3 feet (1 meter) above the ground. The wrestling circle is about 30 feet across (10 meters) and a thick rope is half buried in the floor to mark the ring's perimeter. For some reason there is a dusting of sand on the surface. The aim is to either push your opponent out of the ring or have some part of his body other than his feet touch the ground. The edge of the platform is near the rope boundary (less than a yard/meter) and a potential three-foot drop awaits anyone who gets pushed out. Wrestlers regularly get injured while falling off the platform, and I don't think it would compromise the sport if the three-foot drop was eliminated.

Tradition has a powerful influence in this society, and in some domains, modernization isn't a consideration. The Japanese are world leaders in the age of technology, but many administrative duties are still done the old-fashioned way, with people using pen and paper. Bank tellers don't use computers (as noted before), and when you visit city hall, where foreigners have to visit periodically, you see a mountain of paper and files. Houses are built the traditional way, with inadequate insulation, in spite of today's need for energy conservation. And this is so even though I believe Japan is the leading nation in building earthquake sustainable buildings. It doesn't make sense.

After lunch and another beer, we head to the arena. As we near the main entrance we walk by a side door that has many people waiting around it. I guess this is where the wrestlers enter, and a crowd has gathered to cheer them on as they go in. We stand and watch for a few minutes and soon see a couple of the more famous sumos, ones that I recognize. The sumo champion is like a rock star in Japan. He will get lots of media attention, such as being in commercials and guest spots on the many TV entertainment shows. The Japanese are quite concerned about the state of sumo, because the top-ranked wrestlers are Mongolian.

As we enter the arena we are asked if we have any bottles, and since Ricky has a bottle of beer, he is given a plastic cup to pour it into. I brought a carton of sake for the boys and myself, the traditional Japanese rice wine (I thought it appropriate for watching sumo), so it's not a problem. Our seats are on the upper level, but still good enough. The arena is strictly for sumo, and holds about 10,000 spectators, but there are few spectators here now. Around the ring itself there is some floor seating, then rows of small, elevated platforms gradually rising up to complete the lower two sections. The floor seating and the platforms have no chairs, just cushions on the floor. This is the Japanese custom: in Peppy classrooms we sit on the floor, Peppy apartments have only a low table for floor sitting, and in traditional Japanese restaurants customers sit on the floor. Here each platform is meant for four people, but they are too small to fit four of us. On TV, when one of the top wrestlers is unexpectedly defeated, I have seen the audience throw the cushions into the ring. It makes for quite a sight, but a hazard for the people sitting close to the ring.

We settle into our seats. It is 2 o'clock and the second tier wrestlers are competing. I don't recognize any of the combatants, and the sparse crowd adds to the lull. I find myself reflecting on the nature of societies. On the one hand there are traditions, and on the other there are group events. To explore the latter, they can be sporting competitions, religious events or casual fun, but these happenings are where we lose our sense of time and become engrossed in the experience. And when a group of people are reacting in unison, the effects are compounded (incidentally, this is so with meditation as well). When everyone is cheering for a team, enchanted at a concert or in deep concentration at a group meditation, it becomes a timeless experience. Some examples of such memorable moments are the Olympics, a concert or a New Year's Eve event. Even watching a good movie in a theater is more intense with a large audience. Since these are such powerful experiences, the performers are often glorified, usually without having the spiritual wisdom to act accordingly.

Moments when a society is focused as a group become defining ones for that society. John Kennedy's assassination, the Americans walking on the moon, or the 9/11 terrorist attack are events that have become etched into the American psyche. However, this enduring quality is counter to Zen, so maybe that is a factor as to why our societies still have so many problems. It is powerful to be in the moment with others, but to try to hang on to that moment is taking you out of the "next moment" that is flowing by. I think it is special because we are closer to a godlike experience, where all is One. If a person is truly in the moment, your complete awareness (physical, emotional, mental and spiritual) is absorbed for that instance, and this is the essence of enlightenment. It is the universe's natural state to be totally focused in the moment.

Another important reason to be in the moment is because that is where happiness can be found. Rarely can we be happy and not be present in the moment. And even sad moments are still precious, because genuine emotions are the purest expression of life. If one is willing to feel sadness then one can move on, whereas if one avoids sadness, he or she adds to their energy blockages, which inhibits future happiness. Our consciousness is rooted in our emotional body, so emotions are central to our lives—happy or sad.

However, some emotions cause us *not* to be fully present in the moment; emotions based on the past or the future take us away from the richness of life. It might be helpful to make a distinction between primary and secondary emotions. Primary emotions are directly connected to the events of the present moment. Secondary ones may be influenced by current events, but not exclusively; they are emotions where one of our energy bodies is involved in non-current time. For example, envy involves reflecting upon what we don't have, and so it requires some cognitive processing before we experience the emotion. Primary emotions are the ones we are born into this world experiencing, which may be as limited as happy, sad and contentment. I am not yet a hundred percent sure of this, but I *think* frustration is an early emotion too.

Let's consider the following question: "Is reflecting on happy memories a good thing?" In comparison to other pastimes, recalling happy memories is better than many, but it still takes us away from the present moment. The experience is not what I would call a primary emotion. And if we foster these kinds of reflections, our consciousness is being conditioned to become caught up in old energy patterns, and not all of the old patterns are as benign as happy memories.

As it gets closer to 4 o'clock, the crowd builds. It seems many Japanese fans don't bother watching the lower-ranked wrestlers. Soon it is time for the main event. There are some ceremonial activities before the final wrestling begins. In two separate groups (east vs. west), all the senior sumos come into the ring and bow, and then do a brief "dance." After that, three of the top ranked sumos enter and do another blessing ritual, swinging a sword around. Finally, the wrestling can begin. I'm sure these are old customs that have some significance, but to me they are just quaint. Japan is like that.

A tournament is 15 days, from Sunday to the Sunday next, and today is day nine. There are around 40 wrestlers at the top level and they have one match a day, for a total of 15 during the tournament. The first week's matches are set in advance, but for the second week the matches are arranged according to how well they are doing, so the wrestlers with the best records battle at the end of the tournament.

As the final match finishes, we hang back to avoid the rush out the door, and then it's time to go. It's now 6:15pm. It was interesting and fun, but there were no big upsets, and so no shower of cushions. A couple of the guys are staying in Tokyo for the night, a couple are going to Akihabara (the part of the city that specializes in electronics shops) and a few are taking the local train home. I am the only one going home that is willing to pay for the bullet train. After a day of drinking, it is too monotonous to sit on the slow train for hours. We part ways, and I manage to negotiate the couple of subway transfers to where I can catch the *Shinkansen*. It has been a great day, but now it's time to start sobering up—I have to teach tomorrow.

Before getting on the train I buy some sushi at one of the station's kiosks. I also buy some green tea (Japan's number one drink, hot or cold). Once I find a seat on the train I continue wondering how societies are shaped.

In contrast to group events are traditions. With traditions, it is the connection to the spiritual body that is crucial. A person eats dinner every night, and this is not noteworthy. But if a person says grace before eating dinner, then it is significant. The difference between dinner and grace is the spiritual connection, where grace is a conscious act to feel gratitude and acknowledge a higher power. If the grace becomes rote and the participants don't actually reflect on their good fortune, then the grace slips back into the mundane, routine category.

So traditions are another avenue to connect with the godlike quality of the moment. By consciously making a spiritual connection, we are accessing the Universal Energy and tapping into that godlike perspective. The actions involved in traditions help limit the interference from the personality and our energy blockages. Traditions have this spiritual element as part of their origins, but it is an ongoing challenge to maintain that element. If a tradition loses its spiritual component, then it decreases in value. As North America "de-religifies" Christmas, it becomes more and more of a commercial enterprise. The spending of money and indulgence of Christmas are becoming a new tradition—or more appropriately, a new routine, and its lack of spirituality means it is not enriching. This is contrasted by the festivals in Japan, where the people have a strong sense of tradition, as well as it being a group activity that fosters connecting with others.

After arriving in Fuji, I start the long walk home. Fuji is a big enough city that it has a Shinkansen station, but for some reason it is not near the local train station. Usually the two are together. The long walk home and fresh air are helping me to sober up, and though it was a pleasant but overcast day, the evening is getting chilly. The walk is pleasant, but tiring. The excitement of sumo, drinking during the day and now the trip home have zapped my energy. I decide to get my bed set up and watch TV. Relaxed and satisfied, I will do some channel surfing, but I know it won't be long before I fall asleep.

Chapter 25

Meeting Friends and Strangers

Saturday, October 4

There is a light drizzle coming down as I ride to Mike's house. Today was once again a one-class Saturday, and the lesson went well. My cycling route home takes me within a few blocks of Mike's house, and because of my upbeat frame of mind I took a rare risk and called him to see if he had plans for the evening. Mike said Hank and his girlfriend were coming over to his house later; they are going to hang out at Mike's for a while, then maybe go to a jazz club later. He warmly invited me to join them.

It is just after 6 o'clock by the time I start riding to Mike's house. The sprinkling of rain feels refreshing on my face. It is still early October, and though the days are pleasantly warm, the evenings are cool. The moisture in the air adds to the chill, but the heat generated from cycling keeps me warm. My legs feel strong as I pump the pedals; I like to keep a quick pace going when I ride to make sure I get a cardio workout. It is a mesmerizing sky because even though there is a light drizzle, there are also breaks in the clouds. The effect of the setting sun shining on the patchy clouds gives the holes a brilliant orange fringe, and part of the sky looks like it is on fire. The spectacular evening sky adds to my feeling of anticipation, which encourages me to ride faster.

Stopping at a convenience store, I buy several cans of Chu-Hi and a few beers for Mike. I also pick up a pre-packaged dinner, as I suspect Mike has already eaten. When I arrive, Mike is playing a new computer game he has downloaded—some car chase game. It is not my thing but I don't mind watching as I eat my dinner. Soon, Ayako, Mike's girlfriend, comes through the door, and not long after that Hank and Yuko arrive. The evening is spent watching a pirated version of *I Am Legend*, which, surprisingly, I find to be an entertaining movie. As the evening wears on they decide to skip going to the jazz club. I feel good because I am hanging out with friends, having a few drinks and sharing a few laughs. When Hank and Yuko leave, I decide I should do so as well. The rain has stopped—the weather got worse before it got better—and the ride home is pleasant.

When I get home it is 1am, but I feel energized, so I decide to go to Oz and see if anything is happening there. As I enter, I see several patrons clustered around the bar. After my usual greeting with Muni, I order a beer. Moving around the corner I suddenly see Gerry talking to several women. I am happy to see him because we haven't talked since last Sunday. I grab a coaster from the bar and throw it at him. With surprising accuracy, I get the desired result. Gerry cusses at me in a joking way; I can tell he is happy to see me too.

We have a couple of beers and catch up on our various goings-on, during which time his companions leave and the crowd at the bar thins out. Gerry says he is also going to call it a night and heads for home.

At this point I notice that the young, attractive woman I had been checking out for the last hour is now sitting alone at the bar. My upbeat frame of mind has me thinking of the possibilities. As I've said, I usually don't try to pick up women; I have been much happier since I stopped pretending to be a ladies' man. Also, conversation happens much easier when there are no expectations of the outcome. However, I am willing to challenge my seclusion tonight.

Sex is one area where I still have much healing work to do; I am not very comfortable with myself when it comes to sex. In my intimate relationships I have had periods of being comfortable with sex, and at times it has been great, but overall I have experienced more doubt and confusion than pleasure. After being "cut off" enough times I realized that sex is often the battlefield for unresolved or unspoken relationship issues. Personally I am aware that my ego still runs my life when it comes to sex: the fear of what my partner thinks inhibits me.

My self-imposed seclusion and the recent absence of an intimate lover means I have had little opportunity to apply my now finely-honed inquisitive skills to the energy dynamics of sex. Some practical experience will give me a chance to examine my theory—though I am not kidding myself, I am not pursuing her in the name of science. Part of the mystery of sex is the total absorption of the consciousness during orgasm. Is a person still connected to his or her spiritual body? Are we connected to all four of our energy bodies during orgasm? If so, the involvement of the mental body must be different from the norm as there are no thought processes occurring—it is a non-cognitive experience. There is so much I don't know about the energy dynamics of sex, and I want to understand it.

Paralleling my ignorance are my muddled moral judgments. My confusion is reflective of a general societal misunderstanding of sex. It is certainly one aspect of life where society has lost itself. Sex is so pervasive in our mass media, and it's full of mixed messages, so one cannot help but be confused. Add to the mix that sex generally hits at the core of our insecurities, making it difficult to seek help from others—that is, if you can find someone who has enough wisdom to be helpful. Because society is so confused about sex, and it is an area where I need some personal healing, I intend to write my second book on the subject.

Not surprisingly, I think most religions have gotten the sex thing wrong, but I also think that the New Age spiritual community has done a disservice to sexual health as well. When one attains enlightenment, one has transcended sexual energy; it is part of the human condition, but not part of the soul. Unfortunately this has led some spiritual leaders to omit dealing with it, saying it is a "lower chakra" issue, while they are concerned with the higher energy centers—the spiritual realms. The problem is that one can't just dismiss it without having resolved it. If there are sex-related energy blocks, they need to be healed, not suppressed. And sex blockages are unavoidable since they relate to our life force, a core aspect of ourselves. Having highly developed spiritual energy bodies can give one charisma and wisdom, but many gurus fall into disrepute because they are tempted by greed or sexuality, which stem from blockages in the lower chakras. Part of AlixSandra's wisdom, and how she runs Inner Focus, is that she pushes students to address their lower chakra issues (not specifically sexual issues, but all energy blockages).

There is a quote I like from a spiritual guru named Osho. He says, "That which cannot remain in awareness is sin, and that which grows in awareness is virtue. Virtue and sin are not social concepts, they are inner realizations." I'm not sure sex can grow in awareness, but this quote suggests a different means of determining what are sins and virtues. This mirrors my argument that past masters gave us lessons to learn and not ideas to adopt. I think as long as sex provides some comfort and pleasure to the people involved, and they respect each other, then it is OK, even if the two people are not well acquainted. In spite of trying to take an "enlightened" view of sex, I am not convinced that casual sex is healthy, but tonight I am putting my doubts aside.

Tonight, my upbeat frame of mind heightens my desire for female comforting, and this prompts me to take the initiative. I walk over to the young woman at the bar and sit down. I quickly find out her name is Rise (pronounced Ree-say) but that she speaks only moderate English. Soon my hands and my facial expressions are doing the talking. It becomes evident that we share a common desire; I am now caressing her leg and she is receptive to my forwardness. Everyone else has left Oz and the staff is cleaning up. I make my pitch and indicate my desire for her to come to my apartment. She accepts, and we leave together.

Rise is the perfect person for me in this type of encounter. She isn't aggressive, which is the type of person I usually end up with since I don't take the initiative in seeking these casual encounters. But she is not shy, either; she is keen to interact with me. She seems to trust me, which encourages me to overcome my insecurities and delve into my sexual urges.

Once in my apartment, we begin the mating ritual. First she encourages me to have a shower with her. At least as far back as the 1600s, which is the setting for James Clavell's *Shogun*, the Japanese custom was and is to bathe before sex. After our shower the kissing and caressing moves to the futon, where things continue to progress. But at some point I realize the sexual energy has stopped flowing. We started out passionately, but now it feels like I am methodically going through a foreplay checklist, moving toward intercourse. The energy dynamic shifted, and I wasn't grounded enough to notice how or when. For me, this is becoming the prostitute situation again; I am excited enough to be erect, but the passion has stopped building. She has shut down emotionally and has given control of the situation to me; it is no longer a dance of our sexual energies. Personally, I am not that intent on intercourse, and I am very happy to abandon that goal in the hope of having a mutually enjoyable experience. I know she needs to be more comfortable with me before this becomes a dance of passions again, and I need this experience to be a dance.

I stop my progression, and we lay on the futon for a while. To try to rekindle the passion, I caress her skin. Next I take her hands and place them on my chest. I encourage her to touch me as I want her to feel the power of her caress. I want her to experience that just by moving her hands over my skin she can cause me to twist with tingling pleasure. I want her to explore my body with her hands, with her eyes and with her being. I want her to be curious and become excited with my body. She complies, and her explorations reawaken the passion of our erotic dance.

It is a couple of hours of exploring and pleasuring, which

reaffirms my desire to further investigate my sexual nature. I want to understand the energy dynamics of sex. I want to understand that raw desire for pleasure. I want to understand how the heart is involved even in a casual, carnal encounter.

Rise has gone now, having taken a taxi home, and I am reflecting on the experience. My intimate encounter with this young woman was pleasurable for me, and I believe for her, too. I am pleased, but I am careful to keep my ego in check, as there is a tendency to feel flushed by the conquest. I also need to be wary of my tendency to shame myself; I didn't succumb to naughty urges, but rather I explored natural, sexual ones with a willing partner.

As far as tonight goes, I guess it comes down to what was in my heart during the casual sexual encounter. Or, more important to the moment, what is in my heart now? Is all the baggage I have been indoctrinated with limiting me from seeing this encounter as a caring situation? All the dogma, coupled with the insecurities that I hide during sex, clouds my perceptions.

Most religions try to shame sex, I think for reasons other than knowing that the sex itself is inherently bad. For example, the Catholic Church propagates guilt, which helps keep people enmeshed with the Church. For this and other reasons, people frequently try to avoid being vulnerable during sex, so they hide their insecurities and end up using poor coping skills instead. Certainly, sex, and unhealthy means of obtaining it, has caused immeasurable pain and suffering. Avoiding feelings and using dysfunctional coping skills usually results in being numb or hurt, even after consensual sex. Another aspect of sex that compounds my confusion is that the same sense of wrongness that leads to shame can also be part of the titillation of sex; the forbidden fruit tastes sweeter.

The key to understanding sexual behavior is to become aware of the heart during sex. I noticed tonight that as the passion built, my heart became less involved. The raw desire for pleasure dominated and the caring part of me receded. The more I let my guard down, the more inflamed I became. I don't mean I became rough or crude, but I became self-centered. And I don't think being self-centered is a bad thing, but I haven't explored the truth of this to convince myself it is good. Though I was self-centered, it still felt like a dance of our sexual energies.

I am coming to the understanding that pure moments in life are when our other energy bodies meld with our spiritual body. During sex the focus narrows to the physical sensations, and if the heart is open, then the reduced mental and emotional activity can be channeled into the spiritual body. That is where intimate relationships can be enriching—there is time to develop trust. But that is not always the case—relationships can also create a non-healing, non-nurturing environment. It takes effort and a willingness to face vulnerabilities in order to have a loving, growing relationship.

Alternatively, people that engage in lots of casual sex reflect insecurity about intimacy. And to be fair, some of us who *don't* engage in much casual sex reflect our fears too. So finding an appropriate participant by chance, where you have the trust needed to make a one-time sexual meeting an enriching encounter, is unusual. I think having sex for purely pleasurable reasons soon loses its appeal. We are ingrained with a need to seek a more intimate experience, and if we block this feeling, the casual experience won't be enriching.

It was great having sex tonight, particularly because of the type of sexual experience I just had, but what I long for is intimacy. I crave waking up next to my lover and feeling her naked body curled up against mine, to feel my skin touching her skin. I had some of my needs met tonight, but I am not going to find love in a casual sexual experience, and love is what my heart craves.

This is the crux of the matter; it is not just some indoctrination that leads us to want more, it is our innate desire to be connected. We desire loving relationships because they are enriching and fulfilling. Yes, when spiritually evolved, we transcend this desire, but unless we have committed to a monk-type lifestyle, then we are fooling ourselves to say we don't want loving relationships. And a sexual, loving relationship is possibly the most intense form of love. This is where Osho's idea of virtue and sin is helpful: love in a sexual relationship enriches our heart, and sex in a non-loving relationship doesn't. When done is a respectful manner, casual sex is more of a lessening of a longing rather than fulfilling it. This is not offering a moral perspective, but an energetically functional one. If during casual sex one's heart is open, then it is healthy, and if not, then it is unhealthy. An open heart naturally leads to a feeling of connectedness, which can quickly be translated into a desire for a relationship. If we don't want a relationship, it is easier to close our heart during casual sex, especially if there is no trust.

I let these thoughts go, and soon my tiredness takes over. Now I find my mind drifting with random thoughts, and I know this is a prelude to sleep.

Hours later, I wake up. It is now 2:30 in the afternoon. I feel alert, happy and content. I am hungry, but I can put off eating for a while. Lately, my writing has been sporadic, and if I don't do some writing today it will feel like a wasted day. Still feeling the ego boost from last night's victory, I seize the opportunity and quickly get myself prepared for writing.

Chapter VII, cont. (Healing and Vulnerability)

As mentioned in Chapter VI, over time blockages usually become layered with additional stuck energy. The initial trauma will have more recent, but related, traumas "on top of it," with the habitual avoidance behaviors adding energy as well. Because of this layering of stuck energy, the complete healing of a blockage almost always requires several involved releases, over a long time (likely many years). With each healing, a person gains a more spiritually-wise understanding of the situation. Once healed, the original trauma is still an unpleasant memory, but there are no longer emotional and mental traumas connected to it, and there is no stuck energy pattern to trigger the personality. When the memory is recalled, it is merely a bad memory from the past and not a trigger for the person to avoid the present.

When healing occurs in the Spiritual Body, it releases the judgments contained therein, and this allows us to connect more easily with the wisdom of the Divine Energy. When the judgments are released, then one understands the past trauma as a learning experience; a core trauma is understood to be a life lesson. If there is a perpetrator involved in the past trauma, then that person can be viewed as a troubled individual acting in dysfunctional ways, attempting to meet his or her own needs. That person is driven by the personality and is not spiritually motivated, meaning he or she has many blockages and poor coping strategies. A compassionate wish is for them to get healing, rather than for them to have greater suffering.

Blockages in the Emotional Body stop people from feeling joy, and blockages in the Mental Body mean they have rigid beliefs. This rigid thinking can become a vicious cycle, because a person with many blockages will view his or her life as difficult and unhappy, with little expectation that the future will be much different, and this thinking helps create unpleasant situations. The Soul continues to present that person with experiences that are reminiscent of past traumas, creating situations that could initiate the healing process. But without engaging in healing, this often leads to a loss of hope, which results in a "victim's mentality" towards life. I call this "conditioned helplessness."

With a new sense of accomplishment, I decide to stop my writing. Now with the waning of the ego boost from last night's escapade, I feel my writing at least provides some redemption, which helps ward off my guilt. Past experience suggests that this internal battle will go on for a week or two. I decide to get some fresh air. It is a beautiful day, and as I look out my window I can see Mount Fuji radiating in the sunlight. It reminds me how connecting with nature is also good for my soul. Maybe I will go exploring on my bike; there is a treed hill not too far from my home that I have wanted to check out. This is enough of a plan to spur me into action, so after eating a light lunch, I get ready for a bike ride.

Chapter 26

Struggles In and Out of the Home

Tuesday, November 4

My life sucks. What made me think I could be a writer? My book will never get published, and even if it does, it won't sell. What kind of a life do I have? I'm alone much of the time and my apartment is a mess. I have just eaten a bunch of junk food and I'm getting fat. On top of this it is cold and my body is sore.

It is 11am Tuesday morning, and I am still lying in bed. For the last hour I have been watching TV, and I have yet to see anything worthwhile. My apartment is finally warming up. It is late fall or early winter, I'm not sure which. Fuji City doesn't get snow in the winter, but it does get cold. (Fuji Mountain gets a blanket of snow, of course.) Either way, the nights are chilly, and lately I have been waking up with an achy feeling in my body. A combination of being cheap and the fact that buying too much stuff just creates more hassle when I move back to Canada means I don't have a warm blanket. The portable electric heater is dangerous, and I feel it is wasteful and unhealthy to leave the wall heater on all night.

My motivation to get out of bed is minimal and is based on avoiding negatives rather than an inspiration to do something positive. To try to pacify my agitation, I remind myself that my job is in the afternoon, so I'm allowed to have the morning off. Plus, last week was a tough week of teaching; the students seemed to be particularly active and unfocused. However, this justification for laziness is credible for only a short period, and soon my negative thinking returns.

I should meditate and I should write, both of which have been irregular recently. I need to do *something* because lying here thinking bad thoughts is not good for me! I decide I must meditate; it can shift my mood and help me have a good day. However, first I will do a quick cleanup of my apartment. It is garbage day and a chance to throw out some of the junk that has been accumulating. The papers around my apartment seem to multiply like fruit flies; if there is open space on the floor when I go to bed, then it is magically covered with papers by morning. I gather them up and do a quick sort. Writing stuff goes into one pile, teaching stuff in another pile, nonteaching work stuff in a third pile and garbage in a fourth pile. Some of the papers are in Japanese, so I don't know what I was thinking in keeping them.

Next is the kitchen. My proclivity to save plastic bags has reached a ridiculous stage. I grab a bunch of bags that are overflowing from the storage box and stuff them into one of the bags for disposal. Fuji City seems to have a poor recycling program, and many plastics are not recycled. I do a quick check of the fridge: in spite of it being very small, things still get forgotten in the back. The pineapple and lettuce are looking moist, so into the garbage they go.

The garbage is now three bags, which is good. I take them outside to a spot across the street, which is the collection area. It is just a designated part of the sidewalk where people from the immediate vicinity put their refuse twice a week. The garbage is piled high; it will be collected around noon, even though we are told to put our garbage out before eight. To try to ensure you put it out early, every third or fourth week they collect it shortly after eight. When this happens I have to walk around the neighborhood looking for a dump spot that has not yet been collected. As a foreigner I can get away with this, but I know I am supposed to put my garbage only in my designated spot.

As I add my garbage to the pile, an elderly woman is walking towards me with garbage bags in her hands. I haven't showered and I am wearing yesterday's dirty clothes, so I am not in a sociable mood. The woman greets me warmly in Japanese, and gives me a respectful bow. I am caught off guard by her courteous greeting. I return the bow and say "Konichiwa," one of the very few words I know. We part and return to our respective homes.

This encounter with a stranger has jarred me from my troubled frame of mind; I suddenly notice the weather—mixed sun and clouds with a chill still in the air. Stopping to notice my surroundings and the woman's unexpected greeting prompts some reflective thinking. The woman was *so* respectful; there was no sense she resented a foreigner living in her country. Not all Japanese are so open-minded toward foreigners, though. Japan is struggling to decide the best path in regards to internationalization. The country has a long history of shunning the rest of the world, fueled, I think, by an unspoken sense of superiority. Officially, the government has a policy of globalization, but culturally the sentiment of isolationism is still prevalent, which I think the government unofficially encourages. I have found Japan to be such a fascinating and complex place, and I still haven't figured it out.

This temporary diversion from my negative mood encourages me to do something constructive today. I reaffirm my decision to meditate. I go back inside and quickly settle into my meditation chair, a Japanese-style floor chair with no legs. I sit quietly, and it takes a while to settle my mind, but eventually I do have a few moments of "timelessness." During meditation, time passes slowly if my thoughts wander, but when my thinking is focused, time goes by quickly. Today time passed slowly, but I still feel better for having done it; making the effort to sit and be calm is benefit enough.

Though I am hungry, I know I should strike while the iron is hot, so I get out my computer to do some writing instead. Forcing myself to write will also add to today's good karma.

Chapter VII, cont. (Healing and Vulnerability)

In explaining the benefits of healing, I appreciate that there is a counter view of "get over it." This is the idea that these old hurts are in the past, so we need to forget about them and move on, which does sound Zen-like. If there is no blockage associated with the trauma, then there is nothing to heal. However, if a person has a stuck energy pattern developed in childhood, for example, having an issue about rejection, then there will be a situation later in life when that person finds himself being triggered. The stuck energy pattern doesn't go away, but we learn to ignore it. Unfortunately, this avoidance prevents us from being fully present in some current situations, and it creates long-term health problems.

Furthermore, being emotionally triggered by an old pattern inhibits people from reacting compassionately in that current situation. If one is triggered and simultaneously spiritually connected, then the healing process is initiated, but if one is not spiritually connected, then the compassionate wisdom of the Divine is not being accessed. If one is content to live life in such a limited fashion, then healing is not desirable, but if one has a desire to be whole—to experience all the joys of life, to be fully in the moment, and to have a profound sense of purpose—then healing oneself is required. Once healed there is no inclination to relive the past. If a person is genuinely happy much of the time, then it makes sense for them to continue on as they are doing.

To summarize, healing is the release of stuck energy patterns. They can be released in several ways, such as being dislodged by a new, intense emotional trauma, by a miracle, or by simultaneously connecting the stuck energy pattern with the wisdom of the Spiritual Energy Body. With this latter form of healing, it usually takes several releases over a period of years before a blockage becomes fully released. Once healed, a past trauma becomes merely a bad memory, and it is no longer a subconscious influence on the present. The freeing of stuck energy also allows one to experience a joyous part of oneself that was suppressed by the blockage. The healing of a stuck energy pattern in one of the Energy Bodies also influences the corresponding blockages in the other Bodies. Such multilayered healings result in a deeper understanding of a life lesson, and enable a compassionate perspective of similar situations in the future. With directed healing practices, the personality must be willing to surrender its desire for control; this surrendering is called Vulnerability. The personality is often resistant to surrendering its desire for control, and employs a variety of techniques to avoid connecting with the pain associated with blockages.

That's enough for now, so I let myself off the hook and stop. Having done my writing, I can now tackle my hunger. I will make an omelet for lunch. After lunch I don't want to sit around as I feel the negativity from this morning is still lurking in the back of my mind, so I decide to stop at the bank on my way to work today. I lost my bankbook, so I want to get a new one. Most of my transactions are done with my bankcard at an ATM, but Brad emphasizes having your bankbook updated after a payday to make sure the company deposited the right amount. If problems are found much later, likely the company will not do anything about it—unless they have overpaid.

The weather has soured, and now there is a light rain. When I get to the bank I have a halting conversation with the teller, who then asks me to wait while she gets a manager. When I am called again, I am directed to a small sitting area where we can talk at length. The manager's English is better than the teller's, but still not very good. He understands my wish for a new bankbook and pulls out the appropriate form. I know they have my address on file, but he asks me anyway, and I have to resort to pulling out a slip of paper that has my address on it in English. The manager struggles with this and then excuses himself, returning a few minutes later. He then asks me where I lost my bankbook, and I tell him I don't know. He asks again, so I say somewhere in Fuji City. He is troubled by this answer; he must write something down on the form, but my answer doesn't seem to be sufficient. He tries to elicit more details from me, but I am at a loss as to what else to say. If I knew where it was, it wouldn't be lost.

This back and forth goes on for several more minutes, and I am getting frustrated. The manager may also be getting frustrated, but his manner never changes. After 20 minutes of discussion, we seem to have completed the paperwork. I remembered to bring my passport, which the manager now takes. He then asks me to wait in the general seating area and he will call me again when he is done.

I wait for 30 minutes, and my frustration builds. Time is getting short; this exercise is now cutting into my prep time for my lessons. I don't understand why it is taking so long. This is the first time in Japan where I have found customer service to be sorely lacking. I remember that Brad, my boss, got annoyed when we opened the account, feeling they weren't courteous enough—maybe this is the same manager. I suspect racism may be a part of the problem. I speculate that the manager did poorly on an English test and failed to get into his desired university as a result, so now he has an energy block triggering him. In a situation like this my healing training is to send him compassionate light, as this may soften his tone, but my emotions block this thought and my frustrations turns to anger instead.

Finally the manager calls me back to the private seating area. He has some more paperwork for me. Soon he asks me to "hanko" the forms. (Remember, a hanko is your personal ID stamp and the Japanese equivalent of a signature.) I have rarely used mine, and so I didn't think to bring it. Now we cannot proceed. I don't have time to go back and get it today, so in a less-than-courteous manner I tell him I will have to come back tomorrow. He stands and gives a slight bow as I walk away and head out the door.

Banks are an example of big companies that are stuck in the old ways. Foreign economists consider rigid thinking as one of Japan's shortcomings. Large corporations are another example of uncaring, big companies. I find it odd that they put such an emphasis on customer service, knowing a happy customer is one that is likely to stay, but somehow this philosophy is reversed when it comes to management dealing with staff. It seems treating staff poorly isn't expected to affect staff morale or service. On the plus side, these kinds of fixed attitudes may explain why the Japanese seem more accepting of their personal situations. Their society is based on defined gender roles, such as long work hours for men, and household and family responsibilities for women (which is a more valued role here). In business, the glass ceiling in Japan is strong and low. This suggests they don't desire as much control over their lives. Desire for control is a function of the personality, and the Japanese are raised to consider Japan (or the group) ahead of their personal desires, so maybe they are less motivated by the personality.

However, thinking of the group does not translate into caring for others; the group is un-individuated. They do what is good for society, and not what is good for the members of society. And in contrast, when society members are seen as individuals, they are viewed as competitors, because on a personal level the Japanese are very competitive.

Again this emphasizes my intrigue of Japan with its many contradictions and levels of complication. I hurry off to work because now I don't have much time to prep for my lessons. The bank incident, helped by the rainy weather, encourages more negative thinking.

Chapter 27

Trouble in Paradise — Back Pain

Thursday, December 4

I feel a shiver run through my body just as the lesson ends. My fourth and final class of the day is over, and the last student is walking out the door. I feel a release of pressure, like a weight is lifted off my shoulders. Normally I am not this stressed when teaching, and in fact, today I didn't realize how uptight I was until I felt that shiver. Of course, having my boss here doing a performance assessment is stressful, so it is understandable, but I wasn't conscious of the stress. When I am teaching I am focused on the students.

Another reason I didn't notice the pressure today was because the buildup was gradual. The first class went well and I was on top of my game. It was how teaching should be; I was having more fun than the kids (four and five-year-olds), and I was doing my best to share my joy with them. The second class (six and seven-year-olds) was more of a challenge, and in truth, a little disheartening. Last month when I taught this class (I usually teach each class once a month) I had a profound experience of connection with them. Today I suspect they were feeling so comfortable with me that they forgot their reason for being here. Several of the kids were frequently doing their own thing, and they were not paying much attention to the lesson I was trying to teach.

In the third class (nine and ten-year-olds), one student was being very uncooperative, so much so that I felt the need to confront his behavior. I separated him from the rest of the class for a while to send the message that his conduct was not going to be tolerated. In the end, he didn't change his behavior much, but his temporary separation resulted in the rest of the students being more attentive. They had started to follow his lead and were becoming silly too.

This last class was fine, but because it is our senior-level class (thirteen-year-olds) it is more textbook-oriented. There were no problems with this class, but the material was particularly boring today, and I didn't have the energy to be creative and spice it up.

Brad, my boss, is very enthusiastic with his positive feedback. From the first moment I met him he has been supportive of me, fostered by a shared interest in Zen and drinking. So today is a continuation of the good rapport between us. Brad points out that a good demonstration of effective teaching shows how one deals with problems as well as how to have a fun lesson.

As he talks to me I feel a sharp pain shoot down the back of my legs. It lasts for a few seconds, and then there is a small, residual ache at the base of my spine. Brad and I conclude the discussion of my performance. Normally we would go out for a beer now, but he has other plans, so I must hurry to catch the last train home. I know Mike lives in the area, so I am left wondering if they are hanging out together without me. Emotionally I try to brush it off; plus my attention is being drawn to the dull ache at the base of my spine.

Throughout the rest of the evening I have three or four more episodes of the short, intense pain shooting down my legs, along with the persistent, slight ache. My colitis has been acting up these last few weeks and my intestine feels irritated, so the pain could be related to that, but I have never had this kind of symptom before.

On my way home I reflect that my mood has not been so good lately. I had abstained from drinking for the month of November (actually since the sumo tournament on November 3), realizing that it was too much a part of my life—so no trips to Oz. It's not that I feel addicted or that I can't cope without drinking, and in fact for a while before November I had been drinking only on weekends. I know eventually there is a price to be paid for drinking. Being happy is beneficial to my health, so even if having fun is done in a less-than-ideal manner (i.e. with alcohol), the overall effect can still be beneficial. But as I have explained earlier, drugs and alcohol weaken the energy bodies, and my consistent use of alcohol is adding up. My energy bodies can tolerate some abuse, but the socializing has gotten out of balance. I am drinking to be with others rather than letting the drinking be simply a casual part of socializing. Plus, I am not doing enough healthy stuff to compensate for the abuse to my energy bodies.

During my month of non-drinking I had hoped to find some other social activities to fill my time, but not much has happened. A couple of times I met with a fellow Peppy teacher for day excursions, but she lives a 40-minute train ride away. I am looking for a more convenient friendship that can be more spontaneous. Lately my life has become a struggle; I have felt socially disconnected, my diet has been poor and my intestines are feeling irritated. The worst part of my down frame of mind is that I haven't been doing much writing. I did some a few weeks ago, and even when not formally writing I regularly make notes, but lately I haven't even been doing that. These are my thoughts as I go to bed.

When I wake up the next day there is a more consistent sharp pain in my lower back and legs, but the periodic shooting pains from yesterday are less intense. Taking the day off work and relaxing may be the best thing for me. My schedule today is to team-teach with another Peppy teacher—I don't have any classes of my own. The company arranges team-teaches as a way of developing skills. Canceling a team-teach will not present a problem, so I call in sick. I am more than willing to miss a day's pay to take care of myself (we don't get sick pay).

I go to the local onsen and soak in the various hot tubs. Afterward, I get a massage; it feels great and the pain subsides. I spend the rest of the day relaxing, mostly reading and watching TV.

The next day (two days after my performance assessment), I wake up with a constant, severe pain. Again, I call in sick. This time I am missing my own classes, which means someone will have to cover for me. Brad starts work at 10am, so I wait till then to call him. At his suggestion I struggle to get to a nearby hospital; by now, just standing upright is painful.

Visiting a foreign hospital is a challenging experience, even more so when you cannot speak the language, and coping with this acute pain is an additional hardship. The hospital is a few blocks from my apartment, and I have passed it often, but this will be my first time going inside. It is a small, modern hospital, and not surprisingly it is very busy. I manage to navigate the procedure for registering, though it is awkward explaining my situation by relying on the attendant's minimal English and my gesturing. After registering, I notice a big screen showing the queue of patients' names. I guess which markings are mine and assess that my wait will be over an hour.

In order to cope with the persistent pain and the wait, I decide to meditate, though it will be difficult. Past experience has shown me that there is a point where I can disassociate from physical discomforts. Usually it is an itch or a cough that is the annoying symptom, and in the immediate moment it can be excruciating to *not* react. But if I resist the urge for long enough, suddenly I realize the desire to react is itself an interesting phenomenon. The urge becomes the object of observation, and the physical discomfort becomes secondary. Soon after this shift happens, the initial itch or tickle disappears. Although physical pain doesn't dissipate over time, it is possible to disassociate from the pain with vigilant concentration. Medical drugs, like morphine, mimic the body's natural ability to deal with pain. These drugs block receptors in the brain so the pain doesn't register as it normally would. Meditation may do this too, or something similar.

As I sit in the chair and think about this process, I near the desired meditative state. The periods of feeling disassociated from the pain become longer and my thinking becomes clearer. I focus my mind on the concept of meditation. I believe meditation is crucial for spiritual development. There may be some spiritually evolved individuals that do not formally meditate, but I would guess they frequently attain meditative states by less directed means. As part of my ordination training, I was surprised when reading parts of the Bible how often Jesus took time out to pray. To be consistent with my theory, I would like to say meditation is being connected to all four of the energy bodies, but this doesn't seem to be the case—in fact, as I sit here, I want to use meditation to disassociate from my physical body and its pain.

Maybe the flow of information between the consciousness and the energy bodies becomes reversed; rather than the bodies sending information to the consciousness, it's the consciousness that is sending information to them. During meditation, one decreases the activities of the energy bodies—slowing the heart rate, calming the emotions, quieting the mind and letting go of judgments. I described the consciousness as an echo of the Divine, so limiting distractions to the consciousness is stepping away from the personality and moving towards the Divine. This process also helps the consciousness realize that the energy bodies are like a mirror image and thus reconnect with the original self—the soul.

This is what is so powerful about meditation—the shift from being influenced by the energy bodies, and hence the drama of our lives, to being an observer of our lives—or alternatively, the orchestrator. During my meditations I can assess the events of my life with a wisdom that is lacking when using my normal thinking; I can "unearth" the underlying motivations for many of my choices.

Even though my pain intermittently affects my thinking, the time flows by and I notice my name will be called soon. The subsequent medical procedures include consultations with two doctors. Most of the discussion with the first doctor is done with the aid of a Peppy interpreter conversing over the phone. Fortunately, the second doctor speaks reasonable English. They conduct a series of tests, namely X-rays and analyses of my blood and urine. After the testing I am told the cause of my pain is a herniated disc in my lower back. I am skeptical of this assessment; in my mind, the development of the pain was not a herniated-type onset.

The doctors have done an admirable job in overcoming the language barrier, so even if I could communicate my doubts, I feel reluctant to question their results. Adding fuel to my reticence are stories I've heard of foreigners seeking medical help in Japan. Mike had a misdiagnosed hand pain that resulted in slight but permanent loss of mobility in his hand. I also read a book by an American teaching in Japan, and he felt over treated for a rather benign injury. In both cases, there was a problem of doctors not wanting to change their initial diagnoses.

I decide that if I don't feel better tomorrow, my scheduled day off, I will make arrangements to go home and have my back examined in Canada. Pain this severe and persistent is serious, so I want to feel confident in the diagnosis. Brad had asked me to call him again when I was finished at the hospital, so I inform him of my plan to go home if things don't improve significantly by tomorrow. He is understanding and asks me to call him again tomorrow, even though it is a day off for both of us.

The doctors have prescribed some painkillers, which I take, and then spend the rest of the day relaxing in bed. The pain eases when I lie down.

On Sunday morning the pain has lessened slightly, but is still severe, so I call Brad and let him know I intend to go back to Canada as soon as possible. He advises me to wait till tomorrow (Monday, which is another scheduled day off for me) and then call the head office to get their approval.

On Monday morning the pain hasn't improved, so I call the office and inform them of my need to go home. They say they will get back to me later in the day after they have looked into the options. I have already booked time off for my holiday to Canada in two weeks, but they must see if they can get coverage for my classes for the time between now and then. I am not concerned about whether or not they grant me permission; my mind is made up, but I will let them think I am waiting for their approval.

Next I call the airline. My trip home uses the return portion of my initial two-way ticket that I bought when I came to Japan via Thailand. I am told I can change my ticket to an earlier date, the soonest being tomorrow afternoon. I change my ticket for tomorrow; I am going home!

Reality sets in—I will be going back to Canada, and I am unsure if I will be returning to Japan. When I planned my Christmas holiday home I bought a new return ticket to Japan for January third, but I will have to wait and see what happens with the doctors in Canada to know if I will be using that ticket.

My recent lack of writing is discouraging, but this ailment gives me the excuse to formally put my writing aside. I won't plan to write until I get my health sorted out and I know what country I will be living in. My writing works better with a routine; pretending I will write with this health crisis going on is setting myself up for failure. If I let go of the expectation to write, it reduces my guilt.

As I pack my belongings, I feel a palpable sadness. I am not ready to leave Japan; my adventure here doesn't feel complete. The friends I've made and the ease of lifestyle here entices me to stay. It surprises me how comfortable I feel living here. I wasn't expecting to find Japan such an interesting place. I enjoyed Korea, but I didn't find their culture nearly as intriguing. Japanese culture seems more complex, and this excites me.

In spite of my curiosity about the Japanese psyche, I think a bigger contributor to my sadness is the sense of incompleteness. My book is still in progress, my ideas are still evolving and my personal evolution feels connected to being in Japan. I wasn't expecting to attain Enlightenment, but that was a thought in coming here. Regardless, I was hoping Japan would foster a deeper understanding of living in the moment—and it has—but I feel I can go even further into the subject. I want more compelling insights into the process of living in the moment. Thus, it is saddening to think of not returning to Japan, which may be the case if this back pain is serious.

Several hours later the head office calls and, surprisingly, they are supportive of my desire to go home. I find out they have been talking to Brad, and I am sure he influenced their supportive approach. As I return to packing and sorting my belongings, I decide to take most of my things home with me. What I am not taking I will divide into things that can be given away or thrown out, and things for storage in case I return in a few months. If I don't return immediately after Christmas, I'm sure Mike will store the boxes at his house for the interim till I can return. I'm unsure if Peppy will hold a spot for me, so I may be looking for a different job.

When most of the packing is done, it is still early enough to make some phone calls. It is rare for me to call any of the crew; usually I run into them at Oz. I overcome my reticence and call Hank, Gerry and Mike. I inform them about my back pain and my imminent return to Canada. I also tell them that if the diagnosis is bad, I won't be coming back. I suggest we go out for a beer. It has been a month of sobriety for me, and this is a good justification for having a drink. They all say yes, and Hank offers to pick me up. I appreciate their concern. When we meet, the crew expresses their disappointment and a sincere wish for my return. I am buoyed by their sentiments and try to take them to heart. After a beer, Hank gives me a ride back to my apartment. I say goodbye with doubt and sadness in my heart.

Chapter 28

"Back" to Normal; Seeing Terra

Friday, January 2

Shuffling along with the rest of the crowd, I make my way to the baggage area. The Vancouver Airport is understandably busy at this time of year. At least today I don't have to go through customs; I have come from Penticton to Vancouver, and I will be spending a night here before heading back to Japan.

As it turned out, my back problem was not serious. The specialist told me it was a common inflammation that most adults will experience at some point in their lives. In my case, the inflammation led to some nerves getting pinched, which is why I had the shooting pains down my legs. The remedy is back exercises and rest, which I have had since I've been home, so now I am feeling fine. In fact, my recovery has been good enough that I went cross-country skiing yesterday (a solo, day ski).

The trip home has also given me an opportunity to visit with family and friends. Of course, Terra was in the forefront of my mind. She has relocated to White Rock, a suburb of Vancouver known for its beautiful, sandy beach. She wanted a fresh start as she contemplates a new career. Her move away from Penticton was evidence that I have made big strides in letting go of her because it didn't affect me. Even before my back pain, I had sent out a general e-mail informing family and friends I was coming home for Christmas. Terra replied, inviting me to White Rock for a visit, but she said she would understand if it didn't fit into my plans. She added that she would be happy to pick me up and drop me off at the airport, and that I could even spend the night if it was convenient.

Since *that* day in the park in Japan, we have continued to e-mail each other periodically, although I e-mail more often than she does. Writing helps me sort out my emotions and sometimes releases them, so it is not surprising I write more often. Her e-mails tend to be brief, but periodically she will write a longer e-mail, usually highlighted by some personal struggle she is going through. I rarely know how it resolves itself as she doesn't mention it again in her next e-mail—and I don't ask.

When making my plans, I decided to spend the last night of my vacation with her before flying back to Japan. It will be nice to see her. And though I have made progress in letting go of my hopes for her, spending the night will be a major test. Our relationship has never been sexually intimate, and I expect this occasion to be the same, though I am not sure which would be a bigger challenge—not having sex with her, or having a sexual fling.

As I wait for my baggage, there is no sign of Terra. She has a tendency to be late, as she likes to do several errands at once. It is supposed to be a more efficient way to manage time, but it gives the impression that she is always rushing.

After a few minutes she appears and apologizes for being late. I give her a hug and say it's no problem—my bags haven't come yet. Moments later my bags arrive, and then we head for the car.

As expected, her dog is waiting in the car. Terra has an Australian sheepdog named Apollo. I love dogs, and during the time of our friendship I've had a lot of fun with Apollo. Sometimes I would take him on my night-skiing expeditions. When we get to the car, Apollo gives me a very enthusiastic greeting. Then we start the 30-minute commute south to her new place—a garage that has been converted into a suite.

As we drive, our talking is interspersed with occasional silences. Conversation has never flowed easily with us; it has always been more of a stop-and-go process. For my part, it is because I am guarded with her, never wanting to say something to offend her, and being careful not to expose too much of myself. Sometimes I tell her about my personal thoughts, but I don't reveal any emotions when doing so. I notice I am more relaxed with her this time, but the conversation is stilted just the same.

We do the obligatory descriptions of Christmas and New Year's, and by all accounts, mine was more enjoyable than hers. Then we catch up on news of mutual acquaintances. I answer some of her questions about my life in Japan, but I don't go into a lot of detail. I also mention that my writing has been going well until recently when things have slowed down drastically.

I tell Terra about some of my early memories of White Rock, times during my teenage years when a group of us used to come here on weekends to water ski and party. I make it sound like it was all fun, and a lot of it was, but there were also some sad moments. There were times when I felt like I was on the outside of the fun looking in; those moments have been present during all stages of my life.

As we relax in her new place I give Apollo a good scratching while Terra makes us some tea. It is a quaint place and suits her independent lifestyle. After tea, we decide to go for a walk. She suggests we go to a section of beach that is designated for dogs. As we walk Apollo is in his element, and his enthusiasm is infectious. I suspect sometimes he acts out the underlying attraction and tension between Terra and me.

Vancouver is having a period of pleasant weather this winter, so the day has been mostly sunny, and the temperature is a comfortable 51 degrees Fahrenheit (11 degrees Celsius). There is a gentle breeze and the water is lapping at the shore. I am glad I came to see Terra; it is easier being her friend now. There are still occasional moments where I ponder the "what ifs," but these thoughts no longer have the emotional charge they once did.

Previously she had said she was not physically attracted to me; I think she has cast me in a big brother role in her life. Part of the tension between us was because I was waiting for her to make a conscious decision that a relationship with me would be a good thing. And I think she was waiting for me to break out of my shell and sweep her off her feet. In the end, neither of us changed, so our illusive dance around intimacy continued.

Recognizing our relationship as this dance has helped me move on; now I am OK with my role in it. I rationalize that it would have been greater personal growth for her to make a conscious decision to become romantically involved than for me to come out of my shell. I justify my stance because I had taken some risks in an attempt to change our stalemate, like telling her I loved her. However, the reality is she didn't want to change our friendship. The greatest gift I have gotten from her is a renewed sense that love is a mystery and an adventure. Love doesn't have to make sense, and just having that feeling of excitement when you are with that person fuels the imagination and the heart.

Presently, I listen to her outline some career ideas she is considering, and I give her some feedback. I ask a few pointed questions, trying to get her to think about how some of her personality traits might affect those career choices. Telling her about my good fortunes in Japan emphasizes that a change, for the right reasons, can be great. I emphasize that the important question is whether she is moving in a direction that encourages her to grow. If she is growing, then I believe circumstances will arise that reward her courage. When change comes from running away from something, complications often arise, and she will feel like she is swimming upstream. My philosophy of life is that you can move forward, backward or sideways. Forward is good, backwards is bad and sideways is neutral, but only temporarily. Continuing to go sideways soon changes into a move backwards. When one moves in the direction the soul is laying out for him or her, then that person is in sync with the universe, and things fall into place.

It is not helpful to be preaching all the time—that is, telling everyone how to run their lives—but it is hard not to share my ideas about how the world works. I have come to the realization that it is better to say little about my philosophy unless I am asked. The other person is usually not ready to hear unsolicited advice, regardless of whether it is helpful information or not. After many times of being disappointed when people ignored my advice, it dawned on me that I was sharing the information more for my ego's gratification rather than for their benefit.

After the walk on the beach we return to Terra's place and start making supper. I know Terra likes to do things on her own, and to ask if my help is wanted before trying to be helpful. She declines my offer to help, so I open a bottle of wine, pour us both a glass and go back to patting Apollo.

As I look at her, I realize Terra is also similar to how my father used to be: she is generally distant and nonemotional, with the exception of getting angry when she is stressed, like my mother. Maybe that explains my earlier fixation on her; she encapsulates my childhood misprints of love, including my father's distance and my mother's anger. If we had had a romantic relationship it would have been a chance to heal those misprints from my childhood. And maybe that's why I don't appeal to her; I don't embody the patterns of love that her parents imprinted during her childhood. My ego likes to think that I am too much of a good thing for her to accept, that somewhere inside she doesn't feel she deserves to be that happy (and of course I would make her happy). These are thoughts that Terra and I will never sort out. Our conversations don't explore such intimate details.

As I come out of my reverie, I realize she is asking me to set the table. While setting the table I remember to do an internal check of myself. It seems contradictory to stop and check my internal state as a means of training myself to be in the moment, but it helps. I know in an emotionally complex situation like this it is easy to get caught up in old patterns (or avoid them) and not be tuned into the present. As I look inside I notice the absence of the longing I used to feel around her. This is good. As I look deeper I can sense some sadness, but it is not the old, oppressive sadness. It is not a sadness that will block me from appreciating being with her, from enjoying our friendship.

As the evening wears on and we have a few more glasses of wine, it becomes more apparent that our time to be involved has passed. There are some good reasons why our dance of intimacy has not changed. Months ago I was very willing to minimize the challenges we would face as a couple and say that our love would enable us to work these things out. But now these challenges make me think a relationship with her would be a lot of hard work.

I spend the night sleeping on the couch, and it is a good thing we don't have sex. At this point, having sex would be awkward, full of blocked energies and re-hurting a part of me that is healing. When I see her the next morning I am struck by how pretty she is; it is one last chance to briefly reflect on what might have been, but this is a conscious reflection, and not getting stuck in an old pattern. I have nothing but the best wishes for Terra, and I hope she finds happiness and a loving relationship. She is a wonderful person, and both of us have benefited from having known each other. She hasn't said it, but I believe that, for her, being loved by someone as grounded and supportive as me has made her look deeper into how she sees herself. I hope it has shifted her sense of self-worth. For me, I take solace in knowing that I was willing to stand on the edge of love and fall.

Apollo is lying solemnly by the door. He looks very sad and knows something is up. He can sense the sadness in the air, but I think it is a healthy sadness. Terra and I are friends that won't see each other for a while, and I won't see Apollo either, so it's appropriate to the moment to feel sad.

Terra drives me to the airport, and of course Apollo comes along for the ride. We say our goodbyes without any outward signs of emotion. I feel a little sad, but I am aware that a part of me is feeling pleased; I am moving on from my *stuckness* with Terra. I also feel excited to be going back to Japan, and back to my writing!

Chapter 29

Returning to Japan

Sunday, January 4

Being back in Japan feels great! I landed several hours ago, and I am now hanging out with some of the boys at Oz. My hope was that they would be here, but I didn't know for sure. I almost missed them because I was preparing to head for home when Hank, Rob and Jay came wandering in. I had called Hank and Gerry while taking the train home, but they didn't answer. I am turning over a new leaf; I am going to be more forward with my friendships with the crew.

When I finally made it back to Fuji from the airport and opened the door to my apartment, the mess I had left when I quickly packed for Canada confronted me. The mess, plus the unpacking I have to do, prompted me to go to Oz for something to eat and to see if any of the boys were there. The welcome I am getting from Hank, Rob and Jay is heartening. I left Japan under a cloud of uncertainty, so being back makes the beer taste especially good, and the banter between us more enjoyable. They tell me they are happy to see me again, and I express my joy at being back in Japan and to be hanging out with them again. Eventually we decide to go to Hank's house to relax and have another drink.

I don't know how long I have been up. I left Vancouver in the afternoon and didn't sleep on the plane. Once in Japan I took one train to Tokyo, and then had to transfer to a second train to get to Fuji. Next I spent a couple of hours at Oz, and now I'm at Hank's place. I have missed a night's sleep during all that traveling. I have no sense of time, but it is of no concern to me as I have the next two days off—when I got back, there was a message on my phone from Brad saying he had arranged the extra days off to help my transition back to work.

We have been hanging out at Hank's for an hour or two. Rob left a short time ago and Jay is spending the night here. I have one more drink, share a few more laughs and finally decide to go home while I am still sober enough to find my way. Once I get home, I smile at the mess in my apartment and savor the moment—I am back in Japan. This is where my life is, and I am glad to have it back. Ignoring the mess, I lay out my bed.

Sleep evades me; I must be beyond tired. My mind wanders, and a lingering question arises again: "What was that back pain all about?" In the end, after seeing a neurosurgeon in Canada and having an MRI, it turned out to be common back inflammation. That's the physical story, but what's the holistic story? What are the corresponding emotional, mental and spiritual blockages?

My trip home can teach me a couple of things; one, it serves as a good reminder to live in the moment. But more specifically, it teaches me that I am a likeable person—I received a warm welcome from everyone I visited in Canada. I say I am likeable because the world keeps trying to tell me I am likeable, but I have a hard time truly accepting it. I still have a core belief that holds me back from really believing I am likeable. People can enjoy my friendship, but I question whether they really *want* my friendship. The bottom line is that I still don't trust friends, and I have chronicled my history as to why I have these fears. The layers of this issue continue to unfurl, and I don't know when I will finally clear the core blockage.

What makes me associate the friendship issue with the back pain were the feelings I had leading up it. That was the month I had quit drinking. My social life in Japan primarily revolves around drinking, so during that month my ego was hurt because the "Oz boys" were slow to check up on me. My fear of trusting them inhibited me initiating contact; calling them would have been admitting that I needed their friendship. Over the month of sobriety I did get a call from all of them, but it was slow in coming. I wanted them to go out of their way to make me feel wanted, even though I wasn't prepared to do the same with them. It was during that period of feeling unwanted and dwelling on my issue of friendship that the back pain arose.

Back in Canada, with my back pain diminishing and having a plausible, medical explanation for it, I could enjoy my holiday. During my time in Canada my former coworkers from the Penticton Alternate School, the PAS Posse, went out of their way to show me they were glad to see me again. We had several fun nights and met for lunches. I also managed to get a meeting in with the men's group, which was great, and I went to a service at my old church. The friendship I was shown back in Canada is being mirrored here in Japan. People really *do* want to be my friend! Now the challenge is to heal the core doubt that holds me back from fully accepting their friendship.

Parallel to my internal struggles with friendships was my inertia with writing. It seems like months since I have done any serious writing. Now that I have returned to Japan, I feel inspired to write. It is time to make the final push to complete my book. I am also spurred on by having arranged for an editor while back in Canada. In a file in my storage unit I had the e-mail address for the instructor from the creative writing course I took, so I e-mailed her asking if she would be willing to edit my book. Her name is Luanne Armstrong; she said she remembered me well, and agreed to be my editor. She is a brilliant woman and I feel fortunate she accepted, so I feel buoyed by that as well. These are my thoughts as I finally drift off to sleep.

When I wake up it is 6pm Japan time. I feel sluggish, but I think it is more from the irregular sleeping rather than the aftereffects of last night's drinking. As my mind clears, I feel inspired simply by being back in Japan, and I know exactly what to do next—it is long overdue. I get out my laptop. It is time to write.

Chapter VIII: Initiations

The healing of a core energy blockage leads to a more compassionate understanding of the initial trauma and of the world. When a core energy block is healed, it increases the energy flow within the Energy Bodies. There are special levels of Energy Body fluidity that correspond to certain levels of conscious understanding. The attainment of each level is called an Initiation. An Initiation results in a person having a lasting, more conscious connection with the Spiritual Body, and hence the individual views the world with greater compassion.

I have not explored the Initiation process or its levels, so I am not offering a complete outline of the various stages, but I will provide a brief overview. One early Initiation in our spiritual evolution is "self-awareness," and this happens early in a human's life. A subsequent Initiation is when one accepts that they are more than just a physical being, that there is some kind of Divine beyond the mere physical reality.

Another Initiation is when a person has a sense of a spiritual purpose for his or her life. At this stage, one's purpose is no longer derived from the personality, but is based on a more holistic understanding. The personality is motivated by self-protection and a desire to control. Spiritual motivation is based upon the interconnectedness of the world, and is about surrendering personal control. This Initiation is called a Soul Merge. To use the analogy introduced in Chapter III, the mirror image is starting to remember its relationship with its "original body." There is still more healing that needs to happen before the "person" is whole again, but after a Soul Merge the process of becoming whole has begun in earnest, and one is more consciously aware of the process.

It is also possible to lose the understanding and increased fluidity one has after an Initiation, such as losing one's connection with the Soul. Living life with a connection to the Divine is an ongoing commitment. Having experienced that connection, it is real, and that initial experience serves as a guiding memory of how that spiritual connection feels, but the connection can be lost. This is also true for Enlightenment, the ultimate Initiation. Enlightenment is achieved when one's Energy Bodies are free of all blockages. However, once this understanding is experienced, one is continually challenged to maintain this Divine union. Energy blockages of any kind limit one's understanding, and hence remove one from the enlightened state. The tendency to have beliefs—which is a Mental Energy Body blockage—is a strong one.

So, Initiations are conscious understanding achieved by obtaining certain levels of fluidity in the Energy Bodies. These understandings result in a person having a different view of themselves and their relationship to the rest of the world. By definition, they are profound experiences, but ones that can be temporary. The act of a Soul creating a separate existence incorporates the tendency to create fixed energy patterns, which means a person must make a conscious effort to maintain the understandings gained from Initiations.

Writing about initiations has me wondering about my life and my life lessons. The soul provides a person with situations that force him to confront, and hopefully learn, his life lessons, but the soul has no concern if the person actually learns the lessons. The soul's infinite wisdom means it knows it will happen eventually: whether it is during this life or the next life is not important. The spiritualist community often refers to the "higher self" as an intermediary between the soul and the person. The higher self does try to have a person learn their life lessons during that particular lifetime, and I think my higher self is sending me a message that I needn't fear rejection, that I am a likeable person. However, I know I have not learned this at the core level. The self-knowledge—that I am likeable—must be grounded so that it changes the blockage and my daily life.

There is too much alcohol involved in my friendships here to accurately judge the strength of the friendships. Yes, they are true friends, but the connection must be more personal. The drinking is not healthy, and I don't want my life to be a series of parties. Having fun is good, but the fun needs to be spiritually based and not personality driven. That's the problem: my personality is seeking the friendship via the partying, and I need my friendships to be spiritually orientated—to be based on a heart connection—and not based on the neediness of the personality.

In recognizing that my lifestyle is personality driven, I see it reflects a weakened spiritual connection. I haven't been maintaining my soul merge initiation. Furthermore, my spiritual connection is crucial for my writing, and even more importantly, it is vital for healing myself. My lack of commitment to write is an indicator that my life is not in sync with my ideal path; but there are other indicators as well: my meditation routine, my "Live in the Moment" attitude and my sense of ritual toward the daily chores of life are all missing. Even my emotive midnight walks are a possible avenue for spiritual health, but the drinking inhibits the benefits of this activity too. I have lost my sense of purpose and my healing path. I want my journey to encourage others to heal, and this is what I hope to convey with my writing. I hope I have the determination to get my life and my spiritual growth back on track.

In spite of the awareness that my life is off track, I am able to rationalize to myself that now is not a good time to meditate. My ideal time is in the morning, so I pass on that sudden whim. Going for a walk is an easier option; the cool night air will clear up any cobwebs left from last night. Also, my fridge is empty, so I must get some groceries. I get dressed and head out the door.

Chapter 30

Searching for Spirituality with Yoga

Thursday, January 29

The strain pulls all the way from my feet to my outstretched arms; it is a gratifying sensation. Next I am being directed to form a ball, breathing out as I contract. I hold this pose for a few moments, and then breathe in as I stretch again. At least, I think this is what I am being told to do.

There is a joyful feeling in the room. It is Thursday morning and I am at a yoga class. This is my second visit, and I am enjoying it very much. It is mostly older women... well, actually, *all* women, most of whom are older than me, and several are much older. However, when doing the exercises, every one of them is more flexible and has greater endurance than I do. The sense of playfulness is evident when they occasionally laugh at my attempts to contort into some of the poses. Being the only male, the only foreigner and a foreigner that doesn't speak the native language garners me a certain amount of attention. I like to think these are the reasons why the instructor seems to make an extra effort to help me rather than that I am inept and need a lot of assistance. Regardless, I feel special, and I am very happy to be attending these weekly sessions.

Posing next to me is Aikida; she introduced me to this class. She runs a Buddhist shop near my home, which I visit periodically. I bought several Christmas presents for my friends from her shop. She speaks reasonable English, and she told me she has billeted several foreign women in her home, one of whom was Canadian.

When I returned to Japan after Christmas I wanted to get involved in some kind of spiritual group; ideally I would love to be part of a meditation group, and Aikida immediately came to mind as a person who might know of one. When I asked, she said she didn't know of any meditation groups, but mentioned that she attends a yoga class if I was interested in that. Thinking it might be my best chance to be involved in a spiritually orientated group, and knowing it would be of benefit to my back, I said I would give it a try.

My primary spiritual practice is meditation, but periodically I have pursued other forms of spiritual training. Besides meditation I have done tai chi intermittently, but it has never been for more than a month or two at a time. I learned a "form" (the series of moves that constitute a complete routine, usually consisting of over a hundred moves) at a spiritual retreat center near Campbell River. It is a beautiful form, but without a group to help maintain my enthusiasm I have never made it a consistent part of my life. More out of curiosity, I have taken a couple of yoga classes over the years. One time was when I was attending university, and the second was when I was at the Alternate School. Marsha, one of the teachers and part of the PAS posse, is a yoga instructor, so I attended some of her classes. I enjoy yoga when with a group, but it is not a practice that I have been inspired to do at home.

We are now in the final stages of the morning routine—the instructor likes to end by having us rock back and forth on our backs while curled up in a ball. I find this class much more dynamic than the ones I attended in Canada. The abdominal workout our instructor gives is suitable for a high-level fitness class. We close by saying, "Arigatou gozaimashita," a formal Japanese version of "thank you."

It is a short bike ride home. I feel great! The combination of being involved with a group of regular Japanese folk and doing something spiritually oriented is gratifying. As a physical reminder of today's session, my abdominal muscles feel tender. Collapsing into my chair at home, I consider what to make for lunch. However, since I am not overly hungry, my mind soon begins to wander.

I find myself recalling another spiritual activity that I used to love doing. At the modules for the Inner Focus Healing School, every morning started with a 7am Dynamic Meditation. This meditation routine was developed by Osho, the same man I quoted earlier with regards to virtue and sin. At one time he had a sizable international following, but I am not sure if he is still active. Regardless, he created some very powerful meditation practices specifically designed for Westerners. His thinking was that Westerners are conditioned to use their minds too much (being preoccupied with their mental bodies) and he developed several practices to compensate for this tendency.

With Dynamic Meditation, the first 10 minutes are spent doing a breathing exercise to stir up blocked energy in the body. There are specific movements for this process, which help with the stirring. The second 10 minutes is the release phase, where one moves and vocalizes freely to vent the pent-up energy that has just been incited. This often involves screaming, jumping, moving around or any other safe way you can think of to vent feelings. For me, crying was regularly part of this process. I found it similar to my tire-hitting sessions, but with less focus on the cause of my feelings. The participants are encouraged to express themselves as they feel inclined, without thinking about it or judging it.

After the release, the next 10 minutes are spent bringing in light energy to fill the void created by the venting of the old energy. As you focus on bringing in light, the accompanying action is to say "hu" while bouncing on your heels. The bouncing is done while holding your arms in the air. I would guess Osho's choice of these specific actions reflect his understanding of energy dynamics.

After this active phase of bringing in the light, the next 15 minutes are spent in silence and in a frozen posture. During this stage, one is to continue the intake of energy from the previous activity, but it is done as a mental/spiritual exercise only. Ideally, one is to be a witness to this process and not become consciously involved in it. Then, the last stage is 15 minutes of expressing joy. Often the joy I felt at this point in the process was considerable, and expressing it was fun. The accompanying music during this last part is progressively more dynamic and upbeat, so dancing to it was a creative and inspiring activity.

Like many Westerners, I am overly conditioned to be in my mind, so I found Dynamic Meditations to be an effective and powerful way to bring about healing. It was not something that I looked forward to in the mornings, and in the midst of it I could hate it, but afterwards I almost always felt exhilarated.

In comparison to tai chi or yoga, Dynamic Meditation is designed to facilitate healing, whereas these other practices don't; rather they are a gradual means of integrating the four energy bodies. Nevertheless, with tai chi and yoga, healing will occur if one is committed to the practice. The ad hoc approach of Dynamic Meditation makes it different from the healing practices taught at the Inner Focus Healing School. It avoids the mental body, and thus some beneficial insights from the healing may be missed.

In my case, the dual approach of the irreverent healing of Dynamic Meditation and the directed Inner Focus healing techniques transformed my life. As a student in the healing school, one not only directs healing sessions for others, utilizing the various techniques taught, but one is also required to receive healing sessions too. During this time I released many of my stuck energy patterns—or maybe it is more accurate to say I peeled away layers of blocked energy. Many of my releases revolved around the same traumatic incidents from my childhood, and I know I haven't healed some core blockages yet.

The yoga classes I am now attending in Japan will support my ongoing spiritual growth. If practiced regularly, this gentler approach will gradually bring to the surface some remaining stuck energy, and I hope I will recognize the appropriate time to engage in a more directed healing method to fully release the blockage. In the meantime, yoga will also help me to live in the moment and be connected with all four of my energy bodies. For those benefits alone, it is great.

I will have to remember to e-mail Marsha and tell her I am attending yoga classes here in Japan. I'm sure she will find it interesting. I will tell Terra too, because she is also a yoga person. As I mentally check in, I give myself a pat on the back; Terra just came to mind, and there is an absence of longing, sadness or neediness. It is confirmation to me that I am moving on. I quickly take a moment to mentally send Terra some light. The difference now is that I can send her light with a purer sense of compassion—without an attachment to the outcome—whereas before I think there was an element of hope that sending her light would help bring us together.

Sending someone light is a means of helping someone, or even a situation. On an energetic level, having a small influx of light in the aura can encourage that person or situation to move in a positive direction. Free Will still operates, so the recipient (or people involved in the situation) can easily ignore this bit of light, but on an unconscious level it creates a more favorable, energetic environment that can help a person make a positive choice. Crucial to this process is the intent of the sender: the purer the energy sent, the greater chance it can have a positive effect. And it is this purity of intent that provides the *sender* with a benefit—it strengthens the spiritual connection. It is better to give than to receive. I think, in time, science will shed some light on the process of sending light once it gets over its biases and considers spiritual matters more objectively. Statistically, science knows that focusing one's mind on self-healing (using mental imagery) does help with recovery from an illness, but science has no detailed explanation of how this works, namely the energy dynamics.

I decide to postpone my lunch. This reflection about Dynamic Meditation has put me into a writing frame of mind. I grab my computer.

Chapter IX: Intimacy

This exploration into existence postulates a benevolent Universal Energy which initiates a process of separation to express and experience its Divine love. A Soul is created at some point in the separation process with the intent of experiencing Free Will. When Free Will is used by an individual consciousness to reconnect with its spiritual nature, we come full circle, and the Divine has both expressed and experienced love. Inherent in the energy at all the various stages of separation is the tendency to be whole; this is energy's fundamental state. Love, which can be interpreted as the desire for connection, is a fundamental spiritual condition and is akin to energy being fluid. When the separation process has reached the point of a person having an incarnate experience in the world, the innate desire to be whole gets translated into a desire to be understood. To be understood is the fundamental *human* need. However, the human need to be understood is transcended when the human aspect of ourselves, namely the personality, is transcended. At this point, one is experientially aware of the underlying connectedness of Universal Energy—i.e. Enlightened—or near to it.

At the early stages of an individual's life, the desire to be understood manifests as a desire for acceptance from others. Our early learning and personality development occurs through interacting with others, which results in the pattern of seeking personal gratification via interactions with others. The resulting desire for connection is lessened when one has a sense of acceptance; thus humans learn at an early stage to seek acceptance from others.

This propensity to seek acceptance from others is reflective of the paradoxical nature of the personality; specifically, its sense of individuation keeps one from fully achieving its desire for connection. The personality is, in part, a mental belief system that is predicated on the concept of individuality. The personality's development is greatly influenced by traumas occurring during childhood, so as a result, an active personality has a desire to protect itself, and guards against too much intimacy.

Conversely, if the individual matures and begins to heal old childhood wounds, then he or she can obtain certain levels of understanding. These levels are called Initiations, and reflect a greater understanding of the connection to the Divine. They also reflect increased fluidity in the Energy Bodies. Healing takes us a step closer to realizing our own Divinity. So, as we grow spiritually, the process shifts from the personality looking outward for acceptance and control to the "awakened consciousness" looking inward toward the Soul for Divine connection.

As children mature into adults, the desire for acceptance and understanding becomes the basis for intimacy. As mentioned, Divine Energy is sometimes described as love, and the love experienced in an intimate relationship is a substitute for the direct experience of Divine Energy. If we can find a person who understands us and accepts us, then the innate desire for connection and wholeness is abated. Note that the desire is only abated, and not completely met, as this is done only when we understand the fallacy of our separation from the Divine. Depending upon one's level of Initiation, an intimate relationship serves different purposes.

At a base level, a relationship is a situation where one feels some companionship. In this type of relationship, the sense of acceptance is based upon the fact that someone chooses to be with him or her. It provides a modicum of relief from the mostly unconscious need for acceptance. This type of relationship is not based on trust, and the sharing of inner thoughts and feelings is minimal. The individuals are often ignorant of their own internal states, so they have difficulty being honest with their partners or with themselves. Their internal state can generally be called guarded, and they are frequently triggered; thus, the relationship is not harmonious or regularly joyful. It is more of an escape from loneliness than a move toward happiness, and it often serves as a functional partnership rather than a loving relationship. These individuals are not capable of long periods of being in the moment (too many blockages), so genuine happiness is not frequent. Of course, sharing successes and overcoming challenges together are bonding and enriching experiences no matter what the level of intimacy.

A more intimate type of relationship is one where there is a greater degree of acceptance of each other. In this type of relationship, the two people know some of the underlying issues about the other, though the issues may not be discussed in detail. There evolves an unspoken agreement between the partners to not push each other with regard to certain issues. A balance is struck as to what can and cannot be talked about and what behaviors will and will not be tolerated. This truce is not an unconditional type of acceptance, but more of an unconscious arrangement to be compatible. The benefit of this more intimate arrangement is that it enables the participants to let their guard down. Depending on how much they are willing to trust their partners, a person can learn new possibilities for love outside of the original imprints he or she received in childhood. These people are more capable of living in the moment, though still not consistently.

That's enough for now. My hunger tells me it's time for lunch. The yoga and now the writing have put me in a happy frame of mind. I hope this is an indication that my fortunes are on the upswing.

Chapter 31

Reflections of Japan; Feeling Dis-ease

Friday, February 20

Wow, I am getting some valuable insights! My dream didn't lead directly to these ideas, but it started a flow of connecting thoughts, and now I am reaping the benefits of being connected to the wisdom of my spiritual body. The dream itself reflects an unease I have been feeling recently, and I know that part of it is because my time in Japan is coming to an end (my contract ends in two months, on April 22nd). I think my book is also on target to be completed at that time, so endings and going home have been on my mind lately. Thinking about the future is not living in the moment, but sometimes it is necessary.

Spiritually (and arguably scientifically) everything is One, and time is an illusion, so what is the future? To understand this, let's use an analogy. We know events happen on the other side of the earth, yet for the most part we are ignorant of them. On the other side of the planet, people get up, go to work and live complicated lives without us knowing the details or the truth of what happens. If we traveled to faraway countries, then those distant events would become our reality and we would know the details. So "our reality" is merely where we are focused. Other realities seem less real, but that is a function of our focus and not their validity. Similar to events in a distant land, the future is just other realities, most of which won't be part of our immediate existence, but a few will eventually be part of our reality.

These thoughts remind me of my ministerial thesis where I quote Stephen Hawking, the theoretical scientist. In his book *The Universe in a Nutshell*, Hawking states, "This idea that the world has multiple histories may sound like science fiction, but it is now accepted as science fact." Since multiple histories are fact, multiple futures are also being proposed by scientists. I am suggesting we can help what we will experience from the future by sending light to it, which makes that particular reality more energized and more likely to manifest in our life. This is how we create our reality, so thinking about the future in a spiritual way has its place. The trick is to not get emotionally caught up in imagining the future, but as this morning's dream suggests, I *am* getting emotionally caught up in thinking about my future.

After making a few quick notes about these ideas, I return to my reflective thinking and this morning's dream, now aided by my clear spiritual body connection. In the dream, I was with a lot of my relatives in Canada. I don't know if it was a special occasion, but these relatives would normally get together at family reunions or at special Christmas gatherings. The part of the dream that stands out was that, on a couple of occasions, someone told me I had bad breath! I am not aware of this being a problem for me in my "awake" life, which makes it strange that it was a problem in my dream. One of the people that I distinctly remember telling me of this social faux pas was my aunt. She is my dad's sister (the granddaughter of my great-grandfather, who was the healer) and she practices a type of energy healing called Healing Touch. Her involvement with energy work may have some significance, I am not sure.

It makes sense to me to connect the dream to my struggles with friendships; bad breath seems like a good metaphor for friendship issues. As I have explained, this has been a major problem for me, and this issue has followed me to Japan. I was fortunate to be placed in Fuji City with its ready-made friendship environment—namely, the Oz crew. This has given me the opportunity to address this blockage again. It has been great getting to know Gerry, Hank, Mike, Brad, Jay, Rob and Steve; however, what I am now questioning is if I have been operating under an old self-concept. Over the years I have healed deeper layers of my old wounds, so my need for friendship has evolved too. With this more evolved perspective, I want to reevaluate my friendships here and the purposes they serve.

My quandary with friendship in Japan is *not* reliving an old pattern (not that I have fully healed it, either). I have been misinterpreting my lack of closeness with the "crew" as a repeat of my childhood situation (when I had subconsciously vowed never to trust friends again). However, I now see that a more accurate interpretation is that I have maintained some distance because I sensed that being more enmeshed with them wasn't good for my spiritual growth.

A good explanation of this is to compare it to Buddhism, where there are three pillars for following the practice. One is belief in the Buddha (or of a Perfect Wisdom), two is following the Dharma (or teachings of the Buddha), and three is the *Sangha* (being part of a Buddhist community). It is this latter pillar that is foremost in my mind this morning; I am lacking a spiritual community. It may not be necessary to be part of a group to grow spiritually, but it certainly makes it easier. I will emphasize the word "spiritual" here, because there are religious groups that substitute dogma for spirituality, which inhibits growth.

The Oz crew is not a spiritual support group for me. I don't want to say the "crew" has no sense of spirituality—they do—but it is not a conscious motivation for their lives. I also think that my reluctance to talk about my book has, unfortunately, held me back from sharing more of my spiritual ideas with them. (I still maintain that discussing the book drains the energy from the project.) And when asked about my tattoo I have said it is my way of promoting Zen, but I haven't told them I am a minister. It is not that I am ashamed of it, but my ministry is different from the normal, religious use of the word. If I initially tell others I am a minister, then they immediately judge me and my actions according to common religious standards. I prefer to let people get to know me, and later, when they find out I am a minister, it can foster in them new ideas for what it means to be spiritual.

257

For me, a minister needs to exhibit integrity, honesty, non-judgment and wisdom; it is not about being a moralist. I am a minister of spirituality, not religion. As I see it, it is given that a minister is still a flawed person and is still working on healing his or her issues, and the more honest they are about having flaws, the better. Certainly a minister will have healed many blockages and have a sound spiritual connection, but they needn't be enlightened.

In any event, my being more spiritually open with the crew could benefit all of us. I would be more in sync with my true nature, and it may spark in them some new interests. I must find a better balance between being open and not dissipating the energy from my book. Similarly, my tattoo makes it harder to hide who I really am, but when it comes to people who are not shocked by it (namely, the Oz crew) I have shied away from being who I really am.

The issues surrounding my back pain highlight the state I had reached. The partying tendencies of my lifestyle in Japan had become a focal point, and yet with all this activity I still don't feel a close connection with the Oz guys. What is even worse is that this lifestyle has been interfering with my writing. As I became more active with the crew and partied more, my spiritual pursuits—my writing, my morning meditations and my attitude of self-nurturing—have all decreased, as has my well-being.

How this insight will help me now is that I can feel more comfortable with my partial involvement with the crew. I will still see the guys; they are a support for me, but not of the spiritual kind. If I have any serious issues in Japan, they are the ones I will turn to for help. And seeing them does provide something I am not getting elsewhere: companionship. However, that doesn't mean I need to see them weekly. Using the intimacy levels from my book, my friendship with them is somewhere between level one and level two. There is not an honest vulnerability in our friendships; we do not show who we really are underneath our façades. The real challenge will be not to feel down during the periods when I am not hanging out with them.

My recent involvement with the yoga class emphasizes the benefits of being involved with a group doing a spiritual practice. This is not to suggest the other class members view the practice from a spiritual perspective, and I suspect if they knew me, many of them may not call me spiritual either. Nevertheless, yoga is a spiritual activity and we are all doing it together, and this is good for my spiritual connection. Unfortunately, I am finding that I often have work commitments on Thursday mornings, so attending yoga class is a problem. The Japanese system is to join the organization and then pay fees even if you don't attend, which I am reluctant to pay if I am attending only 50 percent of the time. If I am going to continue then I must pay to be a member of the group.

In thinking about it, support groups have often been a part of my growth, and over the years I have been involved in a number of them. One of the most rewarding ones was when I was living in Campbell River. There was a group that met every Thursday night for a 40-minute meditation. It became special because the numbers dwindled down to a core group of five who sat faithfully every week. That commitment was very bonding and nurturing, like the Buddhist Sangha. Certainly the most colorful group was a gathering of spiritual seekers in Vancouver. I think we met for a couple of hours one evening a month, but maybe it was more frequent. The activities not only included meditation, but also chanting, repeating the mantra "OM," working with crystals and even howling during full moons.

Being a part of the healing school afforded me some of the most joyous moments I have ever experienced! It was an environment where I felt not only accepted for who I was, but encouraged to be my true self. The safety I felt inspired me to show my vulnerabilities, and I felt empowered for doing it. In contrast, when I am with the crew, it is the alcohol that helps me to relax, and even then I am still hiding parts of my true self. I'm sure if we spent the time together doing things that didn't involve drinking I could learn to be more relaxed with them, but our time together invariably involves drinking.

As I lie in bed thinking all this, I get restless. The question arises: "Should I get up now and get on with my day, or continue to let my mind wander and see what other gems I can uncover?" I decide I will stay in bed and let my mind wander some more.

It occurs to me that this dichotomy I have been having with friends is also reflected in Japanese society. It is a country that has every reason to be proud and confident; they have a modern, affluent and dynamic society, and they have a complex and unique culture. Their pride is very evident when on Japanese soil; however, on the world stage, they lack a certain confidence. For example, when traveling, the average Japanese citizen usually chooses to see a country as a part of an organized tour. Not having to arrange hotels, meals, transportation etc. makes traveling easier, but it also limits the interaction with the foreign culture. Japanese travelers tend to be observers, whereas travelers from many other countries—like Canada or the USA— tend to be participants in foreign cultures. The Japanese are more on the outside looking in, which is how I often feel about my life, and it reflects an unwarranted insecurity.

I continue my thinking and notice more parallels between Japan and myself. The indigenous religion in Japan is Shinto, and it is still a predominant influence in Japanese society. Based on my limited observations and readings, Shinto is a prescriptive religion where one performs certain rituals at certain times because of tradition, rather than because it is part of an in-depth ideology. Shinto has neither a prophet nor sacred writings, and it does not attempt to give a detailed explanation of the world or spirituality. Shinto does attribute spirits to many kinds of objects and entities, such as rocks, water, marriage, cars etc., and the Japanese will appeal to these spirits to garner influence.

However, there seems to be much overlap and inconsistencies with the myriad of deities of Shinto, but this does not bother the Japanese. A detailed understanding of the connection to the spiritual realm is not part of the process; the connection is through the heart, and not the mind.

Shinto's limited ideology is consistent with the Zen approach to life. Another reason I think Zen flourished here is because of the passion of the Japanese people. If one observes a baseball game or a sumo wrestling tournament, there is no questioning the intensity of the Japanese people. There are many other examples of their passion, such as a dominant preoccupation with fashion or food—the latter is meticulously prepared and displayed. In fact, name any aspect of life—sports, entertainment or social—and you will find a devout group of Japanese practitioners. Where else do you find intricate customs like the tea ceremony and flower arranging? This passion is reflective of the rigorous Samurai attitude, known as *bushido*. In one book I read, bushido was equated with chivalry. Both are old philosophies of conduct that emphasize doing things for justice and honor, though they have different views of both. These dual influences of segmented thinking and passion, in concert with tradition, have spawned today's society.

And like Shinto, lately I am going through the actions of my life without an integrated, holistic approach. But for me, my heart is not involved and my passion has gotten misdirected. And like the Japanese—where I categorize them as lacking spiritual compassion—I too have lost mine. The socializing is soothing my emotional hurts, but it lacks a spiritual connection, so no healing or growth is happening. However, I am convinced that the Zen practice of living in the moment is a sure path for the integration I am seeking. Where I differ from Zen and Shinto is that I am looking for an ideology to assist me on the path to wholeness. I believe it is beneficial to personal growth to include some mental understandings, such as being aware of the four primary energy bodies. This awareness provides a route back into the moment, namely by consciously connecting with all four bodies. But because I believe energy bodies are ultimately transcended, the ideology is a tool and not a fundamental component of spiritual understanding, in keeping with Zen.

This thinking energizes me, and my desire to get on with my day is stronger. I get up and follow up my inspiring morning by meditating. It is still sporadic, but I am attempting to get back to a daily practice.

After meditation, I know it is time to write.

Chapter IX, cont. (Intimacy)

A third kind of intimate relationship is where the partners actively engage in interactions that are of a healing nature. This type of relationship is distinguished by Vulnerability and by a compassionate acceptance of each other. As this relationship evolves, the partnership is based more upon a conscious choice for companionship and support, and less upon an internal desire for acceptance. One has a sense that the ultimate acceptance they are seeking is an internal process, and a partner can support this process, but not provide the solution.

In addition, this third type of relationship usually features the partners accepting more responsibility for their own emotions and less blaming of the other person for "making" him or her feel a certain way. This is a truth that is difficult for the uninitiated to understand; one is solely responsible for one's own emotions. A person chooses to react to certain situations, or at least allows oneself to be triggered into reacting with certain emotions. It is this triggering process (getting caught in stuck energy patterns) that helps the personality to blame an external source for the resulting emotion. When blaming, one is often trying to prescribe "truths" to the situation, but such judgments are really spiritual blockages.

This leads to what I call *brutal honesty*, which are judgments disguised as so-called "truths" about situations. It is common to hear in spiritual circles, "I am speaking my truth," but what is being said is not a truth; it is a judgment. Speaking one's *real* truth means expressing how one feels internally without referencing the situation that they claim prompted the feelings. *Brutal honesty* is blaming others for causing an emotion—this does not foster Vulnerability, and lacks compassion. Alternatively, this third type of relationship involves compassionate truths, which are truths about internal states without judgments, as they are the only real truths we can have in a situation.

Achieving the perspective of accepting responsibility for one's feelings can be done alone, but it can also be helped by a compassionate partner, and can be hindered by an uncompassionate one. This is because in any relationship, triggering situations arise more often, thus allowing for more healing opportunities; it is a person's choice to react by blaming and judging or by being Vulnerable. It is worth noting that adopting a Zen attitude of living in the moment fosters taking ownership for one's feelings.

This type of relationship also requires renewed commitments, because once major healing work is done, there is a tendency to feel that the relationship has completed its usefulness. If growth is the basis for the relationship, then what keeps the relationship working when the growth abates? Interestingly I've heard in some First Nation traditions a couple must recommit to a marriage every seven years.

As mentioned, the intimacy experienced in a relationship is a substitute for the feeling of Divine wholeness, which is connecting with the fluid nature of the Energy Bodies, hence any blockages one has become highlighted. Being intimate means one is allowing someone else to be important and influential in one's life, so this requires the personality to relinquish some sense of control. If one relinquishes some control, it sparks the healing process, which then forces a person to confront one's energy blockages. Avoiding healing limits the intimacy. This is why the ones that we care about most are often the ones we hurt the most. A person unwilling to show Vulnerability will struggle with intimate relationships because he or she is regularly engaging in dysfunctional coping strategies.

As a cursory note, I will say that sexuality can be a powerful force in an intimate relationship. How this force can affect one's being is complex. One aspect of sexual energy is that it can intensify other emotions, and if a person is not used to feeling his or her emotions in the first place, having them intensified by sexual energy is a challenge. To omit sex completely, however, ignores one of the key elements of an intimate relationship, but I refrain from exploring this matter further because—as mentioned previously—my understanding is limited, and sexual discourse is problematic.

To summarize: all the divided parts of Universal Energy have the innate propensity to seek wholeness. When in the form of a human incarnation, that propensity for wholeness gets translated into a desire to be understood, which is then quickly reinterpreted as a desire for acceptance. When one is older, the level of compassionate understanding one has (level of Initiation) is reflected in intimate relationships. If one has a poor sense of connection with the Divine, then the relationship will be personality driven. This means fear and self-protection influence behaviors, and the partners will regularly use coping strategies. If the partners have a strong sense of connection to the Divine, healing and Vulnerability will be present in the relationship. A key understanding for having a more evolved relationship is accepting responsibility for one's feelings. This understanding is fostered by the Zen practice of living in the moment.

My insights and writing have me in a good frame of mind, so it is easy to forget about the unease I felt this morning when I woke up. Because of the cold weather lately, I could use a new sweater—or at least sweatshirt—so I will leave for work early (I start teaching at 3:45) and check out a few stores on my way to the classroom. It can be another souvenir from Japan.

Chapter 32

Riding the Seawall and Meeting a Friend

Monday, March 2

My muscles feel strong and firm as they exert themselves. Overhead the sun is warm and bright, and there is a mild yet invigorating breeze coming off the ocean. I feel great! I am halfway to my destination, and I will have no trouble reaching it. I am cycling the 20 miles (25 Km) from Fuji to Numazu, the next major city towards the east. There is a seawall that follows the gentle curve of the bay from one city to the other. It is popular with the locals for walking and cycling, but it is actually a tsunami barrier — tsunamis are a real concern in this earthquake-prone country. The absence of cars, the proximity of the ocean and the trees that make up a green belt on the interior side of the wall make the riding ideal. Exploring it has been a desire of mine ever since I became aware of the wall a few weeks ago. I also wish to meet up with Kaori, a friend who lives in Numazu.

Cycling is one of my true pleasures. I have mentioned my passion for mountain biking, but I have also done some major cycle touring as well. I went on a two-month cycling trip through Europe with James, my great friend at that time. James was the exception to my pattern of not having close friends; we used to hang out together all the time, though we have lost contact now. Other extended trips include eight days cycling the big island of Hawaii with Curt (one of the PAS posse) and solo expeditions of the Canadian Rockies, Southern Ontario and Quebec (two Canadian provinces). So long bike rides are nothing new to me.

It is not quite spring, but the temperature is nearing a pleasant 57 degrees Fahrenheit (14 degrees Celsius). It is the type of day that lets me know spring is just around the corner. The exertion of riding generates a lot of body heat, so I feel warm in spite of the ocean breeze. The combination of a scenic bike ride, beautiful weather and going for a picnic with Kaori gives me a sense of elation. I feel as though I don't have a care in the world, and at this moment, I don't. It is a feeling that I have been lacking lately, so I remind myself to focus on the now.

I've gone out with Kaori a few times, and I enjoy her company. Though she is one of the Japanese teachers at Peppy, we met at a beach party in Numazu and not through work. She lived in the United States for six years, so she speaks English well. She is of typical Japanese stature—slim and attractive— plus she has beautiful facial features. It is hard to assess her personality because the Japanese custom is to be nice, and not to express opinions readily.

I am not sure if we have the basis for a relationship, or even if she would contemplate such a possibility, but with my time here coming to an end we won't have a chance to find out. One positive sign is that I feel playful when I'm with her. She has a good sense of humor, and our laughing is part of the attraction. And even without the prospect of a future relationship, it has been nice having a native Japanese friend, and one who doesn't drink.

As I ride, I look inland and notice Mount Fuji. It is a majestic sight, and one worth stopping for to take yet another photo. I have many pictures of Mount Fuji, but the allure of it keeps me taking more. It is an iconic symbol for the heart of the Japanese spirit, and I feel lucky to have had daily views of it. If many people consider something special, then over time that object's aura becomes imbued with that positive energy, especially if the object is worshiped. I agree there is something spiritual about the mountain, and I believe I have benefited from living in the energy of its aura. It has helped me in some way on my spiritual journey.

I marvel that I ended up in a place of such significance because I had no idea where I would be placed. Mount Fuji is also an appropriate symbol for my spiritual mission here; it stands alone as it rises up out of a coastal plain and towers over the rest of the landscape. In Japan, I am alone when I teach, I am alone in my apartment, I am alone with my writing and I have been alone with my spirituality. A major theme for me has been friendship, and when that lesson is fully learned, it will mean greater appreciation of my independence and the value of being alone.

After taking the picture, I have a quick gulp of my sports drink and continue on with my ride to Numazu. Riding alone is a great activity for contemplating, and that is probably why I have been such a keen cyclist over the years. I may have felt alone with my spirituality here, but in a greater sense I am never alone. Universal Energy is always supporting me, and as I think about this it brings to mind one of my healing sessions. It was about connecting with spiritual masters, and it helped propel me along my spiritual path. At the time I had completed my Inner Focus Healing school training in Ottawa, and I was helping staff at a new healing school that AlixSandra and her colleague, Julia, had opened in Vancouver. While I was there I came to know one of the students, Donna, who lived in Kelowna (the city just north of Penticton). I accepted Donna's invitation to be the "recipient" of some of her homework sessions. One healing modality she wanted to practice was Conference Tables.

Conference Table healing is similar to a psychological approach, but with an acknowledgement of—and hence greater emphasis on—energy dynamics. This method gets the client to formulate a question about a major challenge in his or her life. Then the client "invites" significant figures or entities to the Conference Table which he or she thinks might have a subconscious influence on their viewpoint. The client then role-plays these attendees in an attempt to uncover some unconscious biases that may be influencing the decision-making process. Having these biases become conscious empowers the person to determine if the influences are beneficial or not, and whether to heed them or not. For example, we often have a parental bias adopted in early childhood which does not reflect our current beliefs, but unknowingly still affects our thinking—we are still seeking our parents' approval. However, with energy healing, these influences are considered more than psychological issues— they are energetic patterns.

I enjoy Conference Table healing and have found it to be very beneficial for me. With this particular healing technique I am more apt to surrender to the process. When I'm role-playing a particular entity I have a sense that "the voice" is speaking *through* me rather than just my personality speaking the ideas. When allowing a particular "voice" to speak, I feel my body, my tone and my whole presence shift to reflect the persona of that voice. It doesn't matter if I literally believe a "voice" is speaking through me; what matters is that when expressing that attitude I uncover some new insights and liberate my decision-making process.

The particular Conference Table session I am thinking about helped me decide to enroll in the Inner Focus ordination program. The question I proposed was, "Is it in my best interest to pursue the Inner Focus ministerial training program at this time?" The entities I selected to speak were my mother; my father; my brothers (collectively); my grandfathers (both ministers by profession, but spoken as one voice); society (a voice to express the general attitudes of the society that influence me); my higher self; my inner child (an innocent part of me that holds the traumas I experienced in childhood); Jesus; and Buddha. In turn I attempted to speak for each one of these influences, and with Donna's guidance various attendees responded to some of the views being expressed.

The Conference Table was proceeding nicely, with various attendees speaking whenever I felt the inclination to express a particular voice. The views being expressed gave me many insights. Donna reminded me that two voices had yet to speak: Jesus and Buddha. I felt some trepidation and some internal judgments about having these personas speak. As preparation, I reminded myself to ignore my judgments and to do my best to surrender to the process.

First, I sensed that the voice of Buddha wanted to speak. I felt a boundless calm and confidence come over me. When the words came, they were delivered in a simple, sincere and kind manner. There were no judgments being made about my options; rather, it was a benevolent perspective acknowledging that there were no wrong decisions. The voice reminded me that attachments are part of the mind's functioning.

As I heard what this "voice" said, I could sense it would be beneficial to reassess my motivations. I recognized that what I had previously been considering as important factors were only important to my ego and weren't really important to my overall well-being. I could also understand that my choices merely represented different paths, but that ultimately they led to the same place. In thinking about it now, it was more akin to Peter's dramatic decisions to change the management of the youth in the group home: the outcome would be determined by the commitment I made toward my decision.

At this point in the session I again became aware of my normal self and that I was involved in a Conference Table healing. I still felt some residual calmness and confidence, but I was back to my old, doubtful self again. I took solace in knowing that speaking the voice of Buddha wasn't the foolish exercise I feared it might be, and this gave me some confidence to attempt the next voice — Jesus. I thought, "What have I got to lose?" And then I began speaking the "voice of Jesus." I can't recall the specific words said, but what was incredible was how I *felt* while speaking the voice. I felt compassion beyond my comprehension, and in fact, I wept intermittently as I spoke! It was not that the weeping was part of the message, but as a person I was having a hard time staying in character. I felt overwhelmed with the compassion pervading me.

The words were brief, and after a minute or so the message felt complete. I allowed myself another minute or two to adjust from experiencing this immense compassion, and then proceeded with the Conference Table. I returned to being my usual self, but again with a residual feeling of compassion and love. Donna asked me if any of the other voices wanted to speak again. I replied that I felt the Conference Table was complete. She concurred, and led me through the final steps to close the session.

It is worth noting that when expressing these voices of profound wisdom, the words are never a directive. I am not told to do anything specific or to make certain decisions; rather, the words tend to afford me a new perspective with which to view my dilemma. They express a wisdom that I fail to have when considering these problems with my everyday conscious thinking. Conversely, some of the other participants, such as my parents or society, have strong opinions and specific recommendations.

That Conference Table was very powerful for me! It was a major impetus for me in pursuing my ministerial training. Inner Focus is founded on the teachings of Jesus, yet I felt OK about enrolling in the program even though I was ignorant of Jesus and had a reluctance to promote him personally. I appreciated that my ignorance and disposition did not limit me in promoting what Jesus desired—for us to be healed. AlixSandra's wisdom is to allow a broad range of visions as to how to promote healing under the banner of Inner Focus.

I am lost in my thoughts and I don't notice the miles pass by. I arrive in Numazu and start looking for Kaori. My watch says 12:21, so I am a few minutes early for our meeting. I can see our arranged meeting place: a statue of a nude woman. I am reminded of a temporary art display of a nude man in my hometown of Penticton. It caused quite a controversy. Japan doesn't seem to have the puritan dogma of North America. As I approach the statue, I see Kaori looking at me—she is smiling.

There is a nice picnic area in the park that is sheltered from the ocean breeze, both by trees and by the elevated seawall. Kaori has brought a wonderful assortment of Japanese delicacies: sushi (of course), a variety of picked fishes and vegetables, deep-fried chicken nuggets (with real meat, not processed meat), a rice dish and sweets for dessert. Most items have their own particular sauce; the Japanese are very finicky about certain sauces being used only for certain foods. After the ride I am starving, so I dig in, neglecting the formal Japanese custom of coyly refusing several times before nibbling at the food sporadically. Having such self-control must be one reason why the Japanese people are so slender. I hope Kaori's time in America has allowed her to accept my rude behavior.

Our conversation skips around, covering a variety of topics. We both have a keen interest in traveling, so that is always a safe topic. I invariably mention a few ideas about spirituality, but she doesn't offer any insights into her views. I ask a few questions about Japanese customs as they relate to Shinto, but her answers do little to clear up my confusion (it is hard for me to come to grips with Shinto not being a cognitive religion). She is particu-larly interested in my ambitions to be an author; she laughs when I list off the three books I already have planned in my mind. Again, I don't go into a lot of details about my current book.

After lunch we go for a short walk along the beach. Kaori is not a keen outdoors-person, and soon I can tell she has had enough walking. She looks fashionable, but her clothing is too thin to fend off the coolness of the ocean breeze. A few days ago when I called her to set up a date, she informed me that though she was busy later on Monday afternoon, she suggested we meet for a picnic. So her need to leave is expected, but it is a disap-pointment nonetheless. I enjoy spending time with her.

We say goodbye, and being in an upbeat frame of mind, I am looking forward to a leisurely ride home. When I arrive at my apartment, I feel content and happy; I got some exercise, it was a pleasant picnic and I had some lovely company. The feeling of joy has been absent in my life lately, so I try to relish it. Writing has also been absent lately, but I am in a perfect frame of mind to write, so when I get home I grab my computer.

Chapter X: Living in the Moment

Living in the Moment means the consciousness is attuned to all four of the Energy Bodies during that instant (whether it is a fluid part or a blockage). To regularly be connected to the fluidity of all four of the Energy Bodies can be described as "Living in the Flow," or "Being in the Now," as opposed to Living in the Moment. An absence of energy blockages allows one to understand that time is artificial, and that everything and every moment are one. The Now incorporates the expanded awareness of the connection beyond the current moment; in other words, it transcends the current moment. To achieve this state, the personality and its desire for control must be minimal, or nonexistent.

Unless one is Enlightened, each Energy Body will have sections of both fluid energy and blocked energy. If the consciousness is connecting with an energy blockage (i.e. being triggered) and yet stays connected with the wisdom of the Spiritual Body, then at least some degree of healing will occur. If the consciousness is avoiding connecting to a blockage, then one is using a coping strategy, and is not in the moment. If one is connected to fluid parts of the Energy Bodies, then the experience is often joyous, harmonious, relaxing, and compassionate. Hence, persistent Living in the Moment results in either regularly experiencing these positive sensations, or initiating healing.

In part, the personality evolves to avoid emotional pain, and

273

this avoidance creates an illusion of having control over certain aspects of one's life. The propensity to avoid pain also results in learning to live *out* of the moment. If one can stay *in* the moment when starting to experience emotional pain, and resist the inclination to control the situation, then one enters into a state of Vulnerability. In choosing this state, we prevent blockages from forming, or begin to heal ones already formed. Avoiding pain also leads to blaming external factors for the resulting feelings. So an additional benefit of Living in the Moment is that it conditions us to take responsibility for our own emotions.

This is all the focus I can maintain for today's writing. There is an urge to celebrate the day with a drink, but I resist. I sit down to watch some TV, and though I am not hungry, I have a tendency to eat out of boredom. Soon I find myself snacking on some potato chips, thus unconsciously helping my euphoric feeling to fade.

Chapter 33

Feeling Disliked and Having Insights

Tuesday, March 24

This is amazing! I just realized how my fortunes and my life changed so quickly while in Korea—they didn't! It is 3:20 in the morning, and I woke up a short while ago from a horrible dream. I was a teacher in an alternate school, and as one might expect, some of the students liked me and some didn't. As the dream progressed, the kids who liked me disappeared and the ones who disliked me became more confrontational with their attitudes. The pinnacle of the dream came when Brad, my current boss here in Japan—whom I like and have a good relationship with—said he too disliked me.

That was the point in the dream where I lost my façade of calmness. As events unfolded, I could only tell myself so many times that it didn't matter what people said. When Brad rejected me, it was the point when I had to admit it *did* matter what people said! In the dream, I was struggling to not break down and cry. The feeling was so intense that it woke me up.

Then, while I lay in bed trying to make sense of the dream, I started reflecting on recent events and my lifestyle here in Japan. While thinking about these things, I progressed into one of my reflective moods where the ideas flow and intermingle. I suddenly recognized a pattern in my life! My fortunes didn't change that quickly in Korea; it was just that I was ignoring the shift as it occurred, just as I am starting to do so here in Japan. By missing the steps along the way, the major shift that happened in Korea seemed to come out of the blue rather than it being the culmination of preliminary events.

What helped me realize this insight was that I finally admitted to myself that I haven't been happy this last week. Over

275

the last eleven months I've had my ups and downs, but there have always been enough positives to explain away negative feelings. After all I'm living a dream: working in Japan; regularly partying with friends; and writing a book. The worst period was during November when I quit drinking, and that resulted in a severe back pain. I had convinced myself that even this last week wasn't so bad because I wasn't feeling sad, but I just realized I wasn't happy, either. What I have clued into is a pattern of numbing myself. I wasn't feeling sad because I haven't been feeling, *period*—I have been numb!

My teaching schedule has me teach at a particular school for one week, then move to a different school the following week, with every fifth week starting over again. Last week's school was the one with the longest commute (well over an hour), and every day the classes there start at either 2:30 or 3:45. Classes are an hour, with 15-minute breaks in between. My other schools include at least one day, and often more, when I start teaching at 5:00pm or later.

This is significant because I feel rushed if I try to write in the mornings when I am teaching at this particular school. With my schedule of getting home late and having mornings off, I have gotten into the habit of sleeping in. When I write, I prefer to have several hours to do it justice. If I have written in the morning, I will sometimes edit in the evening, but I try not to do creative writing in the evening. I find writing at night leads to problems with sleeping. The result is that I didn't do any writing this last week.

As I considered this further, I recognized the lack of writing as one of several components of my numbing process. If I am not writing, I usually fill the time by watching TV, and I believe TV is a very harmful medium. I can't explain this in detail, but on an energetic level, TV adversely affects one's psyche. Even watching "good TV" only provides some good along with the medium's inherent negativity. I have found by observing myself over the years that when I watch lots of TV, I become less aware of my emotions—it helps me become numb. I suspect spending time on the computer, like surfing the net, is also inherently bad, but I haven't explored this yet. The opposite of TV is music, where it is inherently good, so even bad music provides some measure of good. Just how pathetic my TV watching can be is emphasized by the fact that I have a basic Japanese cable package, and I cannot understand most of what I watch. Yet with such meager offerings, I can still waste a morning or an evening channel surfing.

Contributing to my overall slide is a poor diet: I have been eating out of boredom. Because of my colitis I have become aware of nutritious eating habits, and I try to pay attention to my dietary urges. I am not fanatical about it, so it is easy to go from an occasional indulgence to regular lapses in healthy eating. As with all of us, my willpower is directly affected by my self-esteem, so when I am not happy it is harder to curb my dietary urges.

Adding to this list of numbing habits is masturbating regularly. I am aware that I sometimes use masturbation to avoid my feelings, and I masturbate more frequently when I am emotionally stressed. The relaxed feeling after ejaculating helps suppress unpleasant feelings. In this state, the activity has very little to do with satisfying sexual feelings, and can be sparked by the slightest urge. The dysfunctional benefit that fuels this behavior is not gratification, but rather, the suppression of internal stress.

I have also realized this non-writing week has been sandwiched between weekends of excessive drinking, which is yet another numbing tool of mine. I sometimes use alcohol to access my feelings, but this hasn't been the case recently. The last couple of weekends have been fun, so it is easy to fool myself into thinking things are fine, but I haven't been genuinely happy. My need for friendship can cloud my perception of happiness; I substitute the company of others for genuine happiness.

Put it all together and I have spent a week void of feelings, with the exception of a little drunken fun to distract me. My life here is not bad—in fact, it is very good—but this numbing is how my bubble of light gets dimmer. If I don't focus on the positive and avoid resolving the negative feelings when they do arise, then I am not replenishing my positively charged aura. As this depletion happens, the little negativity I do encounter has a greater impact on me. The struggle with a difficult student, a parent that isn't so appreciative or a store clerk that is subtly racist all start to leave an imprint on me. These incidents leave some kind of residue on me. Before, my bubble of light would transform the residue and I wouldn't feel impacted by such incidents. But if my bubble is not bright, and I suppress these minor negative feelings, then these incidents leave me feeling down—energetically my world gets darker, which in turn prompts me into numbing myself.

When I was in Korea in eight years ago, I think the same pattern developed. Adding to the mix then was the prostitute event. I suspect that event left some major residue on me, as well as working on me from the inside—that is, I felt guilty about the incident. That holiday in Thailand was very intense for me, and back then I wasn't as adept at processing such experiences. That holiday was before my healing school training, and not processing the feelings left my energy bodies out of sync, which caused stress.

So not being able to fully process the effects of my Thailand holiday and my progressive state of numbness in Korea had me set up to play the victim when a major shift happened. That shift came in the form of an immigration official coming to my school in Seoul. If I had been keeping my bubble of light charged, that event could have been a great help (i.e. seeing problems as opportunities). That second job on Cheju Island, which Korea considers to be their Hawaii, was a good one. Cheju may not be the same as

Hawaii, but it is a beautiful island just the same. I think the second work visa could have been obtained if the Cheju immigration official hadn't taken a personal dislike to me and my new boss. On the advice of some other long-term Cheju teachers, I met with the local head of immigration, but he was unmoved by my plea of innocence. If I had made a favorable impression, aided by a bright bubble of light, events may have been more fortuitous.

For me, recognizing this pattern highlights the need to live in the moment. If I am not in touch with my energy bodies as I start the difficult process of winding down my life here, then it's likely to be a hard transition when I return to Canada. In particular I need to pay attention to my feelings. This next month will be my last time to see my students, and after that I will be saying goodbye to my fellow teachers, and of course there is leaving the Oz crew. The busyness of preparing to go home, such as cleaning, packing and discarding my belongings, is an additional diversion from facing these emotions.

Feeling upbeat because of these insights, I decide to get up and write, even though it is now 4am. I get out my computer; it has been too long since I have done any writing.

Chapter X, cont. (Living in the Moment)

In infants, the personality and Mental Body are not yet developed, so an infant does not have the capacity to be out of the moment, thus Living in the Moment is a relearning process for adults. People must retrain themselves once again to Live in the Moment, and to experience the inherent joy of the moment. When we can do this as adults, along with the benefit of developed Energy Bodies, life is harmonious and rewarding. When we are in the moment, our consciousness loses its personality-based perspective and acquires a more Divine perspective. One feels more connected to the innate nature of the world, which in turn satisfies the primal need for being understood. Simultaneously, we can become conscious co-creators of our reality.

It is the inherent joy of the moment that transforms the seemingly mundane—the daily tasks of life—into gratifying moments. Simply washing the dishes, or cleaning one's home, can be experienced as pleasurable moments. When one has cleared the judgments (Spiritual Body blockages) that minimize these tasks, then one can view these chores as nurturing. In some Buddhist traditions, when an initiate joins a monastery, he or she is assigned basic cleaning chores as spiritual training. Though the initiate often perceives this as a test, when they reach a more enlightened state, these tasks represent moments to enjoy the Divine. These moments are no better or worse, even in comparison to watching a beautiful sunset, or hearing a baby cry—every moment is a gift of life. Difficult moments are a chance to practice compassion, but even this separation of the emotional yin and yang is a stepping stone to the enlightened realization of the Universal Energy.

This is not to say life is always an idyllic scene. The Soul, in concert with the Spiritual Body, creates situations to allow the consciousness to learn a life lesson, but the Spiritual Body does not control how the consciousness reacts in those situations. Being connected to the fluid part of the Spiritual Body means one is accessing Divine Wisdom, so one can view difficult situations with compassion. Divine Wisdom recognizes the lesson being presented in all situations, and does not judge people for sometimes trying to avoid the pain of a situation. If one of the participants has poorly devised coping strategies for avoiding his or her pain, it can result in some horrific acts. Understanding this process is not to condone horrific actions, but to comprehend why they can happen, and to wish for healing for the individuals involved. This wish for healing is compassion and it is a reflection of the innate desire for wholeness. No one is served by wishing for more pain in the world. Justice is not having someone suffer for a hurtful act, but rather as that person overcomes their negativity, then the strength or purity of their compassion is a powerful force that rebalances the Divine scorecard. I understand jail as a means to limit an angry person from doing more harm, but ideally a jail would be a place for rehabilitation and not punishment.

It is now 5am and I am getting sleepy again; I have to work later today. I feel great because I have clued into a major pattern in my life. I hope that I can follow through with addressing the issue and not let a brief upswing from having this realization be a substitute for really tackling the underlying pain. If I was back in Canada and I wanted to ensure that I would address the underlying issue, I would call Maria (my fellow I.F. minister) to book a healing session. She is the first one I turn to when I need some intense healing work.

Healing energy blocks doesn't have to be done with the participants in each other's presence; the connection is spiritual, not physical. When I was a student at the healing school there were no other students living near me, so much of my homework was done via the phone. Doing homework sessions over the phone was how Russ and I became so close—he was geographically isolated from fellow students too. I think it is easier to do healings when physically together, but it is not necessary. However, I don't think I can coordinate a phone session with Maria when we are on opposite sides of the planet, plus I can see her when I get back.

When not engaging the help of a healer, there are a few techniques I use for self-healing work. One is Dynamic Meditation (which I explained earlier), another is a healing technique called *Awareness Release Technique* (ART), and a third is to make a concerted effort to let my emotions rise during my sitting meditations. In this last case, I use the spiritual connection that is always present when I meditate and turn the meditation into a release of emotional pain. Unfortunately I don't have the CD for Dynamic Meditation; plus, I wouldn't want to test my neighbor's tolerance, as Dynamic Meditations are loud. So maybe I should try an ART session.

With this technique there are some preliminary steps to create the right energetic setting. Then, one focuses his or her attention inward and begins to mentally scan the physical body, noticing any places where things feel amiss. It could be a tingling sensation, a tense muscle or an actual, minor pain that hadn't been noticed before. Each physical discomfort is connected to some energy pattern. Next the person decides which location is best to work on for this session. This can be done haphazardly or with some spiritual guidance, such as asking the "Higher Self." During my ART sessions I don't usually receive a clear answer as to where to direct my attention, but I trust that where it settles is the best place to work.

Having chosen the physical discomfort to work on, the next step in an ART is to let the mind extrapolate what the discomfort is like. One creates a mental image of that discomfort: how big, what shape, what color, is it hard or soft etc. It is important to not judge the impressions; this is a mental exercise, so the discomfort could be the size of a basketball or a pinhead. This imagining exercise focuses light on the blockage. All stuck energy patterns have an inclination to be released (because fluidity is the natural state of energy), and by focusing one's attention on the stuck energy pattern, one energizes that innate propensity for healing.

The next phase of an ART is to physically express the now-energized blockage, thus allowing it to unravel. Some of the ways this can be done is by shouting, crying, making inarticulate sounds and by moving the body. Whatever safe impulse arises, a person is encouraged to express it. Again, it is important to not judge what is happening.

I think this is why ART sessions have worked well for me: they engage the mind but circumvent my tendency to think too much. It is only after the physical release has naturally subsided that the mental element of the blockage comes into play. Generally, the insight simply arises without having to look for it or think about it. This is part of the magic of this technique: it uses the physical body as a means to access the blockages in the other energy bodies. The "story" trapped in the blockage could be some current drama in one's life; or, if the release was deeper, it may provide some insight into a childhood trauma. The final two stages of an ART are to bring in light to fill the void created, and then to complete the process by expressing gratitude.

I think stuck energy patterns can be accessed through any of the four energy bodies, as they are all affected by the initial blockage. A Dynamic Meditation is similar to an ART because the actions of the physical body are used to access the core blockage.

Feeling very sleepy now, I put the idea of doing an ART into the back of my mind. I let my mind drift. I feel relaxed and contented as sleep overcomes me.

Chapter 34

Crisis Point; Time to Go Within

Sunday, March 29

Here I am again, lying in bed, wasting my day. I had planned to get a head start on sorting some of my things, but I cannot get myself to act. I have been awake for probably an hour playing computer games, and I feel the need to change my frame of mind. It keeps getting stuck on unpleasant thoughts. Just now I was daydreaming an imaginary argument with a store clerk, and before that, with a bank teller. My anger is mounting. As I catch myself in these arguments I try to shift my thinking by focusing on something positive, or by imagining white light surrounding me, but today these methods aren't working. Soon I find myself in another argumentative daydream; I can't seem to shake it. In fact, if I am going to be honest with myself, I have been fighting this negative frame of mind with varying intensity for many weeks.

Today I am desperate enough to try meditation, which I rarely do these days. Hopefully this will ease my troubled state of mind. I put my bed away and clear the clutter strewn about the room— clothes, snack food wrappers and work papers. When I sit and watch TV late at night I will drop things on the floor, meaning to put them away later, but they often get left till morning. Recently, being untidy has become my pattern, and it is both reflective of my internal struggles and a contributor to them.

I light an incense stick and settle into my meditation chair. I do my usual invocation of calling positive Energies into this space. Specifically I call in the Heart of the Earth, the Heart of the Universe, The Ascended Masters of Light and the Healing Angels. Today I feel the need to take an extra step and request the presence of Jesus and Buddha, which I don't normally do. This is followed by a simple mental exercise to clear my place of any negative Energies that may be lingering. After these initial steps, I allow my mind to settle on what it deems relevant for this day's sitting. It is not a matter of making a conscious choice, but of surrendering to the process. It is an act of faith to let the issues or ideas most pertinent to my present life come to the fore. Usually there is a gradual transition from having fleeting thoughts to focusing in on a particular issue.

Today I find my mind is again being drawn to negative thoughts. Why can't I shake this negativity? Exasperated, I confess that this must be some deep-seated anger that has been simmering away for weeks and needs to surface. The time has come to finally address this anger. I ask myself, "What is at the heart of this matter?" When asking this type of question during meditation, the answer will sometimes come drifting in, and often it will be an answer I don't want to hear.

However, today I do not get an answer, which is indicative of why my negative mood has been lurking for so long. Obviously I have a strong aversion to really addressing this issue. I know anger is frequently a defense for avoiding an underlying hurt, so I decide to change my tactic. I will shift this meditation into a healing session. To do this, I will focus on the emotional energy body and allow it to express itself. And since I am confident that the core of this issue is sadness, I will let myself cry.

I try to find some past pain that will allow me to tap into the familiar well of sadness inside me, but I can't find a trigger. After a few minutes of failing at this, I decide I should try something else. This is a time when hitting a tire with a baseball bat or a Dynamic Meditation would be ideal, but in Japan I don't have these outlets. Instead, I will vent my anger on my pillow, so I grab it and begin hitting. At first it feels awkward, but after a few hits I start to lose my inhibitions. The hitting become more forceful and soon I add some sound to my actions. There are no specific thoughts at this point. After a minute of this, I clutch the pillow and use it to smother a scream. I am swearing so loud that my voice is straining.

These tricks haven't broken through my wall of self-protection, but they are helping. I can feel the sadness getting closer to the surface. With my emotions welling up I feign crying, as I have found this to be another helpful technique to connect with underlying pain. The crying is forced and artificial, but I can already sense a part of me—a hurt part—preparing to step into this role-playing. An emotional blockage wants to connect with my physical body, and it wants to be crying in earnest. I just need to get my personality out of the way.

As this shift of energy bodies occurs, my crying starts to take on a "richer" tone, and tears start to build. Within moments I am genuinely crying, and it is not long after this that the crying becomes a wailing. I grab the pillow again and use it to muffle the sounds. It is a deep guttural expression of pain, and now the tears are pouring out. With what little objective awareness I have left, I try to stay with the pain and let it flow out.

Time loses its meaning in these states, but I am guessing this goes on for a minute or two. Then the intensity of my wailing subsides and my expression of pain recedes to sobbing. With my consciousness recovering its self-awareness, I am able to consider the source of this pain. This is a mentally passive process; I don't have to do anything except allow the mental component of this pain to come into my consciousness. A clear and distinct thought comes to mind: I am mourning the loss of other possibilities in my life. I am mourning for that part of me that wanted to be married. I am mourning for that part of me that wanted to have children. I am tired of spending so much time alone.

As I allow these thoughts to surface I can feel another wave of emotion building. By acknowledging these regrets, I am soon in the midst of another outpouring of pain. I try to let it flow and release without restraint. I am wailing into the pillow again, and the sound has that same deep guttural quality to it. The sound vibrates throughout my whole body.

As this second episode of intense pain subsides, more insights come to the surface. This time my thoughts astonish me; I am mourning the loss of God! It is God abandoning me that is at the core of this pain. As soon as this thought has registered, there comes a fuller explanation: God did not abandon me, it was I who turned my back on God!

As my body settles back into a meditative pose, the thoughts keep flowing. God is that life force that permeates all things. God is the Universal Benevolence that surrounds every situation, every place and every thought. It takes effort on our part to tune out God's love, but it is easily done, and it is done often. God is the flow of energy that constitutes everything that exists, and to tune it out we must stop the flow of energy. We must create stuck energy patterns.

So it is not even that I abandoned God, it is the very act of becoming a soul; the process of creating a separation from the Divine means we identify ourselves as "not God." God is the concept we use to describe the external part of the Divine; God is the externalization spirituality. It is the belief that we are separated from the Divine, but in the bigger picture, God is a false concept. *Everything* is the Divine! Our selves and God are one and the same!

I get an image of swirls in a flowing river. As flowing water encounters a blockage, swirls form in the water around it. In real rivers the blockages are rocks or stuck logs, and the swirls are called eddies. I envision energetic eddies as the Universe's way of bringing the required solutions to blockages. We cannot create blockages in the natural flow of energy without creating its counter-influence as well. These energetic eddies exert a subtle but persistent pressure for blockages to unravel.

As I turned my back to God, believing I was separate from the Divine, the Universal Benevolence immediately began to create situations in my life where I could re-experience that Infinite

Benevolence. Every scene of nature I've witnessed, every compassionate act I've encountered, every loving thought I've been exposed to are all ways the Universe encourages me to be fluid again. And the rewards of being fluid are boundless! When we understand the Universal Benevolence, life cannot be anything but movement toward harmony and joy. "In the moment" there is only flow. We can try to step out of the flow and be *out* of the moment, but the moment is always present, and it is our way back *into* the flow. When we are in the moment and free of blockages, we are relaxed, joyful and compassionate. And to "Live in the Flow," rather than just the moment, is to take a higher perspective and realize life is a game; it's a dance we perform to experience the Universal Benevolence anew. We play at life to rediscover our own Divinity.

I am not really thinking these thoughts; I am having a non-cognitive understanding of how the world works. To actually *think* this would slow the process down; the step-by-step procedure of mental understanding would clog the flow of energy. I am just intuiting this information.

Along with these revelations I feel a sense of expansion, elevation and love. I am in a state of joyous reverie! Having a physical body doesn't begin to describe where my "being" is contained. I envision myself as a compassionate being, emitting Light out into the world. It is pouring out of every part of me! I imagine a stream of light coming from my heart and going to the Middle East, going to America, going to Africa, and finally I imagine it encompassing the planet.

This expanded state is suddenly accompanied by an urge to ground this experience. I want these incredible realizations to change my life, to change my being! I don't want to go back to being that old John. I consider opening my eyes but this might break my magical spell; nevertheless it could also ground the experience. In preparation for opening them, I take a moment to visualize my surroundings. Then, as I open my eyes, I see the love in every item around me. The few pieces of simple art hanging on my wall represent the work of caring artisans. Art is another way to express the Divine. I see my clothes, which may not have been made in an idealized manner, but the essence of clothing is to create a warm and loving layer to nurture us. The plant sitting on my window shelf radiates the benevolence of nature. It is the embodiment of peace and harmony.

The plant's essence is part of the web of life, and it fulfills that role no matter what external events are happening. A plant channels the basic elements of air, water, earth and sun and melds them into an expression of life. If the plant dies, it is merely taking part in a greater rejuvenation process. It doesn't have the capacity to view itself as an individual life, as a greater expression of life than other life forms. Its purpose is to express life in its unique way for as long as it has a life. A plant has no means to be out of the moment; it can only be part of the Universal Benevolence.

I decide to get up and move around. What a pleasure it is to feel the intricate movements of my body! I am aware of my muscles as they tighten and relax, generating motion as they do. I take a moment to feel my heart beating, moving blood through my veins and spreading life throughout my body. The sensory nerves in my skin are receptive to all kinds of gentle stimuli: my clothes, the air, the floor under me. It all reminds me of how alive I am!

The sun is streaming in through the window and it is calling me outside—to commune with nature. No sooner do I have this thought than another one comes to mind: I know it would be wise to bring closure to this healing before doing anything else. I am not sure if this awareness is because of my training as an energy healer or if it is a higher wisdom I am accessing, but I know closure is important.

I sit down again and close my eyes. I have released a lot of negative energy today, and in doing so I have created a void in me. I have liberated a part of me that held the belief that I am separate from the Divine. Though much of the filling of this void happens of its own accord, it is important to consciously fill in the hole with positive light. I don't understand the details of this process, but I know conscious intent is an integral part of energy dynamics. I set my intention to bring in White Light. I imagine this Light surrounding my body, permeating every part of me. I imagine it filling every pore and reaching every molecule in my body. I am infused with White Light.

In the midst of this process I have a vision of myself as a little boy. I have no specific features in my vision, but there is no doubt it is me. I see this youthful "me" sitting with three other beings. One is Jesus, one is Buddha and one is an older, wiser me—my Higher Self. The four of us hold hands, and soon our hands become indistinguishable; there is a flow of white energy circulating from one being's heart to the next being's heart, forming a big circle of Light. The boy—me—feels completely safe and loved, and I know I am forever part of this Greater Presence. Never again does he need to feel alone; never again do I need to feel alone. After a minute of envisioning this image I start to lose my concentration, which indicates that the process is complete. I then ask the Universe to continue to surround my physical being with healing light throughout the rest of the day.

Now I am ready to express my gratitude. This was the final stage of all the healing techniques AlixSandra taught. Again I don't understand the details, but I know the state of gratitude is a very significant spiritual state. It is a state of appreciation that encapsulates both humbleness and self-respect. Today, no effort is required to achieve this state—I am already there! I am truly grateful, and I feel incredibly blessed. A few tears seep out of my eyes, but this time they are tears of joy.

I verbally express my gratitude to the Heart of the Earth, the Heart of the Universe, to The Ascended Masters of Light, to the Healing Angels, and specifically to Jesus and Buddha. I give thanks to the part of me that held that stuck energy pattern of separation. That person, the younger me, showed great courage in being willing to face his fear and release it. Again I imagine that little boy, that previous stuck part of me, being surrounded by Light and sitting peacefully with Jesus, Buddha and my Higher Self. I also give thanks to myself—the John, sitting in his meditation chair in his apartment in Japan. I also showed great courage.

I close with an unspecified thank you. Now the healing is complete. I feel pure elation! I feel energized and vibrant, and I want to be with nature. There is also a fragility to my state, like things are still happening on an energetic level. I am not fully back to my daily consciousness and cannot function well in the real world right now. I need to be alone, but I am keen to go for a walk in the park. Soon I head out the door to be with nature, and to be with God; feeling nature's Divinity reinforces my own sense of Godliness.

Chapter 35

Preparing to Leave

Sunday, April 12

How important is this shirt? Do I take it home or do I give it to the second-hand store? These are repeating questions as I pack my things for shipping; I am going home in two weeks. It is almost fun to objectively watch my attachments in action as I ponder the fates of all the items I have accumulated.

It has been a few weeks since my amazing healing, and I still feel the high of that experience. I am back to feeling like a bubble of light, positively influencing all that I encounter. Everything I do I approach with a sense of spirituality. The less-than-ideal things in life, like packing and cleaning, I view with compassionate understanding because of my stronger connection with the Divine. Everything is part of a benevolent whole. It has been a magical few weeks!

My insights have been plentiful since that healing, aided by meditating regularly. Now I clearly understand my reluctance leading up to the healing—it was fear, which I hid with anger and numbing. It was a multitude of fears: of the unknown, of change, of being alone and of being all that I can be. By transcending that fear I think I've had another initiation. As AlixSandra says, spiritual initiations clear away deeper levels of fear, and that is what I have done. This initiation is about believing in my own Divinity, about having a deeper realization of the fallacy of my separation from the Divine. In concert with this I am liberating myself from my personal will and aligning myself with Divine guidance—a Spiritual Will.

My Spiritual Will is connected to my Soul where it is aligned with the Universal Goodness of the Divine. I refrain from calling this a Divine Will, because I think "Will" arises at some point during the separation process, but it does not exist in the higher realms of the Divine. As an incarnate person we are free to react in situations in accordance with our wisdom, or alternatively with the influence of the personality. The Spiritual Will I am talking about embodies the counter-influence of energy blocks— our life lessons—that are stored in the Soul. Life lessons influence which experiences come our way, so the Spiritual Will is how we influence the physical world via energy dynamics, as opposed to physical action. We energize the future reality that embodies our ideal spiritual path.

This Will has parallels in science where the strange laws of subatomic particles operate, or in the extreme reality of black holes—the places where time is malleable. For example, science theorizes that even in a vacuum, minute particles randomly appear and disappear. They are called virtual particles. These virtual particles give the vacuum a potential energy which has real world influence. This is akin to the background influence of the Spiritual Will. Furthermore, when this Will is directed by pure consciousness, it can trigger the energy dynamics of the universe. This is the process of manifesting thoughts and intent into reality. However, it has to be consistent with the Divine Benevolence, and the power of those dynamics is a function of how pure our intent is. A troubled person cannot muster much Will force; an active personality will hinder the connection to the Spiritual Will; whereas a wise person has few blockages impeding the power of the Will force.

Another way to consider this is to think of the Divine Will as the map of how a perfect world looks, and we as individuals can allow it to unfold or impede the map from opening. So in this sense it is not a Will, but the natural order of things. In contrast, our Personal Will has the ability to create or to heal blockages— inhibiting or allowing the map to unfold. The blockages affecting the personality motivate the Personal Will to seek control, which in turn hinders the influence available via the Spiritual Will.

Spiritual Will is not a power *over* me, it is a power *within* me. And surrendering is the key; as my book asserts, the state of vulnerability is pivotal to transforming our blockages. Free Will is also a key; my theory is that souls create incarnate experiences for the purpose of having a different experience of the Divine. Only by having Free Will can the drama of an incarnate life be enacted. In one sense, Free Will is an illusion, but it is more appropriate to say it is a concept that has meaning only in the realm of an incarnate life. Like Newtonian physics vs. Einstein's physics, Free Will applies only to circumstances that are a limited part of a greater whole. As I say in my book, it is similar to willfully standing: eventually a person will have to sit down, but the moment they decide to sit is still a free choice. With this latest initiation, I'm using my personality's belief of Free Will to accept my Divinity, which in turn minimizes the personality because it is accepting the limitations of Free Will—the personality surrenders its desire for control. This is connecting the Divine world with the physical world and the loss of perceived separation.

I've also developed another analogy—or expanded an old one—with regards to the distinction between lessons vs. beliefs. The masters have climbed up the mountain and they have described the journey and view from the top. Their descriptions are like rocks on the way up the mountain. The rocks have been retrieved and used to build a structure in the valley in the shadow of death. I've always thought the "valley in the shadow of death" is a cool piece of scripture and now I have found a place to use it, even if it is a little overdramatic. The building in the valley may show the beauty of God (external spiritualism), and it can also be a place of comfort and inspiration, but a structure eventually ages and crumbles, which is nature's way of keeping things fresh. Zen has taught me that belief structures ultimately limit us so I even consider my theory of energy bodies, consciousness and healing to be a structure that will crumble.

Religions take the structure and make it a church, and religions fear aging and crumbling, so they patch and repair and even rebuild the church. However, this removes us from the wisdom of the masters and adds layers of interpretation. The structure, and religions, can provide some benefits, but it is believing that the *religion* is an ultimate Divinity that holds us back. The best use of the building is to train us to be climbers, and not as a substitute for climbing. Fluid wisdom (lessons) empowers people, while fixed beliefs limit people. Instead, the rocks' origins are ledges on the mountain that are resting places and stepping stones for the climb to the top. One must stop and reflect on the lesson in order to obtain the wisdom as it relates to an incarnate life. As one transcends each lesson it enables the climber to move further up the mountain.

In spite of this most recent healing and all my subsequent insights, I still haven't been writing. I have made all kinds of notes, but I wanted time to reflect on them before deciding if I should incorporate them into my book (and how I might do so). I have also been busy preparing to go home, but I suspect the real reason I have been slow to translate these insights into my book is because it means the completion of the book, and I have a fear about completing it. Fear of completion has been another recurring theme in my life, and one I am now starting to understand. For example, it took me ten years to complete my university degree (which is normally a four-year program), and I left the Zen workshop before it finished. Initially I thought my fear of completion was fear of the unknown, but now I know this isn't accurate; it is fear of being all I can be. If I truly believe in myself then the unknown is an adventure, and not a risk. Belief in myself keeps my heart open, which makes the unknown a harbinger of good fortune; I co-create my future.

As I continue sorting my belongings, I have a sense that time is precious. There is a lot to do as I prepare to move back to Canada, and I only have two weeks. The process of ending my life in Japan is a compelling diversion from my joy. Part of the trap is the looming prospect of reestablishing a life in Canada, but I know the fears I have about the future are based on imaginings, and are not valid. Instead, I keep reminding myself to focus on the present moment. With joy, the heart opens, and with fear or worry, the heart closes. The return to daily meditation is also a big help in staying "present," and in keeping in touch with my emotions as they arise.

The intensity of this last month is validating the benefits of my approach to life. I understand the sentiment others may have, that it is easy for me to talk about living in the moment because I don't have the responsibilities and complications of a more conventional life. I am single, I do not have children and I do not have major financial obligations, but for others—those with these responsibilities—it is not so practical to "live in the moment." In sympathy with that criticism, it has been a challenge to keep myself in the moment these last few weeks, but it can be done. In fact, these last few weeks emphasize the need to live in the moment. Being conscious of staying in the moment has been the key for me to be happy during the process of ending my life here. As I have taken care of the many tasks and faced up to my feelings, I have maintained a sense of spirituality.

Busyness is a practical way of avoiding some unpleasantness in people's lives, like confronting stuck energy patterns. People running on the societal treadmill are, in part, running to avoid facing their pain. It requires courage to face and heal old wounds, and it seems simpler to avoid them. However, once a pattern is healed, we can enjoy moments that previously triggered us and enjoy the parts of ourselves that were hidden by the blockage.

Committing to *living* also alters one's priorities; many things that are thought to be important become less pertinent, and many desires are recognized as unnecessary complications (like drinking for example). Part of the calling of this journey is to look deeply inside oneself to find what is truly meaningful. Our parents, society, media, religion, our personalities etc. shape our desires, and looking inside changes those priorities. Healing gets us closer to our spiritual nature and our Divine purpose.

As I think this, I continue sorting and come across the last of my T-shirts. It has a picture of Jesus on it. When I saw it in the store, I felt compelled to buy it. For me, the nonsensical English phrases on most of the T-shirts in Japan adds charm to them. My Jesus shirt reads, "Have you finished your work yet? I will help you. I have just finished milking the cow." These words are superimposed over a faint image of Jesus. Under the image and in bolder print, it reads, "In Your Jesus Christ Pose." I have no idea what it means, but I like it. I put the shirt into my "take home" pile.

Finally, I have finished sorting my clothes; that is another project completed. Next I will take some personal time and make some tea, and then I will do some writing. My procrastinating has to stop; it's time to complete the book.

With my cup of tea in hand, I grab my notes and sit down to write.

Chapter X, cont. (Living in the Moment)

So, even in the midst of traumatic events, one can still have a sense of calm, clarity and compassion by being attuned to the four Energy Bodies. However, to do this requires a spiritually mature person; a person must have very few blocks in their Energy Bodies to not be triggered in challenging situations. When a person can be very compassionate in difficult situations, their compassion radiates so strongly that it can actually influence the processes around them. The compassion of spiritually evolved beings is felt, and is effectual. This temporary, intense involvement of the Divine energy can have a miraculous effect, causing healing or cleansing of the uninitiated people involved, resulting in them acting in surprisingly out-of-character ways—namely, with benevolence.

One thing that tends to happen for most people, even in moderately emotional situations, is that the consciousness is drawn to an energy blockage. Something in those circumstances reminds them of a past trauma, and the people are triggered into—at least partially—reliving those old experiences. Spiritual Energy blockages, namely judgments, stop us from keeping an open heart when confronted with challenging situations. Alternatively, an intense event that is not processed can have such an emotional impact that people add layers to existing blockages or create new blockages. A second reaction that limits compassion, either in conjunction with triggering or independently, is that the personality intervenes.

It is worth noting that, as mentioned in Chapter III, a person with a strong connection to their Soul has a more conscious involvement in creating the situations they encounter. The Soul orchestrates situations for one to learn life lessons, but if one already has a good understanding of these lessons, the person chooses their situations for other reasons. With an evolved person, the personality's involvement is diminished, so many spiritually wise beings living on the planet live almost reclusive lives as they have nothing to prove or learn. They will share their wisdom with those showing a determined effort to acquire it, but generally they will let others learn their life lessons as their Souls direct them. They understand that the unification of yin and yang is inevitable. However, the mere existence of these evolved Souls in human form raises the consciousness of the planet as a whole and provides a foundation for others that are aspiring to this state.

To summarize, Living in the Moment means the consciousness is attuned to all four of the Energy Bodies during that instant. This is our state when we are born, so it is a natural one. If the connection is to fluid parts of the Energy Bodies, the experience is often one of relaxation, joy, harmony, and compassion. If there is an unconscious connection to a blockage in any of the Energy Bodies, the person is not in the moment. If it is a conscious connection to an energy blockage, and it includes a connection to a fluid part of the Spiritual Body, then a healing process is initiated. One learns to be out of the moment because, during early human development, one does not know how to process emotionally traumatic events. And in shifting the consciousness out of the moment, the personality develops a false sense of control. And when the consciousness stays in the moment during challenges, it can seem threatening to the personality.

Other benefits of being in the moment are finding a joy in the previously experienced mundane aspects of life and accepting responsibility for one's own emotions. Being in the moment means one can view situations with at least part of the wisdom of the Divine Energy. However, one often gets triggered when confronted with emotionally challenging situations, and hence is no longer Living in the Moment. Living in the Flow is the state of being regularly connected to fluid parts of all four of the Energy Bodies, and when the Energy Bodies are free of all energy blocks, it is the state of Enlightenment.

The End

I make myself another cup of tea. I feel satisfied; writing this book has been an amazing journey! In fact, what I feel is a much stronger feeling than simple satisfaction. Completing the book makes me feel complete, too. I am in sync with my world, and I know my place in it. My sense of longing and searching has abated.

Again I feel the exhilaration of my life aligning with a higher purpose, when everything fits together and makes sense. This feeling of life "falling into place" is echoed by an e-mail I got from Russ the other day. Russ and I met at Inner Focus, cemented our bond by performing healing sessions with each other and then became ordained together. And now, as my ministerial vision becomes clearer, so is his; in his e-mail he said he is opening a church in Little Rock, Arkansas. He has toyed with this idea for a while, and now he is moving ahead with the project. It is reasonable to think that as each of us clarifies our vision, we have helped set the stage for the other to make a similar shift. We don't directly affect each other, but I think others that are closely connected to us and function on a similar wavelength automatically receive positive energy when one or the other heals a core blockage. That's good, but more than this, I want to consciously help others. That's why writing the book was important—it is part of my mission to help others.

I am confident things will fall into place in Canada, too, so I needn't fret about it. Having finished sorting my clothes, and now having finished my book, I feel exhilarated, and it is important to stay conscious of this feeling. I decide that going to the park and communing with nature will be an ideal way to both focus on, and maintain, this state. I can do some more cleaning later. I shut off my computer and head out the door.

Chapter 36

Quiet Endings

Thursday, April 23

Tomorrow I go home to Canada, but for tonight, once I finish the last of the packing and cleaning, I will go to Oz for a final visit. Even if some of the crew are there, tomorrow morning they will go to work and I will catch the train to the airport, so it will be a low-key night. The boys and I had a celebratory send-off last weekend. For me it wasn't a party night. I felt it important to bring some closure to our friendships, but the appeal of drinking has worn off. Now if I have more than two drinks I am aware it has a negative impact on my well-being: not so much physically, but spiritually.

I have had some insights into my drinking habits. I've realized that when I drank, my wall of separation tended to come down. I lost the perspective of looking at the world from the outside, and I became part of my situation. I recognized this pattern when I thought about times of hanging out with the Oz crew. Drinking enabled a part of me to surface—the part that could easily joke and be playful—without worrying about how others might view me. Ironically, during those times, I cared less about others' approval, and this made me more likable. As I move forward, I should be able to achieve this state more often without the use of alcohol.

The energy blockage affecting my social behavior and drinking has its roots in my emotionally-troubled teen years. The time I started drinking semi-regularly was while I was hanging out with my neighborhood friends again—the ones that taunted me—but I never allowed myself to trust them as friends again. I would socialize with them physically, but emotionally I was not part of their group. However, when I drank, I forgot about my

301

emotional separation from them and I felt we were true friends once more.

It would have taken a wiser person than me to sort out those complex dynamics between my friends and me. The basic energy pattern was that I distanced myself to protect me from being hurt again. It is a pattern that has persisted into my adult life, but I hope that, as of a few weeks ago, I won't need drinking to feel connected to friends. Now I feel things are different. I suspect I will soon stop drinking altogether, but I haven't made that final decision just yet. As for the crew, they helped me confront my issue of separation, and for that I am very grateful. We also had a lot of fun, and that was good too.

Somehow it feels right to just quietly walk out of Oz for the last time without a lot of hoopla. A quiet ending at Oz seems appropriate because I don't view my life as dramatic. My life has changed from having dramatic moments to a life with intense, periodic moments. I think the difference is that intense moments tend to be part of a greater process, having a buildup and a subsequent integration. Dramatic moments are more sudden and tend to leave a person feeling at a loss afterwards. I leave Japan with many intense experiences, but not so many dramatic ones. A quiet departure from Oz, and from Japan, means my involvement here has ebbed and flowed, and now the tide is out.

I had hoped for an even more intense spiritual conclusion, such as Enlightenment, but I am at peace without it. I am leaving Japan with a clearer connection with my spiritual body. Enlightenment could have made me into some guru and helped me make lots of money, even though both ideas are inconsistent with Enlightenment. Yes, I want to make a comfortable income, and I believe I have something to say that is of benefit to others, but my desire is not for wealth, and the real success I seek is to believe in myself. Ultimately, peace comes from total self-acceptance, which is an inward expression of the outward idea of the interconnectedness of everything. I am still working on even greater self-acceptance, but I am leaving here with a more profound sense of trust and inner peace.

I started my ministerial journey wondering, "What is my mission as an ordained minister for Inner Focus Church?" and "What is a spiritual life?" I feel my writing is my mission, and having a book come into reality has been an amazing process. Actually, it is not the books that are my mission. The books will be a means of *achieving* my mission. Rather, my mission is to live a more joyful, rewarding life, and in so doing, help others get there too. This is not based on a desire to be a savior—the only thing I have power over is me—but I want to help others understand life, and especially spirituality, in a more practical and useful way so they can be empowered. And I have come to the conclusion that a spiritual life is following the Zen practice of "Living in the Moment," and not just following the dictates of some religious belief system. I hope others can understand this too. We are all part of an integrated whole, and the peace we each achieve helps all of us. If we all live in the moment, then we are all living as one, and the world will certainly be a better place.

It is the stuck energy patterns encoding old traumas from the past that take us out of the moment, so part of my mission is to promote healing. Healing is the part of the Inner Focus Church that connects me directly to Jesus. In a very practical way, he wished for people to be healed and he taught others the art of healing. As children, we do not have the understanding or sufficiently developed energy bodies to process traumatic events. And usually, our parents or caregivers do not have the understanding to help us. So the traumas create a desire to be out of the moment, to avoid the emotional pain, and thus we develop the capacity to disconnect from our energy bodies. The personality develops through this avoidance process, and it orchestrates our ongoing avoidance.

So life is unavoidably about creating blockages and then hopefully using our Free Will to heal and release those old patterns. In doing this we have chosen to be closer to our true spiritual nature, and to embody more of our "Godliness" — we are climbing the mountain. This cycle of creating and consciously healing blockages is the process underlying human life, and mirrors the cycles of nature as well as having parallels in modern scientific theory.

Both the opportunities to encounter these patterns and to release them can be accomplished by living in the moment and with meditation. And by combining more directed healing practices with these techniques, the Zen attitude becomes more accessible for the layperson. Zen acknowledges that emotional releases happen as one undertakes its traditional practices, but they do not encourage one to seek these releases or to try to understand the messages encoded in them. For Zen, getting caught up in the emotional and mental complications of events is an impediment to Enlightenment.

Contrary to this, I am suggesting that understanding the dynamics of energy bodies helps people learn to live in the moment. I am suggesting that recognizing when one is not connected to their energy bodies can help individuals learn to be present in the moment. I want to incorporate the mind, our emotions and a conscious desire for healing to augment the Zen pursuit of Enlightenment and make it more accessible. However, I am not going so far as advocating the detailed structure of Buddhism or any other religion; we do not need a belief system. Rather, I am suggesting that energy bodies and healing are just tools, just as living in the moment is a tool. We can use a building in the valley of the shadow of death, but in the end, it must crumble.

Jesus' lessons are about love and compassion, and specifically, he did healing. Buddha's lessons are about non-attachment and a search for meaning, and he specifically taught "live in the moment" and meditation. Using Buddha's techniques lead to healing, but I think it is more effective when consciously done, and in a structured way, which is Jesus' gift. By uniting the lessons of these two masters with Zen wisdom, we can realize our Godlike nature and heal the world. When Divine Energy flows through us unimpeded, then we are Enlightened; we no longer experience ourselves as separate from Universal Energy. Ultimately, we cannot describe the state of Enlightenment, but Enlightenment is coming full circle in the process of believing in separateness, and then, with our Free Will, choosing to re-experience the interconnectedness of all.

I put the last few pieces of clothing into my suitcase. If I can close it, then I am ready for tomorrow's departure. My life will begin anew. I will return to Canada with the awareness of what a spiritual life looks like, and with an ongoing mission to promote healing, so that I and others can have joyous and harmonious lives. But I also return to Canada with a deeper understanding that joy and harmony are to be found in each moment.

With some forceful persuasion, my suitcase closes. I head out the door for my last trip to Oz. As I walk, I check in with myself and feel an inner peace. I look for signs of sadness, but I can't find any. Though my world is changing, I feel comfortable with the change and with myself—or at least I do in this moment.

The End

Closing Comments

When I moved to Japan, my parents were elderly but still enjoying life. However, they did have some health challenges so it would not have been a surprise if one of them became seriously ill and died. With that thought in mind, I sent a copy of my book to them when I thought it was nearing a finished state (however, I later realized it needed much revising). Yes I was still looking for their approval, but there was also a genuine desire to share my passion with them. My dad was in the later stages of rethinking his views on God, religion, love and life. My manuscript prompted an enjoyable e-mail exchange between us about these subjects. A few years later my dad died, choosing to leave this world in the same pragmatic fashion as he had lived his life.

Many people have said to me that my parents were a model for how they hoped their marriages would be. So my mother's strength and grace came to the fore as she transitioned from being part of a wonderful marriage to being a content, happy, single elderly person. I have been able to show her a more polished and readable copy of my manuscript. Understandably, one of her concerns was how John's mother comes across in the book. I reminded her that it is a work of fiction. However, her comments did make me realize that the book doesn't convey the love and support that was around me as I grew up, and continues to be. Maybe because I wanted the book to show a period of life where some real issues are healed, it is slanted towards the struggles John goes through. I also know that some of the walls I had built around me limited me from really appreciating and enjoying the love and happiness that surrounded me.

Finally, I feel I should also say something about Japan. I make some strong statements about the country and culture, but because I don't speak the language I only have a glimpse of their true nature. It is a complicated country with a long history and complex society, so I don't doubt I would qualify my statements if I knew more.

About Healing

I think the best and quickest way to heal, both personally and globally, is to engage in directed healing practices. I will stop short of saying that this must be done with the aid of a healing practitioner, but I highly recommend it. Inner Focus is a real organization that does train healing practitioners. Can I ensure that all Inner Focus trained healers are competent? No. Am I saying that *only* the Inner Focus approach to healing is worthy? No. But I can say Inner Focus' intentions and methods are sound. One needs to decide if a healer is able to deliver his or her healing service while guided by a spiritually pure source. A competent healer is not a "pure" individual, but is able to keep his or her own issues from interfering with the healing session. Inner Focus teaches healers to connect with both their own soul and the client's soul as a way of creating a pure healing environment.

Finding an appropriate healer is a process of listening to your heart. You must trust the healer enough to let yourself be vulnerable. Note that doubts may not always be your heart telling you that this person is not right for you; it may be that your personality is afraid of addressing deep-seated issues and is trying to avoid healing work. But in the end, the distinction between wise caution and avoiding your issues must be your own realization. And while a healer might be appropriate at one juncture in your life, that does not mean that person will always be appropriate. Be open to changes. Know that opportunities will come your way to help you learn your lessons, but don't be overconfident that you know what lessons are being learned.

The most important step in helping humanity as a whole is to release our own stuck energy patterns, and by healing ourselves, we jointly heal the heart of humanity.

If you are interested in checking out Inner Focus Church and School, their webpage is: www.innerfocus.org.

If you are interested in checking out my cousin's organization in Thailand, you can find Rev. Al Purvis at World Mission Continuum, www.wmcontinuum.com.

Timeline for John Alexander

45 yrs., Ordination – Inner Focus Church

44 yrs., Enroll in Inner Focus Church Ordination Program

43 yrs., Complete involvement with Inner Focus Energy Healing
    Schools
43 yrs., Healing session with Maria – communion

42 yrs., Join the Men's Group

38 yrs., Major healing at Mod. 1, join Inner Focus Healing
    School

37 yrs., Return from Korea, Relocate to Penticton, Travel with
    Lib

36 yrs., Met Lib in Korea and become involved with her
36 yrs., First holiday in Thailand
36 – 37 yrs., Living and working in Korea

34 – 36 yrs., Work for John Howard Society at Youth Detention
    Center

33 yrs., Program Higher Self Workshop in Vancouver with
    AlixSandra
33 yrs., Involved in meditation group in Campbell River

30 yrs., Zen Workshop and my Kensho

29 yrs., Move to Campbell River to work in group home with
    Peter

28 yrs., Graduate University – B.A. Philosophy

27 yrs., Involved in spiritual seekers group in Vancouver
27 yrs., Anger work with my spiritual teacher Helen (venting
      my anger and affirmations)

17 yrs., Graduated High School

11 or 12 yrs., Fight with my brother – quit raging
10 yrs., 6 mos., Rejected by School friends

Age 2, Trying to fit in with my older brothers
Early Childhood, Problems eating
Infant, Mother uses formula

Born May 9

BOOKS

O is a symbol of the world, of oneness and unity; this eye represents knowledge and insight. We publish titles on general spirituality and living a spiritual life. We aim to inform and help you on your own journey in this life.

Visit our website: http://www.o-books.com

Find us on Facebook:
https://www.facebook.com/OBooks

Follow us on Twitter: @obooks